The Hidden Welfare State

PRINCETON STUDIES IN AMERICAN POLITICS:
HISTORICAL, INTERNATIONAL, AND
COMPARATIVE PERSPECTIVES

SERIES EDITORS

IRA KATZNELSON, MARTIN SHEFTER, THEDA SKOCPOL

A list of titles

in this series appears

at the back of

the book

The Hidden Welfare State

TAX EXPENDITURES AND SOCIAL
POLICY IN THE UNITED STATES

Christopher Howard

PRINCETON UNIVERSITY PRESS
PRINCETON, NEW JERSEY

Copyright © 1997 by Princeton University Press
Published by Princeton University Press, 41 William Street,
Princeton, New Jersey 08540
In the United Kingdom: Princeton University Press, Chichester, West Sussex

Library of Congress Cataloging-in-Publication Data

Howard, Christopher, 1961–
The hidden welfare state : tax expenditures and social policy in the United States / Christopher Howard.
    p.   cm.—(Princeton studies in American politics)
Includes bibliographical references and index.

ISBN 0-691-02646-7 (cl : alk. paper)

1. Taxation—United States.   2. United States—Social policy.   3. Tax expenditures—United States.   I. Title.   II. Series.
HJ2381.H684   1997   336.2'06'0973—dc21   96-50044

Portions of this book previously appeared in somewhat different form in "The Hidden Side of the American Welfare State," reprinted with permission from *Political Science Quarterly*, vol. 108, no. 3 (1993): 403–36; "Testing the Tools Approach: Tax Expenditures versus Direct Expenditures," reprinted with permission from *Public Administration Review*, vol. 55, no. 5 (1995): 439–47; and "Happy Returns: How the Working Poor Got Tax Relief," reprinted with permission from *The American Prospect*, no. 17 (Spring 1994): 46–53, © New Prospect, Inc. Chapter 7 is a revised version of "Protean Lure for the Working Poor: Party Competition and the Earned Income Tax Credit," *Studies in American Political Development*, vol. 9, no. 2 (1995): 404–36, © 1995 Cambridge University Press (reprinted with permission from Cambridge University Press).

This book has been composed in Galliard

Princeton University Press books are printed on acid-free paper and meet the guidelines for permanence and durability of the Committee on Production Guidelines for Book Longevity of the Council on Library Resources

Printed in the United States of America
by Princeton Academic Press

10 9 8 7 6 5 4 3 2 1

Contents

PART FOUR: *Conclusion*

Tables

Acknowledgments

ABOUT A YEAR into this project, the head of the department where I was a graduate student gave a talk about writing a dissertation. She offered some good pointers about keeping the literature review short and not waiting until we finished our research to start writing. What I remember most, though, was this piece of advice: choose your topic carefully, for it may be with you for at least a decade. Ideally, she said, we would take a few years to research and write the dissertation, another couple of years to refine (i.e., shorten) the dissertation into a book, and then spend several years basking in the glow of professional acclaim or rebutting our critics. Her advice elicited some nervous laughter, particularly from a certain graduate student who started imagining the next ten years of his career as a painting entitled, "Still Life with Tax Expenditures." Yet here I am, squarely in the middle of the sequence she laid out.

No one in his right mind would choose to study and write about tax expenditures (better known as tax loopholes) knowing in advance that it entailed a ten-year commitment. Investigating the ins and outs of the byzantine U.S. tax code is simply not its own reward, which is why many people pay lawyers and accountants good money to do it for them. If someone were going to study tax expenditures for longer than a day or two, he or she would need to come upon the topic by accident. Over time, that someone might develop a curious affection for tax expenditures, much as one does for a stray dog or cat that keeps hanging around the house. Even then, one would have to remind oneself constantly that studying tax expenditures was not the ultimate goal but a means of saying something interesting about a larger issue, like U.S. social policy. At least that has been my experience.

Even in the best of circumstances, making a long-term commitment to study tax expenditures requires a great deal of support. I have been fortunate to receive such support from the very start of this project and want to acknowledge a number of individuals and institutions for their help. A good place to start is with the library staffs of various institutions, including the Massachusetts Institute of Technology (MIT), Harvard University, the College of William & Mary, the Library of Congress, and the National Archives, all of whom provided me with knowledgeable, prompt service. By the same token, this study could not have been written without the cooperation of several policy makers and experts who taught me much about tax expenditures during a series of interviews. Although their names are listed in an appendix to this book,

I want to single out Wendell Primus and Gene Steuerle for being especially generous with their time and offering thoughtful comments on my work.

Early on, as I fumbled around for an argument, fellow graduate students Larry Best, Erin Flynn, Steve Page, Simona Piattoni, and Jim Shoch provided useful suggestions and much-needed encouragement. Their friendship remains one of the greatest rewards I took away from graduate school. The Boston-based Workshop on American Political Development allowed me the first chance to share my findings with an audience outside my own department. Attracting scholars from Boston College, Boston University, Brandeis, Harvard, MIT, and Northeastern, this workshop consistently forced me to see familiar topics in a new light, including the topic of this book. That experience led to a series of conference papers and journal articles. Here I must acknowledge those journals that graciously allowed me the opportunity to tell the world more about tax expenditures and social policy in the United States: *Political Science Quarterly, Public Administration Review, Studies in American Political Development,* and *The American Prospect.*

Since those articles appeared in print, I have refined my argument in several substantial ways: adding the case of the home mortgage interest deduction; saying less about the actual implementation of tax expenditures in order to focus more on their origins and development; updating the data and narratives through approximately 1995; and streamlining the conclusion. Loyal readers who eagerly await my latest thoughts concerning tax expenditures and social policy therefore have every incentive to buy this book.

Toward the end of my work, the College of William & Mary provided generous financial support in the form of a summer research grant that allowed me to add to and refine the project. David Kerstetter and especially Sarah Dickerson proved able research assistants, even with little direction. My colleagues in the Government Department at William & Mary deserve special mention, for they have shown by example that it is possible to be productive scholars while still maintaining a strong commitment to undergraduate teaching. Princeton University Press located two anonymous referees whose comments were enormously helpful in simplifying and strengthening my arguments. They took what I thought was a decent manuscript and uncovered a number of stylistic and methodological weaknesses that I then worked hard to remedy. Whether I succeeded can be judged later; what matters most is that two colleagues rendered me a tremendous service with their comments.

In contrast to those who appeared early or late, a number of people have been with me during this entire process. Michael Lipsky and Theda Skocpol were mentors in the truest sense of the word, advising me on this project as well as inviting me to collaborate with them on other research. Their record of publishing with graduate students and younger scholars speaks for itself, and I am lucky to have been one of their students. Ellen Immergut and Rick Valelly offered a great deal of sound advice, both conceptual and practical, and I found myself acting on suggestions they had offered years earlier as I prepared the final draft of this manuscript. All four of these individuals proved time and again that constructive criticism is not an oxymoron. By treating me and my ideas seriously from the beginning, they also helped me make the all-important transition from student to professional colleague. That debt goes well beyond this book.

My parents, brother, grandparents, and in-laws showed far more interest than I had any right to expect, and I am grateful for their encouragement and understanding. Few people would take such pride in telling themselves and their friends that their (grand)son was spending some of the most productive years of his working life writing a book about tax expenditures and social policy. I only wish that my grandmother had lived long enough to see the final product.

My wife Dorothy Holmes gave me the greatest help of all. She listened to me think aloud, read some of my work (even some truly awful first drafts), worked to put a roof over our heads and food on the table, left me alone at all the right moments, and, best of all, brought our first child into the world. Our son Stephen was born just as I was finishing up, and I discovered that chronic sleep deprivation can make one a very efficient editor. I also discovered that being a father offers joys that even a published study of tax expenditures and social policy cannot match.

Abbreviations

AARP	American Association of Retired Persons
AFDC	Aid to Families with Dependent Children
CBO	Congressional Budget Office
CETA	Comprehensive Employment and Training Act
CRS	Congressional Research Service
EITC	Earned Income Tax Credit
ERISA	Employee Retirement Income Security Act
FAP	Family Assistance Plan
GAO	General Accounting Office
IRS	Internal Revenue Service
JCT	Joint Committee on Taxation
NJTC	New Jobs Tax Credit
OMB	Office of Management and Budget
PBJI	Program for Better Jobs and Income
TRA	Tax Reform Act of 1986
TJTC	Targeted Jobs Tax Credit

PART ONE

Overview

Introduction

MANY AUTHORS fear that events will somehow conspire to invalidate their research as soon as it is published. One of my goals in writing this book, oddly enough, is to hasten the demise of my subject. If I do my job well, the hidden welfare state will start to disappear. The various programs may continue, but their politics will no longer be so mysterious.

This study throws new light on the American welfare state by examining a powerful but poorly understood tool of social policy—tax expenditures. Tax expenditures, popularly known as tax loopholes or tax breaks, are "departures from the normal tax structure . . . designed to favor a particular industry, activity, or class of persons."[1] They can take the form of tax deductions, tax credits, preferential tax rates, tax deferrals, or outright exclusion of income from taxation. They subsidize a broad range of activities, from oil exploration to the rehabilitation of historic buildings. The focus of this study is tax expenditures with social welfare objectives, meaning those that parallel direct expenditures for income security, health care, employment and training, housing, social services, education, and veterans' benefits. Familiar examples include tax deductions for home mortgage interest and charitable contributions. Altogether, tax expenditures with social welfare objectives cost approximately $400 billion in 1995.[2]

Despite their impressive size and scope, tax expenditures with social welfare objectives are largely invisible to citizens, policy makers, and academics who study U.S. social policy. Many people are unfamiliar with the term *tax expenditures* (though they recognize the terms *tax loopholes* or *tax breaks*) and are unaware of their magnitude. Few people connect tax expenditures with social policy, believing instead that these loopholes benefit only powerful corporations and wealthy individuals. Few studies of social policy have ever drawn attention to the importance of these tax expenditures. For these reasons I refer to tax expenditures with social welfare objectives as the "hidden welfare state."[3] Programs like Social Security, Medicare, and Aid to Families with Dependent Children (AFDC, now Temporary Assistance to Needy Families) constitute the visible welfare state of direct expenditures.

Intuitively it may seem strange to equate the failure to collect taxes with government spending, yet most public finance experts consider tax expenditures to be "conceptually equivalent" to direct spending.[4] They portray tax expenditures as a simultaneous exchange of cash: taxpayers write a check to the government for their full tax liability, and the government issues them a check to cover those activities exempted from taxation. The major government organizations responsible for tax policy accept this line of reasoning. According to the Senate Budget Committee, tax expenditures "may, in effect, be viewed as the equivalent of a simultaneous collection of revenue and a direct budget outlay of an equal amount to the beneficiary taxpayer."[5] They "are considered to be analogous to direct expenditure programs, and the two can be viewed as alternative means of accomplishing similar policy objectives,"[6] says the Joint Committee on Taxation. Policy makers certainly have no trouble understanding the concept of tax expenditures. In the words of Russell Long, then chairman of the Senate Finance Committee, "that label don't bother me . . . I've never been confused about it. I've always known that what we're doing was giving government money away."[7]

Some people, mostly conservatives, do not accept the equivalence between direct expenditures and tax expenditures. Their main argument is that "the concept of listing uncollected taxes as an expenditure is rooted in the notion that all income belongs to the government and only the generosity of the government allows us to have the income we produce."[8] One reason the recent Commission on Entitlement and Tax Reform was unable to agree on a set of recommendations is that a few of the most conservative members refused to discuss cutting tax expenditures as a means of reducing entitlement spending or raising taxes. Many of the liberal and moderate members insisted just as strongly that tax expenditures be on the table.[9] Conservatives' opposition to the concept of tax expenditures is dismissed here mostly because it is a minority view with little support from academic experts and little effect on government practice. Moreover, conservatives' defense of tax incentives contradicts their principled opposition to government interference with market forces. Tax incentives inevitably favor certain groups and activities, which means that government is selectively influencing individual and corporate behavior. My strong suspicion is that what conservatives are really opposed to is government spending, and they see tax expenditures as an expedient (if second-best) means of choking off tax revenues for programs they dislike. That is a separate debate.

The central question of this study is how the hidden welfare state changes our understanding of social policy in the United States, an understanding until now based solely on the visible welfare state of direct expenditure programs. In particular, this study analyzes the politics of creating, expanding, and retrenching social programs. Answers to this question are based primarily on four case studies of tax expenditures: home mortgage interest, employer-provided retirement pensions, the Earned Income Tax Credit (EITC), and the Targeted Jobs Tax Credit (TJTC). Evidence from other tax expenditures is introduced periodically to give readers a general sense of the size and scope of the hidden welfare state and to reinforce some of the key findings from the four cases. This two-pronged approach is driven partly by necessity, to compensate for the fragmentary nature of the evidence, and partly by choice, to give readers a richer understanding of the hidden welfare state.

THE NEED FOR THIS STUDY

The hidden welfare state is part of a larger blind spot in the academic literature. By defining the American welfare state as the sum of direct expenditure programs like Social Security and AFDC, scholars have ignored indirect tools of social policy such as loans, loan guarantees, and tax expenditures.[10] As a result, they have overlooked dozens of indirect spending programs costing hundreds of billions of dollars. Although the most important of these indirect tools are tax expenditures, one can easily imagine a similar study of loan guarantees for housing and education.[11] These latter programs have been instrumental in making home ownership and higher education available to millions of citizens.

The exclusion of indirect spending is impossible to justify. Every commonly accepted definition of the "welfare state" and "social policy" makes room for both direct and indirect social spending. It does not matter whether one defines the welfare state as an instrument of social control or social betterment; as a part of the state or a particular stage in the development of capitalist states; as a minimal safety net for those in need; social insurance for the middle classes; or everything the government does to improve the well-being of individuals and families.[12] None of these definitions stipulates *how* these various goals are to be accomplished or what *form* these goods and services must take. Scholarly convention, not reality, dictates that we equate the welfare state with direct expenditures. In fact, governments can and do use a variety of direct and indirect tools for promoting social welfare. Some welfare states, notably the United States, appear to rely heavily on indirect spending. Although this study focuses solely on the United States, cross-national studies of indirect social spending could prove quite interesting.[13]

This study is not the first to make connections between tax policy and social policy. That distinction belongs to a provocative essay written in the 1950s by the British sociologist Richard Titmuss. Tax expenditures, according to Titmuss, constituted a system of "fiscal welfare." This system was conceptually distinct from the social welfare system of direct public spending and the occupational welfare system of fringe benefits.[14] This insight was largely ignored until the 1980s, when a few scholars began to acknowledge the existence of tax expenditures and occasionally hint at their importance. Tax expenditures, according to Flora and

Heidenheimer, constitute "the third and often neglected method" of providing welfare benefits, along with transfer payments and in-kind services.[15] That said, the authors then proceed to omit tax expenditures from their influential explanation of the development of modern welfare states. In their sweeping survey of U.S. social and economic policies, Amenta and Skocpol draw a provocative analogy between contemporary tax expenditures and nineteenth-century patronage policies, but they do not elaborate.[16] A few scholars, notably Abramovitz, Lampman, and Peterson, compare aggregate expenditures for direct and indirect social programs without examining concrete examples of tax expenditures. Nor do they compare the politics of direct versus indirect spending programs.[17] Among students of social policy, Rein and Rainwater and the Gilberts have written the best theoretical analyses of tax expenditures. Probably the most detailed empirical work belongs to Stevens, whose study of employer pensions in the United States helped to animate my own research.[18] None of these studies, however, systematically compares the politics of tax expenditures and direct expenditures or generalizes about policy making in the hidden welfare state.

Tax expenditures have received closer scrutiny by students of taxation and budgetary politics.[19] A relatively small group of tax lawyers, economists, and political scientists has tried to make tax expenditures more visible, principally to academics and policy makers interested in budgetary reform. Their studies typically list the theoretical advantages and disadvantages of tax expenditures versus direct spending as tools of public policy. They show that the benefits of tax expenditures accrue disproportionately to more affluent citizens and powerful corporations. Some chart the impressive growth of tax expenditures over the past quarter of a century. And some of these studies describe the unusual institutional setting in which tax expenditures are created. The consensus is that tax expenditures are bad public policy: they are economically inefficient; they complicate the tax system; their growth is uncontrollable; and, because they are rarely deliberated over or reviewed, they lack the legitimacy of direct spending programs. The message of these studies is clear. If policy makers wish to control the budget deficit and make sound policy decisions, they have to exert tighter control over tax expenditures.[20]

For the purposes of this study, the tax policy literature is limited in several respects. The conclusions drawn are based on evidence from tax expenditures that favor wealthy individuals, specific companies, specific industries, or business generally.[21] To the extent that these exemptions are justified at all, the stated rationale is usually promotion of economic growth. The mass media perpetuate this equation of all tax expenditures with the rich and powerful, in part because the gyrations required to tailor the tax code to a single firm or a single individual make such good copy.[22] Tax bills are often referred to as Christmas tree bills because of legislators' habit of decorating them with tax expenditures targeted at their favorite special interests. Though important, the attention devoted to these tax expenditures in the media and in Washington is disproportionate to their size. Many are one-time exemptions (i.e., transition rules), and those provisions that are permanent cost the government less than one-third the revenues lost through tax expenditures with social welfare objectives. The prevailing wisdom therefore rests on a narrow empirical foundation that excludes the majority of tax expenditures. The four cases in this study indicate strongly that the patterns described by these authors do not apply to many tax expenditures.

Second, these authors discuss tax expenditures in the context of tax policy and budgetary reform, not social policy. They are interested in the ways in which tax expenditures affect decisions about raising revenue and appropriating funds. They are not interested in investigating how tax expenditures change our understanding of the American welfare state. Third and equally important, they seldom explore the *politics* of individual tax expenditures. A few authors may explain how tax expenditures are created, but they ignore the subsequent politics of sustaining and administering tax expenditures. Once enacted, tax expenditures are allegedly removed from politics because they are immune from the annual appropriations process and insulated against other mechanisms of audit and oversight; this insulation is part of their appeal. Students of tax policy do not investigate the politics of tax expenditures because they believe that none exists.

As a result, the hidden welfare state occupies a sort of no-man's land between the social policy and tax policy literatures. This study begins to chart that territory.

Admittedly, the prospect of slogging through the notoriously complex U.S. tax code in order to gain a better view of the American welfare state may strike some readers as a slightly perverse academic exercise, of interest only to a small number of specialists. Nothing could be farther from the truth. Tax expenditures have become central to contemporary debates over fiscal and social policy, and this study helps shed light on those debates as well. The most obvious link is to the deficit. Policy makers have become increasingly concerned about the negative consequences of persistent peacetime deficits over the last decade. One approach is to reduce or eliminate tax expenditures, thereby increasing tax revenues without increasing tax rates.[23] A desire for deficit reduction, as we shall see, had an impact on the development of several cases in this study. As this book went to press, the 1996 presidential election was shaping up as a duel between competing packages of tax cuts and tax credits, with each candidate insisting that his proposal would not increase the deficit. Similarly, debates over comprehensive tax reform, such as those leading up to the Tax Reform Act of 1986 and more recent flat tax proposals, almost always lead to debates over tax expenditures.

Tax expenditures have moved to the center of debates over social policy. One widely accepted goal of welfare reform is to "make work pay" for the poor, and one favorite approach is the Earned Income Tax Credit. When congressional Republicans tried cutting the EITC in 1995 in order to lower the deficit, they were roundly criticized for undercutting welfare reform and punishing the working poor. Much of the recent debate over family policy has revolved around tax credits and tax deductions for child care. The bipartisan National Commission on Children, for example, recommended expanding the EITC and creating a refundable tax credit worth $1,000 per child in 1991. Rather than sign legislation mandating unpaid parental leave, President Bush endorsed tax credits for companies who offered employees this benefit. With respect to employment policy, the Los Angeles riots of 1992 rekindled interest in using tax incentives to lure employers into the inner cities, where decent jobs are scarce and unemployment is distressingly high. To foster a better-skilled, more flexible workforce, Labor Secretary Reich recently proposed tax incentives for employers who retrain their workers.

Tax expenditures have played a central role in debates over health care reform. The existing tax subsidy for employer-provided health benefits has been blamed for rising health care costs. Critics claim that this program has made consumers less price conscious than they would be in a "pure" market. They wish to reduce or eliminate this program, which costs the government tens of billions of dollars, and perhaps use the savings to extend coverage to the uninsured. In contrast, a number of moderate and conservative policy makers view tax expenditures as the key to making health care more available. They propose creating tax credits to offset the costs of purchasing health insurance (e.g., by subsidizing individual Medical Savings Accounts). Their arguments are similar to those offered earlier in connection with welfare reform, family policy, and employment policy: tax expenditures are a less intrusive, less bureaucratic alternative to government regulations or direct expenditures. They work with the market rather than against it. These arguments tend to be asserted in the abstract and are generally not supported by concrete evidence.

At a more general level we need a better understanding of who gets what from government.[24] There is, still, a misconception that U.S. social programs primarily benefit the poor. That is not true for the visible welfare state of direct expenditures, and it is an absurd claim to make about the hidden welfare state. Tax expenditures, as we shall see in the next chapter, flow overwhelmingly to citizens with above-average incomes. By the same token, it is common to underestimate how many people depend on government for employment and income. Government bureaucrats are easy to spot. Less visible are the networks of third-party service providers who deliver health care, child care, housing, and job training to eligible citizens. Their presence creates an additional constituency for social programs and raises questions of democratic accountability. These networks are even more prevalent in the hidden welfare state than in the visible welfare state.

In short, policy makers have started to recognize tax expenditures as an integral tool of fiscal policy and social policy. Their actions, however, have usually been based on some mixture of anecdote, atypical cases, and sheer speculation. For purely practical reasons, it is essential that we understand why tax expenditures were created, who supports them once they are created, and what factors have contributed to their growth or retrenchment.

THE ARGUMENT IN BRIEF

Simply because the hidden welfare state is unexplored territory is no guarantee that its terrain is unfamiliar or unique. Conceivably, tax expenditures with social welfare objectives might mirror traditional social programs in all important respects. When I started this project, I did not care how close a resemblance I might find. If the hidden welfare state looked much like the visible welfare state, then existing generalizations about the politics of social policy in the United States would be that much more powerful. If the hidden welfare state was sui generis, then these generalizations would have to be confined to direct spending programs. In either case we would gain a better understanding of U.S. social policy.

As I examined the overall structure of the hidden welfare state and became more familiar with the politics of four separate programs, I was repeatedly struck by the distinctiveness of the hidden welfare state. The contrasts were so numerous that I decided to devote most of my efforts to describing them and offering explanations for them. The most important differences include:

1. the relative ease with which tax expenditures are enacted;
2. the role of moderate and conservative politicians in creating and sustaining the hidden welfare state;
3. the near absence of interest groups representing the nominal beneficiaries of each program, leaving third-party providers as the core societal advocates;

4. the institutional arena, comprising congressional revenue committees, the Treasury Department, and the Internal Revenue Service (IRS);
5. the ability of some targeted tax expenditures to grow during the 1980s and 1990s, despite escalating budget deficits, Republican administrations, and heightened criticism of traditional "welfare" programs; and
6. the difficulties facing policy makers who wish to influence the size and distribution of benefits conferred in the hidden welfare state.

In effect, the hidden welfare state illustrates a greater range of political possibilities for social programs in the United States than we are accustomed to seeing.

The distinctive politics of the hidden welfare state mean that we must approach the subject from a new angle. Virtually all students of the American welfare state equate social spending with direct expenditures, and most of them implicitly or explicitly invoke comparisons with European welfare states. Much of their analytic energy is therefore devoted to explaining what did not happen in the United States but did happen in other advanced industrial nations. Their primary task is identifying the major barriers to welfare state formation and expansion in the United States. Once we include tax expenditures, see how common their introduction has been, and note their impressive growth, we become less interested in barriers. We start to search instead for those features of American politics that create possibilities for a different type of social program. That search reveals a curious paradox: some of the same features that inhibit the creation and expansion of traditional social programs unintentionally promote the hidden welfare state. These features help us account for the differences listed above.

The most important feature is Congress. Congress has typically been portrayed as an impediment to the American welfare state. This barrier results partly from the fragmentation of authority within Congress and partly from the historical prominence of conservative southern Democrats, who often block or dilute social welfare legislation.[25] Congress is in some respects better designed to enact new tax expenditures than new direct expenditures, and the same conservative legislators who oppose direct expenditures often support tax expenditures. Primary emphasis is placed on the two revenue committees, Senate Finance and House Ways and Means, that have exclusive jurisdiction over tax expenditures. The second feature to note are political parties. Though parties and party competition are usually considered irrelevant to social programs at the national level, tax expenditures are different. Because tax expenditures are tied closely to tax policy, and tax policy is a common site of party competition, parties matter in the hidden welfare state.

The importance of Congress, conservative legislators, and parties is rooted, to some extent, in certain properties of tax expenditures as a policy tool. Tax expenditures are incentives rather than commands. Like school vouchers, they are believed to promote individual choice and consumer sovereignty; like "green taxes" and emissions trading programs, they are thought to be a more flexible, less bureaucratic tool of public policy. They are more compatible with the classical liberal values of limited government and individual liberty, values some argue have inhibited the growth of the visible welfare state.[26] As a market-like tool, tax expenditures appeal to moderate Republicans and conservative Democrats in ways that direct expenditures do not. "My natural inclination," said Sen. Pete Domenici (R-N.Mex.) in 1977, after proposing a new tax credit for the elderly, ". . . is to let people do the problem-solving rather than the government."[27] A related benefit of this tool is the potential for avoiding government bureaucracy. Relying on individuals and corporations to make policy, however, limits the ability of public officials to control the subsequent development of tax expenditures. Everything from changes in tax rates and inflation to collective bargaining agreements over fringe benefits can have a sizable impact on these programs. Public officials, much less those officials formally responsible for tax expenditures, have great difficulty influencing many of these factors. More so than Social Security or Medicare, tax expenditures are the embodiment of "uncontrollable spending."

Perhaps the more important attribute of tax expenditures is their *ambiguity*. Tax expenditures can be defended politically on at least four distinct grounds: as aid to some needy category of citizens; as a subsidy to third-party providers in the private sector, who furnish most of the goods and services underwritten by the tax code; as tax reductions; and as alternatives to traditional government programs (i.e., direct expenditures and regulation).[28] These various objectives are not mutually exclusive. Policy makers can and do support tax expenditures for more than one reason. Such ambiguity helps proponents of new tax expenditures forge broader coalitions of support than proponents of direct expenditures are typically able to do. In particular, such ambiguity helps conservative Democrats and moderate Republicans to support tax expenditures more strongly than they do direct expenditures.

To understand the development of tax expenditures, we must therefore understand how their distinctive properties affect policy making. This line of reasoning is a familiar one in political science. James Q. Wilson, for example, describes how the perceived distribution of costs and benefits affects patterns of policy making. Theodore Lowi argues that developmental, regulatory, and redistributive policies develop in distinctly different ways.[29] My argument is that the differences between direct expenditures and tax expenditures as policy tools affect the nature of political support for each type of spending. These policy attributes determine the politics of tax expenditures less, however, than the attributes highlighted by Wilson and Lowi. The historic links to tax policy and the inherent ambiguity of tax expenditures increase the significance of historical contingency.[30] They increase the likelihood that individual programs will experience significant discontinuities as a result of unpredictable events occurring elsewhere in the polity. It is, in short, harder to predict the future path of tax expenditures than it is for other types of public programs.

Readers familiar with prevailing schools of thought in the social sciences will recognize the basic approach of this study as institutional.[31] My argument emphasizes the ways in which specific institutions—particularly Congress and the structure of tax expenditures as a policy tool—influence the politics of the hidden welfare state. Institutional approaches to politics are often criticized for being overly "statist," for ignoring developments in civil society. While this criticism can be overstated, it contains a grain (or two) of truth. Readers will discover that it is impossible to understand the hidden welfare state without accounting for economic variables and interest groups, two key elements of civil society. Indeed, a central part of my argument is that the structure of tax expenditures places real limits on the capacity of government officials to influence these programs. This approach is consistent with recent institutional analyses that emphasize the complex relationships among state structures, public officials, and societal actors.[32]

The approach of this book is also decidedly historical.[33] The use of history is helpful in analyzing tax expenditures because evidence for any single year or interesting episode is often spotty. It also gives added leverage to the case study design: by tracing the development of programs over a longer span of time (in two cases almost a century), we can start to recognize patterns of policy making.[34] A historical approach is particularly appropriate in a study of U.S. social policy. Most of the important works in this field have been explicitly historical, concerned either with a decisive, early moment of creation (e.g., the New Deal) or with a period of development spanning several decades.[35] They have tried to answer a common set of questions—How are new social programs created? Who or what is responsible for their subsequent growth?—using inductive reasoning and a wealth of empirical evidence. In order to facilitate comparisons between the hidden welfare state and the visible welfare state, it seemed wise to adopt a similar approach and ask a similar set of questions.

THE PLAN OF THIS BOOK

One advantage of a book based on several case studies is that it can be read in parts or from cover to cover. Readers who want a general introduction to the hidden welfare state can focus on the first and last parts of the book, Overview and Conclusion. They should also read the introductions to the the two middle parts of the book, Origins and Development, which contrast what we might expect and what we actually observe in more detail than is found in the concluding chapter. This format is somewhat unorthodox in that it presents several of the main conclusions before providing the supporting evidence. The advantage, though, is alerting readers to certain key themes that run through the cases so they will not lose the forest for the trees. Those who are interested in a particular program should read the relevant chapters in part 2 (Origins) and part 3 (Development).

Chapter 1 is a general introduction to the hidden welfare state. Assuming that most readers are unfamiliar with this topic, I compare the size and scope of tax expenditures that have social welfare objectives with their direct spending counterparts. These comparisons are revealing and suggest that in several ways the structure of the hidden welfare state is as distinctive as its politics. In addition, this chapter indicates that the four cases chosen for in-depth study are "typical" tax expenditures in several important respects.

The origins and development of tax expenditures are discussed separately in parts 2 and 3 because scholars have increasingly found that these two processes require different kinds of explanations.[36] This pattern holds as well for the hidden welfare state: tax expenditures receive broader support and are more clearly "political" after their enactment than before. Each part opens with a brief summary of the received wisdom, primarily concerning U.S. social programs and secondarily concerning tax expenditures. This summary creates a baseline against which evidence from the four cases can be compared. Part 2, which includes chapters 2, 3, and 4, accounts for the origins of the tax expenditures for home mortgage interest and employer pensions, the EITC, and the TJTC, respectively. These chapters describe the timing of new programs, the specific actors responsible for enactment, and the larger political, economic, and social conditions associated with enactment. Part 3 (chapters 5 through 8) follows the same format in accounting for the development of these four tax expenditures after their enactment. Particular attention is paid to the scope of conflict and to program size. Scope of conflict is defined broadly to include the number and range of actors who work for or against the program, how often the program is amended, and the magnitude of changes to the program's structure.[37] Program size refers to the program's estimated cost.

Chapter 9 generalizes about policy making in the hidden welfare state. It summarizes common themes from the four cases and includes evidence from other tax expenditures that are consistent with these themes. The resulting patterns are fairly clear, and I offer some explanations for them. As mentioned above, two of the most important reasons for the distinctive politics of tax expenditures involve Congress and certain attributes of tax expenditures as a policy tool.

THE FOUR CASE STUDIES

Because four case studies form the heart of this book, it is important to choose them with care.[38] In doing so, I tried to strike a balance among cases that are somehow typical, that are important in their own right, and for which evidence is available. Knowing little about the relevant differences among tax expenditures, I chose cases based on previous research into traditional social programs. Whatever their disagreements, and there are many, students of social policy agree on one central fact. Two kinds of social programs exist in the United States: inclusive programs, which are usually structured along social insurance principles (e.g., Social Security and Medicare),[39] and means-tested programs, which are targeted at the poor, the most notorious being AFDC. Each type exhibits a different kind of politics. The former enjoys widespread support, provides decent and uniform benefits, and treats recipients with respect. The latter is morally and politically suspect. It conjures up images of "welfare fraud" and "the dole." Benefits vary considerably by state, are seldom adequate to lift recipients out of poverty, and can be difficult to obtain. Two of my cases, home mortgage interest and employer pensions, are inclusive programs. The other two, the Earned Income Tax Credit and the Targeted Jobs Tax Credit, are means-tested.[40]

A second distinction commonly found in the literature is between cash transfers and in-kind benefits. In the visible welfare state, cash transfers (e.g., Social Security and unemployment insurance) were generally created before in-kind benefits (e.g., Medicare and Medicaid). The two types of programs also differ in their bases of political support, with third-party providers rallying around in-kind benefits they deliver but not around cash transfers. Two of my cases, employer pensions and the EITC, qualify as cash transfers; the other two, home mortgage interest and the TJTC, provide in-kind benefits.

One can thus imagine a simple two-by-two matrix with inclusive/targeted on one axis and cash transfer/in-kind benefit on the other (Table I.1). Each case in this study corresponds to one of the four quadrants.

TABLE I.1
The Four Case Studies

	Cash transfer	In-kind benefit
Inclusive	Employer pensions	Home mortgage interest
Means-tested	Earned Income Tax Credit (EITC)	Targeted Jobs Tax Credit (TJTC)

The tax expenditure for employer pensions is an inclusive cash transfer to retirees, closely akin to Social Security.[41] It allows companies to deduct certain contributions to pension plans from their adjusted gross income, thereby lowering their corporate income taxes. The investment income from these contributions is not taxed until it is actually disbursed to retirees, when most face lower tax rates, and this deferral lowers individuals' income taxes. The home mortgage interest deduction is an inclusive in-kind benefit that is restricted to consumption of a specific good, namely, housing. There is no counterpart to it among traditional housing programs; its closest analog is Medicare.

Both the Earned Income Tax Credit (EITC) and its direct spending counterpart, Aid to Families with Dependent Children (AFDC), transfer cash to families with dependent children who fall below a certain income threshold.[42] The EITC works by reducing the income tax burdens of the poor and near-poor and often generating a tax refund. For families with two or more children, the EITC equaled almost 36 percent of the first $8,600 in earned income (known as the phase-in range) in 1995, a flat $3,110 for incomes between $8,600 and $11,300, and $3,110 minus twenty cents for every dollar earned between $11,300 and $26,673 (the phase-out range). Families with one child are eligible for a smaller tax credit, and those without children have been eligible for a tiny credit since 1994. The EITC was also selected because it was one of the few tax expenditures to generate widespread interest among policy makers and the media when this project started. The fourth and final case is the Targeted Jobs Tax Credit. It subsidizes employment and training for select categories of disadvantaged workers by allowing employers to deduct 40 percent of the first $6,000 in workers' wages from their corporate income taxes, providing the individual had remained with the company for a minimal period of time. The TJTC parallels direct spending programs covered by the Job Training Partnership Act (JTPA).

A WORD ABOUT SOURCES

Perhaps by design, tax expenditures leave a fainter paper trail than comparable direct spending programs. Although their low profile can be a decided advantage for the programs' advocates, it presents problems for researchers. A study such as this one must therefore piece together evidence from a variety of sources, as a casual glance at the endnotes will indicate. Piecing together a coherent account of tax expenditures, I discovered, was much like reconstructing a crime scene or a very bad accident. As secondary sources, I refer to the social policy and tax policy literatures in the introductions to part 2 (Origins) and part 3 (Development) in order to generate a series of hypotheses about the politics of the hidden welfare state. Assorted economics, public finance, law, industrial relations, public policy, and political science journals sometimes contained articles concerning tax expenditures but seldom about their politics. Government documents proved more useful. Cost estimates for tax expenditures are generated by Congress's Joint Committee on Taxation (JCT) and by the Office of Management and Budget (OMB), in conjunction with the Treasury Department. The Congressional Budget Office (CBO), Congressional Research Service (CRS), and General Accounting Office (GAO) occasionally issue summaries of major legislative changes to individual tax expenditures. The *Congressional Record* and transcripts of congressional hearings provide clues as to who is supporting individual tax expenditures, the reasons for their support, and how well the program is working. *Tax Notes, National Journal,* the weekly and annual publications by Congressional Quarterly, Inc., and major newspapers often report not only the major provisions of tax bills but also the details, which is where tax expenditures often lurk. Trade journals like *Nation's Building News, Mortgage Banking,* and *Nation's Restaurant News* offered insights into the political activities of third-party providers. These written records were supplemented with personal interviews of current and former congressional staff, current and former Treasury staff, tax lawyers, academic economists, and interest-group advocates (see the appendix). These individuals provided me with an indispensable education in the theory and practice of tax expenditures. Their help was particularly crucial in analyzing the development of the two targeted programs, the TJTC and EITC, where written records were often lacking.

CHAPTER 1

Sizing Up the Hidden Welfare State

THIS CHAPTER offers an aerial view of the hidden welfare state. The purpose is to show readers the general lay of the land before investigating four regions in greater detail. How big is this hidden welfare state? What are its distinguishing features? How has it changed over time? To put these features in context, comparisons are made periodically between tax expenditures and direct expenditures. This overview raises several interesting questions about the politics of the hidden welfare state—such as who has authority over these programs and who has an interest in their continuation and expansion—that are addressed in subsequent chapters. It also demonstrates that the cases chosen for closer examination capture important differences between tax expenditures in addition to important differences between traditional social programs.

This chapter reinforces some beliefs about the structure of the American welfare state and challenges others. On the one hand, once tax expenditures are included, known strengths in retirement income become more pronounced. Programmatic fragmentation, long a hallmark of U.S. social policy, is even more pervasive. The notion that benefits flow mainly to the poor becomes even harder to sustain. On the other hand, perceived gaps in housing and family policies begin to disappear after we take into account tax deductions for home mortgage interest, property taxes, and child care. Agencies thought to be irrelevant to social policy, notably the Treasury Department and its Internal Revenue Service (IRS), emerge and take center stage. Perhaps the most striking finding is how much larger the entire American welfare state looks after including tax expenditures. The hidden welfare state is almost half the size of the visible welfare state, making the United States appear less a welfare state laggard than many cross-national studies claim. The United States may not spend less on social welfare than other countries do; it may just spend similar amounts of public monies in different ways.[1]

Readers should exercise a degree of caution when reading the following map of the hidden welfare state. Experts familiar with the intricacies of the U.S. tax code find it hard to measure tax expenditures precisely. They disagree about which provisions should count as tax expenditures and how best to express their cost. Even when the Treasury Department/Office of Management and Budget and Congress's Joint Committee on Taxation (JCT) use the same method to estimate future costs, they rely on different assumptions about the economy and produce different numbers. Moreover, although policy makers try to group tax expenditures in the same categories used for direct expenditures—thus facilitating comparisons between the two types of spending—plenty of judgment calls are needed, and some programs switch categories over time.

Nevertheless, these disagreements are less of an obstacle than they appear. Many of them concern tax expenditures that lie outside the hidden welfare state, and others affect truly minor programs. The most important issue to keep in mind is the impact of different methods of estimating the cost of individual programs. Where possible, I provide a range of cost estimates. This approach seems reasonable considering that the basic purpose here is to explore a large and overlooked realm of government activity and not to provide a detailed map of the entire terrain. Whether the tax treatment of employer-provided retirement pensions is expected to cost $69 billion in revenue losses or $76 billion in budget outlay equivalents in 1995 is not so important. What matters is that public spending on retirement income is tens of billions of dollars greater than most people realize and that the national government helps subsidize pensions usually considered to be purely private.

SIZE AND STRUCTURE

Sizing up the hidden welfare state and then comparing it to the visible welfare state requires a series of judgments about which programs to include and how to calculate their cost. Because these judgments influence my findings, it is important to make them as transparent as possible. One of the first choices concerns the operational definition of "social policy" or the "welfare state." If one thinks of social policy only in terms of programs targeted at the poor, then few tax expenditures qualify. Readers who equate social policy strictly with a residual safety net of income and services ("welfare" in its pejorative sense) will not find their view of the American welfare state challenged in this chapter.[2] The overwhelming majority of tax expenditure dollars benefit individuals well above the poverty line. Nevertheless, such a definition excludes programs like Social Security and Medicare that policy makers, academics, and ordinary citizens routinely mention when they discuss social policy or the welfare state. To most people, social programs guarantee a minimum standard of living *and* protect citizens against losses of income beyond their control, especially losses caused by retirement, sickness, disability, or unemployment. The welfare state contains a public assistance component and a social insurance component. It serves both the poor and the middle class.[3] This more inclusive definition is employed here.

A second choice involves specifying which programs count as social policy, meaning which ones have social welfare as their primary (but not exclusive) objective. The usual approach, both in government documents and academic studies, is to equate social welfare with a specific list of government functions. Virtually everyone can agree to exclude certain government functions like national defense, energy, commerce, and transportation. These omissions are important, for they eliminate many well-known and lesser-known tax expenditures from consideration. One can, for instance, rule out the accelerated depreciation of machinery and equipment, a major incentive for corporate investment. One can do the same to multiperiod timber growing costs that are incurred, no doubt, from IRS-approved trees.

The U.S. government typically counts spending for income security, health, housing, education, employment and training, social services, and veterans' programs as social welfare expenditures. Academic studies generally accept this framework and sometimes distinguish between functions at the core and the periphery.[4] Core functions usually include income security, health, employment, and job training. These functions share several features: the need for them is rooted in the dislocations created by industrialization; they tend to be structured as social insurance programs; and they tend to have been the first social programs enacted in Europe and North America. Housing, social services, education, and veterans' programs usually occupy the periphery.[5] Some scholars count only core programs to be social policy; most count core and periphery. Although I employ the broader definition of social policy, I will present the data in such a way that readers who prefer a more restrictive definition can make the relevant calculations and comparisons.

Likewise, I have chosen not to limit social policy to those programs that promote income equality.[6] Redistribution from rich to poor may be an admirable goal, but it does not accurately reflect recent experience. Since World War II, the distribution of income has not become significantly more equal in modern welfare states and has steadily become less equal in the United States over the last two decades. Social programs are designed to redistribute income more across generational lines than across income lines. To remain consistent with prevailing definitions of social policy and the historical record, this chapter includes programs that do little to promote income equality among classes.

Along with deciding which beneficiaries and functions to include, one must determine which provisions count as tax expenditures. The official government list seems like a good place to start, except that there are two official lists. The Treasury Department's list of tax expenditures (used by the executive Office of Management and Budget, OMB) is

TABLE 1.1
The Hidden Welfare State: Major Programs, 1995 (billions of dollars)

Budget function and program	Revenue loss	Budget outlay equivalent
INCOME SECURITY		
Net exclusion of pension contributions and earnings		
Employer plans	$69.4	$75.9
Individual retirement plans	8.4	8.9
Keogh plans	3.1	6.0
Exclusion of untaxed Social Security and railroad retirement benefits	23.1	22.4
Exclusion of capital gains at death	12.7	37.7
Exclusion of investment income on life insurance and annuity contracts	11.1	13.6
Maximum 28% tax rate on long-term capital gains	9.1	8.2
Exclusion of miscellaneous fringe benefits	4.9	NA
Exclusion of benefits provided under cafeteria plans	3.8	NA
Exclusion of workers' compensation benefits	3.9	4.5
Earned Income Tax Credit (EITC)	3.5[a]	5.7[b]
Exclusion of other employee benefits		
Group term life insurance	2.0	3.7
Accident and disability insurance	0.2	0.2
Additional standard deduction for the blind and the elderly	1.9	1.8
Deferral of interest on savings bonds	1.3	1.4
Special tax provisions for Employee Stock Ownership Plans (ESOPs)	0.9	2.6
Exclusion of cash public assistance benefits	0.5	0.6
Deductibility of casualty and theft losses	0.1	0.6
Exclusion of special benefits for disabled coal miners	0.1	0.1

TABLE 1.1 (*cont.*)

Budget function and program	Revenue loss	Budget outlay equivalent
Exclusion of employee awards	0.1	NA
Tax credit for the elderly and disabled	(*)	0.1
Exclusion of employer-provided death benefits	(*)	(*)
HEALTH		
Exclusion of employer contributions for medical insurance premiums and medical care	45.8	77.3
Exclusion of untaxed Medicare benefits		
Part A—hospital insurance	8.0	NA
Part B—supplementary medical insurance	5.1	NA
Deductibility of extraordinary medical expenses	4.1	3.7
Deductibility of charitable contributions to health organizations	1.7	2.0
Exclusion of interest on state and local government bonds for private nonprofit hospital facilities	1.6	2.2
EMPLOYMENT AND TRAINING		
Exclusion of income earned by voluntary employee beneficiary organizations	0.5	(*)
Targeted Jobs Tax Credit	0.2	0.4
HOUSING		
Deductibility of mortgage interest on owner-occupied residences	53.5	51.3
Deferral of capital gains on sale of principal residences	14.8	17.1

TABLE 1.1 (*cont.*)

Budget function and program	Revenue loss	Budget outlay equivalent
Deductibility of property tax on owner-occupied homes	13.7	14.8
Exclusion of capital gains on sales of principal residences for persons aged 55 and older ($125,000 exclusion)	4.9	6.4
Low-income housing tax credit	2.2	2.3
Exclusion of interest on state and local government bonds for owner-occupied housing	1.9	2.6
Depreciation of rental housing in excess of alternative depreciation system	1.7	1.3
Exclusion of interest on state and local government bonds for rental housing	0.9	1.3
Exclusion of rental allowances for ministers' homes	0.3	0.3
SOCIAL SERVICES		
Deductibility of charitable contributions, other than education and health	14.3	25.0
Credit for child and dependent care expenses	2.7	3.9
Exclusion for employer-provided child care	0.6	0.9
Expensing of costs for removing architectural barriers to the disabled	(*)	(*)
Credit for disabled access expenditures	(*)	(*)
Exclusion for certain foster care payments	(*)	(*)
EDUCATION		
Exclusion of charitable contributions for educational institutions	2.5	2.3
Parental personal exemption for students aged 19 to 23	0.9	0.9

TABLE 1.1 (*cont.*)

Budget function and program	Revenue loss	Budget outlay equivalent
Exclusion of interest on state and local government bonds for private educational facilities	0.8	1.1
Exclusion of scholarship and fellowship income	0.7	0.9
Exclusion of interest on state and local government student loan bonds	0.3	0.4
Exclusion for employer-provided education assistance benefits	0.3	0.1
Exclusion of interest on educational savings bonds	0.1	(*)
VETERANS' BENEFITS AND SERVICES		
Exclusion of veterans' disability compensation	1.6	2.0
Exclusion of veterans' pensions	0.1	0.1
Exclusion of GI bill benefits	0.1	0.1
Exclusion of interest on state and local government bonds for veterans' housing	0.1	0.1

Sources: U.S. Congress, Joint Committee on Taxation (JCT), *Estimates of Federal Tax Expenditures for Fiscal Years 1995–1999* (Washington, D.C.: Government Printing Office, 1994), for revenue losses; Office of Management and Budget (OMB), *Analytical Perspectives, Budget of the United States Government, Fiscal Year 1996* (Washington, D.C.: Government Printing Office, 1995), for budget outlay equivalents.

Notes: (*) denotes less than $50 million. NA means that OMB does not consider this program to be a tax expenditure. In a few cases, budget outlay equivalents are smaller than revenue losses because OMB used more recent data and different assumptions about economic growth and marginal tax rates than did the JCT.

[a] Figures reflect tax revenues not collected; additional refunds total an estimated $18.6 billion in 1995.

[b] Figures reflect tax revenues not collected; additional refunds total an estimated $16.8 billion in 1995.

shorter than that used by Congress's Joint Committee on Taxation, largely because the two organizations use slightly different definitions of the tax baseline and tax expenditures.[7] Treasury and OMB define the tax baseline more broadly and hence recognize fewer tax expenditures than does the JCT. Although many of the differences do not affect the hidden welfare state, occurring in such categories as Commerce and National Defense, some do. The most notable omissions from the Treasury's list are untaxed Medicare benefits and miscellaneous fringe benefits.[8] Reasoning by analogy, it is hard to see why the Treasury would count untaxed Social Security benefits and corporate health insurance benefits as tax expenditures, but not untaxed Medicare benefits. The same goes for its decision to count employer-provided retirement pensions, health insurance, and life insurance but not miscellaneous fringe benefits. The JCT list seems to make more sense and is used wherever possible in this chapter.

We can now offer an initial description of the hidden welfare state. Table 1.1 provides a list of tax expenditures with social welfare objectives for 1995, grouped by traditional categories of income security, health, employment and training, housing, education, social services, and veterans' benefits and services.[9] Anyone who thought the tax code was used solely to raise revenue may be surprised to discover just how many different functions it has, even after eliminating many tax expenditures for commerce, energy, natural resources, and agriculture. They range from providing special benefits for disabled coal miners to fostering home ownership and underwriting a variety of employment-based fringe benefits. The cost of individual programs ranges from less than $50 million to more than $75 billion. In terms of size and scope, the hidden welfare state looks much like the visible welfare state. The sheer number and variety of tax expenditures drive home once again the extent of programmatic fragmentation in U.S. social policy.

This table offers two estimates for the cost of each program. Revenue loss refers to the reduction in income tax liability that results from a given tax expenditure and is the method favored by the JCT. These numbers do not necessarily equal the amount of revenue the government could expect to generate by repealing that tax expenditure. One reason is because tax expenditures are interdependent: repeal of one provision could cause the value of another to change. For instance, eliminating or reducing the home mortgage interest deduction could deter individual taxpayers from itemizing all deductions, as their total would no longer exceed the standard deduction. Other itemized deductions for charitable contributions and extraordinary medical expenses might then decline. Second, tax expenditures are incentives, and the reduction of any one provision may or may not affect the behavior of taxpayers in a simple, linear manner. Readers should also note that the estimated revenue loss is based on individual and corporate income taxes only. Tax experts have found it too difficult to estimate the effects on social insurance and excise taxes, though they believe some effect must exist. That omission implies that these figures may underestimate the true cost of tax expenditures. The revenue loss method has been used since the late 1960s.

Budget outlay equivalence, in contrast, did not appear in government documents until the early 1980s. It estimates the value of a traditional budget outlay "required to provide the taxpayer with the same after-tax income as would be received through the tax preference." Depending on the individual provision, this figure is either greater than or equal to the revenue loss figure. It is larger "when the tax expenditure is judged to function as a Government payment for service. This occurs because an outlay program would increase the taxpayer's pre-tax income." In cases "when the tax expenditure is judged to function like a price reduction or tax deferral that does not directly enter the taxpayer's pre-tax income," the two estimates are the same.[10] The term does not imply that policy makers would in fact replace a tax expenditure with an equivalent budget outlay. It only indicates how much it would cost to deliver the equivalent goods and services through direct expenditures. The difference between revenue loss and outlay equivalence can be significant for individual programs (e.g., employer-provided health benefits).[11] The effect on the overall size of the hidden welfare state is dampened somewhat by the major tax expenditures for housing and retirement income in which the two estimates are nearly identical.

Regardless of how one estimates cost, the hidden welfare state must be quite large—at least a couple hundred billion dollars. Adding tax expenditures, however, is no simple matter. Although some analysts claim that "the differences between an additive summary of tax expenditures and a summary that controls for interactive effects are not large," others are more cautious.[12] The net effect of eliminating one or more tax expenditures simultaneously could have unpredictable effects on other parts of the tax code, as the above example concerning itemized deductions illustrates. But tax expenditures are not unique in this respect. Cuts in direct spending programs can have similar second-order effects elsewhere in the budget. For instance, cuts in disability insurance may prompt more claims for Supplemental Security Income (SSI).[13] A conservative approach would therefore be to consider the sum of tax expenditures as a good ballpark estimate of their overall magnitude.

In 1995 the U.S. government spent approximately $400 billion on social welfare via the tax code. The sum total is $346 billion in revenue losses and $438 billion in budget outlay equivalents (Table 1.2).[14] The

TABLE 1.2
The Hidden and Visible Welfare States, 1995 (billions of dollars)

	Tax expenditures		Direct expenditures	
Budget function	Revenue loss	Budget outlay equivalent	Budget function	Budget outlay
INCOME SECURITY	$160.2[a]	202.7[a]	INCOME SECURITY	$481.3
Employer pensions	69.4	75.9	Social Security (OASI)	294.6
Social Security and rail-road retirement benefits	23.1	22.4	Disability insurance (DI)	41.6
			Federal civilian employee and disability benefits	37.5
			Supplemental Security Income	27.5
			Food Stamps	26.6
			AFDC	17.3
HEALTH	66.3	99.3	HEALTH	272.4
Employer health insurance	45.8	77.3	Medicare	157.3
			Medicaid	88.4
HOUSING	93.9	97.4	HOUSING	24.1
Home mortgage interest	53.5	51.3		
Deferral of capital gains on sale of principle residences	14.8	17.1		
SOCIAL SERVICES	17.7	30.1	SOCIAL SERVICES	15.5
Charity, other than education and health	14.3	25.0		
EDUCATION	5.6	5.7	EDUCATION	32.1
VETERANS	1.9	2.3	VETERANS	38.4
EMPLOYMENT AND TRAINING	0.7	0.4	EMPLOYMENT AND TRAINING	32.2
			Unemployment insurance	23.8
TOTAL	346.3	437.9	TOTAL	896.0

Sources: JCT, Estimates of Federal Tax Expenditures for Fiscal Years 1995–1999; OMB, Analytical Perspectives, Budget of the United States Government, Fiscal Year 1996.
[a] Does not include EITC refund.

beauty of numbers this large is that they could be somewhat overstated and the hidden welfare state would still reflect a huge commitment of public monies and still demand investigation. The right side of Table 1.2 depicts the visible welfare state of direct expenditures, grouped in the same functional categories as the tax expenditures on the left.[15] The visible welfare state cost almost $900 billion in 1995. Depending on how one estimates the cost of tax expenditures, the hidden welfare state is therefore 38 to 50 percent as large as the visible welfare state. This simple comparison suggests that talking about U.S. social policy without mentioning tax expenditures is much like discussing the visible welfare state without mentioning Social Security and Medicaid. You can do it, you just cannot do it well.

To give added perspective to these numbers, consider that in 1995 the hidden welfare state was more than twice as large as all corporate income taxes collected at the national level. The U.S. government spent roughly one dollar on the hidden welfare state for every four dollars it collected from all revenue sources, including payroll taxes.[16] The hidden welfare state was larger than the entire defense budget and far larger than the national deficit that year. It was larger than all means-tested social programs combined. Viewed from any angle, the hidden welfare state represents a massive commitment of fiscal resources.

Within the hidden welfare state, certain functions and certain programs within each function are clearly more important than others. Regardless of how one estimates cost, income security is the single most important function in the hidden welfare state. The national government spent $160–$200 billion on income security via tax expenditures in 1995, making it roughly half the hidden welfare state. The overwhelming majority of monies spent in this category are for retirement income. The tax expenditures for employer-provided retirement plans, Keogh plans (for the self-employed), Individual Retirement Accounts, and Social Security benefits total approximately $110 billion. Employer pensions stand out as one of largest programs in the hidden welfare state; within the visible welfare state only Social Security, Medicare, and Medicaid cost more. The significance of retirement income is similar with regard to direct expenditures, where the combination of Social Security, federal civilian employees' retirement benefits, and Supplemental Security Income equals $400 billion.[17] This finding gives added credence to the claim that retirement income has been one component of social policy in which the United States has been relatively generous compared with other welfare states.[18]

Housing and health are the next two largest functions in the hidden welfare state, and again a few programs dominate the picture. Subsidies for home ownership comprise almost all housing tax expenditures, to the tune of $90 billion per year. Tax subsidies for rental housing and

TABLE 1.3
Distribution of Selected Tax Expenditures, 1994

Tax expenditure	Total amount	*Percentage of total dollar amount claimed by income class*				
		$10K	*10–30K*	*30–50K*	*50–100K*	*100K+*
Home mortgage interest	$51.2B	0.0%	1.9%	10.1%	43.9%	44.2%
State and local income and personal property taxes	23.7	0.0	0.5	5.2	31.9	62.3
Social Security and railroad retirement benefits	22.2	0.3	35.4	46.8	16.3	1.3
EITC	19.6	26.2	71.0	2.6	0.1	0.0
Charitable contributions	16.5	0.0	3.1	10.4	34.3	52.1
Real estate taxes	13.1	0.0	2.1	10.3	44.4	43.2
Extraordinary medical expenses	3.8	0.1	9.9	25.6	44.2	20.2
Child and dependent care	2.7	0.0	20.7	27.8	42.3	9.2

Source: JCT, *Estimates of Federal Tax Expenditures for Fiscal Years 1995–1999.*

Notes: Percentages may not total 100% because of rounding. Dollar figures reflect revenue losses, not budget outlay equivalents. Comparable figures are unavailable for most tax expenditures. Ideally, figures for personal property taxes would be reported separately from state and local taxes, but they are not in source tables showing distribution of benefits. The figures for EITC includes refund.

low-income housing come to a few billion dollars at most. This picture is the reverse of direct expenditures for housing, which are primarily aimed at subsidizing rental housing for the poor and seldom at home ownership for anyone. In absolute terms, the United States spends more than twice as much on one tax expenditure—the home mortgage interest deduction—as on all traditional housing programs, including Section 8 rental vouchers and public housing. Although the tax subsidies for home ownership may be good public policy, their sheer size undercuts the prevailing image of "subsidized housing" as housing for the poor. Moreover, the size of these tax expenditures challenges the usual verdict in the social science literature that the U.S. government, at least in a cross-national perspective, spends very little on housing.[19]

Tax expenditures for health are spent primarily on two programs. The exclusion of employers' contributions for health insurance premiums from corporate income taxation is a huge subsidy. It and the tax expenditure for employer pensions are the largest single components of the hidden welfare state. Both programs enable employers to write off the costs of providing benefits to workers as a business expense. The favorable tax treatment of Medicare benefits, analogous to those for Social Security benefits, costs another $13 billion.

Among the remaining tax expenditures, social services represents the largest budgetary category. The combination of deductions for charitable gifts and the tax credit for child and dependent care exceeds all direct spending for social services (e.g., child care and foster care). That feat is a little less impressive than it first appears, if only because the U.S. government appropriates relatively little to social services. Tax expenditures for employment and training, education, and veterans, the final three categories, are less important in absolute and relative terms. Most of these programs are rather small, costing less than $3 billion. They are consistently dwarfed by their direct spending counterparts, even though the national government plays a small role in financing education and, apart from unemployment insurance, spends little on employment and training.

In sum, with the important exception of housing (and perhaps social services), the basic structure of the hidden welfare state resembles that of the visible welfare state. Both represent sizable commitments of public resources. The top priority is income security, especially for the elderly. Health care is quite important at the national level; education is not.[20] In both cases, a handful of large programs account for most of the spending. There are also dozens of smaller programs, scattered across different functions, that contribute to the prevailing image of fragmentation. In these ways the hidden welfare state is a smaller-scale version of the visible welfare state, which means that previous generalizations about the structure of the American welfare state apply to a broader range of programs than before.

The limits of the received wisdom become more noticeable as soon as we stop focusing on general functions and start asking more specific questions about who has formal authority over these programs and who benefits. The Joint Committee on Taxation is such a good source of information because it helps the congressional committees with jurisdiction over the hidden welfare state. The JCT is a special committee in that it lacks formal jurisdiction over any policy domain yet possesses a large and technically competent staff. Its main function is to coordinate and inform the actions of the Senate Finance and House Ways and Means committees in Congress. Tax expenditures therefore accentuate the importance of these two committees, which already have jurisdiction over Social Security, Medicare, and unemployment insurance. What really distinguishes the visible and hidden welfare states are the bureaucratic agencies responsible for administering their respective programs. Most direct expenditure programs are administered by the Department of Health and Human Services (e.g., Medicare and AFDC) and the newly independent Social Security Administration. Others are administered by the Departments of Labor (job training), Housing and Urban Development (subsidized housing), and Agriculture (food stamps). The Treasury Department and Internal Revenue Service, on the other hand, are responsible for *all* tax expenditures.[21] One could argue that the size and broad scope of tax expenditures make the IRS, rather than Health and Human Services, the most comprehensive social welfare agency in the United States. That is clearly not the way most people have thought about either the IRS or social welfare agencies.

The benefits of tax expenditures flow in different ways. Most tax expenditures are financial incentives designed to encourage employers and individuals to purchase goods like health care, housing, and child care. There are, of course, a few exceptions. Some tax expenditures subsidize public programs, such as Social Security and Medicare, in which participation is mandatory for virtually all wage earners. In at least one instance (the Earned Income Tax Credit), the Treasury provides cash directly to individual taxpayers with no restrictions concerning the type of good or service individuals can purchase or when they can use the cash. But, for the most part, the government uses the tax code to entice market actors to consume in socially desirable ways.

The most important of these actors are employers. Judging from the complete lists of tax expenditures furnished by the government (not shown), the insurance and energy industries are particularly favored. Other tax expenditures are described so obliquely (nondealer installment sales, like-kind exchanges, possessions source income) that the real beneficiaries are hard to identify—a good indication of politically savvy actors at work. However, the most important subsidies are for benefits that private companies and government organizations offer their workers.[22] The extent to which the national government subsidizes employer benefits—in the range of $128 to $170 billion per year—is one of the more striking implications of Table 1.2. This figure is roughly equivalent to the sum of all corporate income taxes collected by the national government. Conceivably, these tax subsidies mean that the government has helped create a constituency for "private" welfare programs among more affluent citizens, thereby curbing demands for new or expanded forms of direct spending.[23] If true, this finding could resolve one of the major debates in the welfare state literature: why such a wealthy nation as the United States has lagged behind other nations in (direct) spending for social welfare. What is clear already is how much overlap exists between public and private programs. Tax expenditures for retirement pensions, health insurance, and other fringe benefits demonstrate that the line separating public and private is not a rigid barrier. Most of these supposedly private programs are heavily subsidized with public monies. It does not make sense to portray government and corporate welfare programs as wholly distinct realms of social welfare.

The contrast to the visible welfare state is subtle but important. True, the U.S. government often relies on third parties to deliver goods and services financed with direct expenditures, but there the similarity ends. Employers participate in traditional social programs either because they are required to by law (Social Security, Medicare), or because they expect to profit from providing goods and services that are publicly financed (job training). In both cases, citizens are eligible for benefits based on criteria such as income, age, employment, and health status that corporations cannot change. Workers in the hidden welfare state are not so fortunate. They must rely on their employers to offer a retirement or health plan in order to benefit from the government's tax subsidy. This difference makes coverage more erratic and less comprehensive than in traditional social programs.

Heavy subsidies for employer benefits are one reason that more affluent citizens are the main beneficiaries of the hidden welfare state. As a general rule, these benefits are most likely to be available to workers in larger companies, unionized industries, and better-paying occupations. In addition, some tax expenditures reward behaviors that less affluent taxpayers cannot afford to engage in (e.g., owning a home). The final explanation for this skew in benefits is ironic. Essentially, the more progressive the tax rates, the more upper-income taxpayers benefit from tax expenditures: as the tax bite increases, so does the value of avoiding taxation. Without some deliberate effort to cap benefits, a progressive tax system will always contain regressive tax expenditures.

Table 1.3 shows the distribution of benefits by income for selected tax expenditures. The income groupings are intended to reflect, as much as the source material allows, major economic divisions in society. Lower income is defined as less than $10,000 in income per year, which is near the poverty line for two persons; lower-middle income, commonly referred to as the working poor, here equals $10,000 to $30,000; middle income ranges from $30,000 to $50,000, which is above and below the median household income; upper-middle ranges from $50,000 to $100,000; and upper income refers to those reporting more than $100,000. The individual provisions for which data are available constitute about a third of the hidden welfare state's total cost, so they offer a fairly representative portrait. The most obvious inference to draw from Table 1.3 is that the majority of tax benefits go to people who earn more than the median income, often well above.[24] Over 85 percent of

the tax benefits for home mortgage interest, real estate taxes, and charitable contributions go to people earning more than $50,000 per year. In
more than a few cases, those earning more than $100,000 account for
the largest single portion of spending. The one exception to these patterns is the Earned Income Tax Credit, which is explicitly targeted at
people below or near the poverty line.

The tax expenditures shown are all programs that lower individual
income taxes. The JCT has found it technically difficult to calculate the
distribution of tax expenditures that lower corporate income taxes. That
hurdle helps explain why the major employer fringe benefit programs are
absent from Table 1.3. One can, however, find estimates from other organizations. A recent study by the Employee Benefit Research Institute
calculated that in 1992, the tax expenditure for employer pensions was
distributed as follows: 0.1 percent of total benefits to individuals earning
less than $10,000; 8.5 percent for those earning from $10,000 to
$30,000; 28.1 percent for those earning from $30,000 to $50,000;
42.8 percent for those earning from $50,000 to $100,000; and 20.0
percent for those earning more than $100,000. A 1983 study by the
Congressional Budget Office found that "88 percent of tax-free employer contributions [for medical insurance premiums and medical care]
went to households with annual incomes over $20,000. The median
household income that year was $20,885. The tax benefit averaged
$622 per household in the $50,000–$100,000 income range, but $83
per household in the $10,000–$15,000 range."[25] A more recent analysis by Eugene Steuerle estimated that the value of this tax expenditure
was worth $270 for people in the lowest-income quintile and $1,560 for
those in the highest quintile.[26] These figures are entirely consistent with
the data in Table 1.3, and it seems reasonable to infer that the distribution of all tax expenditures for fringe benefits follows a similar pattern.

The benefits from direct social spending are less skewed. Although
comparable data are unavailable for many direct spending programs, important contrasts can be seen. Probably the easiest comparison involves
the mix of public assistance programs available only to the poor and social insurance programs available to (virtually) all citizens. The mix of
direct expenditures is roughly one-quarter public assistance and three-
quarters social insurance. For every dollar spent on programs like AFDC
that are targeted at the poor, the United States spends three dollars on
inclusive programs like Social Security. In contrast, only the Earned Income Tax Credit, Targeted Jobs Tax Credit, low-income housing tax
credit, and exclusion of public assistance benefits are strictly aimed at the
poor and near-poor. Even including the EITC refund, they account for
less than 10 percent of the hidden welfare state.

Of course inclusive programs like Social Security also serve the poor, so the above measure may understate how well the poor fare in the visible welfare state. The Congressional Budget Office estimates that in 1995, 15.5 percent of all Social Security and disability (OASDI) benefits will go to those earning less than $10,000, 46.5 percent to those earning between $10,000 and $30,000, and 22.3 percent will go to those earning between $30,000 and $50,000. Those classified as upper-middle or upper-income will receive 12.3 and 3.5 percent, respectively.[27] According to the Kaiser Foundation, 77 percent of Medicare recipients have incomes of less than $25,000, 18 percent have incomes between $25,000 and $50,000, and 5 percent have incomes of more than $50,000.[28] Thus, although the poor may not receive the majority of benefits in the visible welfare state, neither do the affluent. Most benefits go to citizens with average or slightly below-average earnings. At bottom, the visible welfare state serves a far greater proportion of individuals below the poverty line, and below the median income, than does the hidden welfare state.

By now we have enough information to question a core claim about the structure of the American welfare state, namely, that it has two separate tiers.[29] The upper tier consists of inclusive social insurance programs like Social Security and Medicare. These programs are widely viewed as entitlements and enjoy broad political support. Benefits are financed by contributions from wage earners and are proportional to past wages. Redistribution across income lines occurs but is hard to detect. Beneficiaries are treated fairly well: eligibility criteria are uniform nationwide, receipt of benefits is considered socially legitimate, and bureaucratic discretion is kept to a minimum. Benefit levels are high enough to lift most recipients out of poverty, and benefits are indexed to inflation to keep those above the poverty line from falling below it in the future. This tier might be considered the "male" tier of the American welfare state because the programs are designed primarily for wage-earning men and their families.

The lower tier consists of means-tested programs like AFDC and Food Stamps. By definition, these programs serve the poorest segment of the population. Benefits are financed out of general revenues rather than payroll taxes; they are not "earned" like Social Security benefits. The combination of targeting and visible redistribution renders these programs politically vulnerable. Recipients are treated relatively poorly. Eligibility criteria and benefit levels vary considerably from state to state, and administrative hurdles are often high. Receipt of benefits is often stigmatizing and at times dehumanizing. Benefits are seldom indexed for inflation and leave many recipients below the poverty line. This tier might be considered the "female" tier of the welfare state to the extent that single mothers and their children are the principal clients.[30]

Tax expenditures do not split into corresponding tiers. For one, the public assistance component looks more like a thin veneer than a full-fledged tier. To the extent that tax expenditures are targeted, it is the rich who benefit and not the poor.[31] One usually needs to have considerable means to buy a home so expensive that it makes sense to itemize the mortgage interest and property taxes rather than take the standard deduction. "Means testing" in the hidden welfare state refers to an abundance and not shortage of means. Another difference concerns financing. Like the lower tier of means-tested programs, tax expenditures are financed out of general revenues rather than contributory payroll taxes and dedicated trust funds. Yet tax expenditures are structured as open-ended entitlements. No annual ceiling is placed on spending; everyone who meets the eligibility criteria is entitled to benefits. Despite the absence of payroll taxes and trust funds, receiving these benefits does not entail social stigma. Policy makers and pundits do not warn of the dangers of "tax deduction dependence." The sum of these differences means that the two-tiered image of the welfare state needs to be confined to direct expenditures.

CHANGE OVER TIME

So far we have seen a static map of the hidden welfare state circa 1995. We have a decent sense of its overall size and major regions and how it compares with the visible welfare state of direct spending. What happens when we examine how this terrain has changed over time? As mentioned above, the oldest method of estimating costs is revenue loss, used since the late 1960s. At that time there were about fifty tax expenditures, with and without social welfare objectives, costing a total of $36 billion. Despite these limitations, three decades of data are enough to establish some interesting trends. The upper half of Table 1.4 charts the growth of the hidden welfare state between 1967 and 1995, adjusted for inflation. Viewed simply on its own terms, the hidden welfare state has grown rapidly over the last few decades. Its overall size has increased at a real annual rate of 4.8 percent. Over a span of almost three decades, the size of the hidden welfare state has almost quadrupled.

The overall trend, as often happens, conceals some interesting variations at lower levels of aggregation. Some functions, like health (6.7 percent) and housing (6.4 percent), grew faster than the overall rate and hence became more important components of the hidden welfare state between 1967 and 1995. Their absolute size grew by a factor of 6, a testament to the power of compound interest. Although income secu-

TABLE 1.4
Growth of the Hidden and Visible Welfare States, 1965–1995 (average annual growth rates, adjusted for inflation)

The Hidden Welfare State of Tax Expenditures				
Budget function	1967–95	1967–75	1975–95	1980–90
Total	4.8%	5.9%	4.3%	3.9%
Income security	4.2	5.7	3.6	2.6
Health	6.7	6.1	6.9	6.0
Housing	6.4	7.7	5.9	6.7
Other	1.8	4.6	0.7	0.2

The Visible Welfare State of Direct Expenditures				
Budget function	1965–95	1965–75	1975–95	1980–90
Total	5.9%	11.4%	3.2%	3.1%
Income security	5.2	9.6	3.1	3.4
Health	12.6	24.1	7.2	7.0
Housing	8.3	24.9	1.0	1.9
Other	3.1	10.4	-0.4	-1.8

Sources: JCT, *Estimates of Federal Tax Expenditures*, various years; Office of Management and Budget, *Budget of the United States Government: Historical Tables, Fiscal Year 1995* (Washington, D.C.: Government Printing Office, 1994); U.S. Department of Commerce, Bureau of the Census, *Statistical Abstract of the United States, 1993* (Washington, D.C.: Government Printing Office, 1994); OMB, *Analytical Perspectives, Budget of the United States Government, Fiscal Year 1996.*

Note: Figures for tax expenditures are based on cost estimates.

rity, consistently the largest category of spending, grew somewhat slower than average (4.2 percent), it still managed to treble in size. The smaller categories, collectively referred to in this table as "other spending," grew more slowly. Social services and education have about doubled in size (meaning real growth of 2–3 percent annually), and the veterans category declined slightly. Employment and training, the smallest category for much of this time period, decreased considerably.

The picture is much the same at the level of individual programs. Employer-provided retirement pensions, the mainstay of income security, increased at a rate of 6.3 percent between 1967 and 1995. The major housing program, the home mortgage interest deduction, grew even faster (7.1 percent). The major health program, employer-provided health insurance, experienced a dramatic growth (8.6 percent) that eventually produced a program ten times its earlier size. Several new programs were enacted during this era. Some of them, like the Earned Income Tax Credit, started small and grew; others were soon eliminated (e.g., adoption expenses). At the other end of the spectrum, certain tax expenditures barely kept pace with inflation and others were eliminated. For instance, the tax expenditure for unemployment benefits was eliminated by the Tax Reform Act of 1986. In 1985 this one program accounted for three-quarters of the total spending for employment and training. Its termination accounts for the overall decline in spending for this function.

If we equate rapid growth with political success and elimination with political failure, then the experience of tax expenditures has been quite varied. Once embedded in the tax code, some tax expenditures have remained concealed from public view and grown like topsy, and some have not. It is generally true, however, that the largest programs have experienced the most rapid growth, suggesting that once tax expenditures reach some threshold size they become less vulnerable to cutbacks.

The lower half of Table 1.4 presents comparable trend data for direct expenditures. Although it is hard not to be impressed by the growth of the hidden welfare state, this additional evidence places that growth in perspective. The visible welfare state of direct expenditures appears to have grown much faster than the hidden welfare state—5.9 percent versus 4.8 percent, annually. That gap may not seem small, but compounded over a period of three decades it translates into large differences in absolute size. Nevertheless, this gap is heavily influenced by the selection of 1965 as the starting point for direct expenditures. The total for this year does not reflect much if any spending for Medicare, Medicaid, or the so-called war on poverty. If we then move the starting point forward to 1970 and allow these programs to get off the ground, the growth rate for the visible welfare state drops to 4.7 percent, virtually identical to that of the hidden welfare state.

The comparisons become more complex if we break the time series into meaningful segments. For instance, there is a general consensus in the welfare state literature that the rate of (direct) social spending declined starting in the mid-1970s. Slower economic growth meant that nations were able to collect fewer revenues and distribute fewer benefits. Or, to be more precise, they could not collect and distribute as fast as they could in the 1950s and 1960s. If this is true in the case of the United States, we would expect faster rates of growth before 1975 than after. The potential impact of economic growth is clear with direct expenditures, which grew at an 11.4 percent clip annually between 1965 and 1975 and 3.2 percent between 1975 and 1995. The recent history of the visible welfare state is therefore one of a decade of truly remarkable growth followed by two decades of considerably slower growth. The impact of slower economic growth on tax expenditures was more muted. The hidden welfare state grew at a rate of 5.9 percent between 1967 and 1975 and 4.3 percent between 1975 and 1995. Interestingly, the hidden welfare state has grown faster than the visible welfare state since 1975. Relative to direct expenditures for social welfare, tax expenditures have gained in importance over the last two decades.

The other time period worth examining is the 1980s, the supposed era of welfare state retrenchment in the United States. Led by Republicans, and particularly during President Reagan's first term (1981–85), the United States cut spending for some social programs. Most of these cuts were targeted at the poor; the bulk of spending, for inclusive programs like Social Security and Medicare, continued to escalate. The overall effect was significantly slower growth in direct expenditures (3.1 percent, half the rate of the entire 1965–95 period), but real growth nonetheless. The growth of tax expenditures declined less between 1980 and 1990, to 3.9 percent per year. This figure is somewhat misleading, for the first five years were a period of rapid growth (10 percent annually)—coinciding exactly with Reagan's "war" on the welfare state—and the second five years featured the only sustained decrease in spending on record (negative 3 percent annually). There is no comparable span since 1965 in which the visible welfare state shrank. According to the Congressional Budget Office, the most likely culprit was the Tax Reform Act of 1986, which reduced some tax expenditures and eliminated others outright. More important, the Tax Reform Act lowered marginal tax rates, thereby reducing the size of the remaining loopholes.[32] The often unintended effects of major tax bills such as this one on the development of the hidden welfare state will be explored further in later chapters. The reductions created by the 1986 Act were not enough to change the basic picture for the decade. In a potentially hostile political environment, the hidden welfare state fared better than the visible welfare state.

There is, in short, a lot going on in the hidden welfare state—or, to use the language of social science, there is much variation to be explained. Total spending has grown faster in some periods than others, and some categories of spending have grown much faster than others. It would be interesting for future researchers to investigate why. Compared with direct expenditures for social welfare, tax expenditures appear less sensitive to major changes in the economy and in political leadership, and they are somewhat better suited to "hard times." Again, it would be helpful to know why.

DISCUSSION

The primary objective of this chapter was to generate a basic map of the hidden welfare state. Readers should now be familiar with its size and composition and how these features compare with the visible welfare state of direct expenditures. Readers should have a sense for how these features have changed over time. These comparisons helped achieve a secondary objective of this chapter, which was to indicate in what ways the four cases chosen for intensive study might be typical not only of important categories of traditional social programs but also of important categories of tax expenditures. As mentioned in the introduction, my choice of cases was initially guided by previous research regarding the visible welfare state. The basic typology of programs was a simple two-by-two matrix of inclusive versus means-tested programs and cash versus in-kind benefits.

After surveying the surface of the entire hidden welfare state, we can now see that these cases capture much of the variation within it. Employment-based pensions is one of several tax subsidies to employers that provide benefits to their workers, an important segment of the hidden welfare state. Its history may offer clues into the tax treatment of health insurance, life insurance, and other fringe benefits. The home mortgage interest deduction is one of several tax expenditures for home owners, which are in turn one of the largest categories of spending in the hidden welfare state. This deduction is not tied to employment, allowing us to see what actors besides employers and workers may be politically salient. The size of these two programs contrasts nicely to the EITC, which has become a moderate-sized program, and to the TJTC, always one of the smallest tax expenditures. Variations in size will presumably be correlated with variations in visibility and in support. Furthermore, the first comprehensive list of tax expenditures in the late 1960s included home mortgage interest and employer pensions, but not the EITC or TJTC. The first two programs must have been created at some prior point and the latter two sometime after this list appeared, thus enabling us to see whether variations in the timing of new programs matter politically.

There are ways in which these four cases may not be representative. The present study contains no examples of tax expenditures for public programs like Social Security. That omission raises the possibility that the study will overstate the role of third-party providers in the private sector in lobbying on behalf of tax expenditures. Perhaps the most important source of bias is the skew in favor of programs targeted at the poor. Although the EITC and TJTC constitute two of the four cases, means-tested tax expenditures are but a tiny fraction of the hidden welfare state. Still, these two cases have other merits. They may become more representative in the future, given the growing interest in using tax expenditures to help disadvantaged citizens purchase health insurance and secure employment. There is simply more information available concerning the TJTC than many medium- and large-scale tax expenditures, making that case more "do-able." And it is hard not to include the EITC after all the claims policy makers have made about its ability to reform welfare, improve access to child care, raise the wages of the working poor, and add fairness to the tax code. The overrepresentation of programs targeted at the poor is countered to some degree by the choice of home mortgage interest and employer pensions, two of the largest programs in the hidden welfare state. Any generalization about the hidden welfare state—and all tax expenditures for that matter—must account for those two programs. With these caveats in mind, we can now begin to explore the origins of tax expenditures with social welfare objectives.

PART TWO

Origins

TWO QUESTIONS have long puzzled students of the American welfare state. The first is why new social programs were created primarily during two brief periods in the 1930s and 1960s—the two "big bangs" of welfare state formation.[1] The programs we know now as Social Security, Unemployment Insurance, and Aid to Families with Dependent Children all trace their origins to the Social Security Act of 1935. Public housing dates from 1937. Several decades later, the Economic Opportunity Act of 1964 created a variety of educational, employment, and social service programs aimed at the poor (the so-called war on poverty). In 1965 Congress passed Medicare and Medicaid, which President Johnson then signed into law. Outside these narrow windows of opportunity, new social programs have been few and far between. Why? The second question is why the United States was relatively late in enacting nationwide social programs. Germany introduced the first such programs in the 1880s, and most European nations followed suit by 1920. The United States waited until 1935 and has never created national health insurance—why?

Agreement on the questions worth asking is important, for it enables us to make educated guesses about the origins of the hidden welfare state. New tax expenditures should be created during the 1930s and 1960s and not before. We might also expect that new cash transfers preceded new in-kind benefits. The first wave of traditional social programs provided cash assistance for the elderly, the unemployed, the blind, and poor children of single mothers. The second wave provided in-kind benefits such as medical care, job training, and day care to the elderly and the poor. If these patterns hold for the hidden welfare state, then the tax expenditure for employer pensions and the Earned Income Tax Credit should originate before the home mortgage interest deduction and the Targeted Jobs Tax Credit. The former are more open-ended cash transfers whereas the latter are restricted to specific goods (housing) and services (employment and training). We would not expect much difference in the timing of inclusive and targeted programs because both were enacted in the visible welfare state during the 1930s and 1960s.

Most scholars have treated the questions of why so rare and why so late as two sides of the same coin. The basic problem is to identify those features of U.S. politics that usually thwart the introduction of new social programs but that diminished enough in the 1930s and 1960s to permit some programs to go through. Nothing approaching a scholarly consensus exists as to which features matter most. For some scholars, the answer lies in classical liberal values of limited government and individualism. Others point to the representation of interests: strong business groups and relatively weak labor unions; the lack of a durable labor or socialist party; the historic power of conservative southerners in Congress; the occasional outburst of popular protest; or the recent explosion in the number and variety of interest groups, none capable of representing a sizable fraction of citizens across a range of issues. Still others believe that the answer is rooted in the peculiar nature of U.S. institutions. Madison's "compound republic" fragments political authority among different levels of government and among national institutions. Further fragmentation within Congress may have given committee chairmen veto power over many initiatives. The sequence of democratization and bureaucratization may have rendered government agencies weak and political parties unable to organize around substantive platforms.[2]

It will be useful to keep this laundry list of suspects in mind when analyzing how new tax expenditures are created. Given the polarization of scholarly opinion on this issue, it is unlikely that even a strong pattern among four cases will be enough to settle this debate.[3] What may be more useful is to identify commonalities among these explanations and see if new tax expenditures share those traits. For instance, although scholars disagree over which obstacles have been decisive, all agree that the obstacles to new social programs have been substantial. Overcoming these obstacles requires some extraordinary event, like a Great Depression or a landslide election favoring liberal Democrats. Even under the most favorable circumstances, debates over enactment are quite public and contentious. The scope of conflict, to use Schattschneider's phrase, is broad.[4] Passage of the Social Security Act and Medicare are two classic examples. If new tax expenditures do not trigger a comparable level of controversy and debate, then their creation would be distinctive.

The next three chapters challenge several of the most firmly held beliefs about the origins of U.S. social programs. The home mortgage interest deduction (1913) and tax expenditure for employer pensions (1914–26) appeared years before the Social Security Act. Admittedly, neither tax expenditure could have cost much or benefited many taxpayers at first. But the significance of new programs is seldom measured in terms of their initial size or impact, for many start small and grow over time. Social Security initially paid no benefits, and barely half the workforce was covered. What matters is that these tax expenditures were created by the national government and were available to individuals in every state. The Earned Income Tax Credit and Targeted Jobs Tax Credit also did not originate when expected. Both were created in the

1970s, at least ten years after the second big bang ushered in Medicare and Medicaid. A skeptic might argue that all generalizations have their exceptions; perhaps the tax expenditures in this study represent aberrations as well. Chapter 9 presents evidence concerning the timing of other tax expenditures with social welfare objectives to show that their introduction has not coincided with *any* specific period in U.S. history.

By the same token, cash benefits did not precede in-kind benefits. The home mortgage interest deduction was one of the very first tax expenditures, and the Earned Income Tax Credit is a relatively recent program. If any pattern emerges, it is that more inclusive tax expenditures were created before those targeted at low-income citizens. Chapter 9 offers additional evidence for this pattern.

The process of enacting new tax expenditures was extraordinary because it was so routine. These programs were not automatic responses to an economic crisis: no great decline in home ownership preceded the home mortgage interest deduction; no great surge in the numbers of the working poor triggered the Earned Income Tax Credit. Nor was control of government by liberal Democrats decisive. The home mortgage interest deduction and TJTC appeared when the Democrats had unified control of the government, the tax expenditure for employer pensions appeared when the Republicans had unified control, and the EITC emerged under a divided government. Even when the Democrats had unified control, it is hard to argue that liberal Democrats had anywhere near the power in 1913 or 1978 than they did under Roosevelt or Johnson. None of the social movements of the 1970s (the antiwar, the women's, and the environmental movements) advocated anything resembling the EITC or TJTC; the plight of the working poor was not on their agendas. Such movements were less potent in the 1910s and 1920s and just as peripheral to tax expenditures. The one time that organized labor participated in any of these cases (the Targeted Jobs Tax Credit), its preferences were ignored. Groups representing beneficiaries and service providers appeared only after the fact.

The role of business interests deserves close scrutiny, for both the corporate liberal wing of the social policy literature and the tax policy literature predict that business should be instrumental in building the hidden welfare state.[5] The connection appears plausible considering that three of these tax expenditures effectively lower employers' labor costs and the other subsidizes the housing and lending industries. Nonetheless, the one instance in which employers participated directly, they failed to have much of an impact. Business interests were divided over the New Jobs Tax Credit (NJTC), the immediate predecessor of the Targeted Jobs Tax Credit. Larger, capital-intensive firms favored an increase in the investment tax credit whereas smaller, labor-intensive firms favored the

NJTC. A year later the same business interests that pushed for the NJTC failed to prevent Congress from changing it into the Targeted Jobs Tax Credit. The National Federation of Independent Business, a leading representative of small business, argued unsuccessfully that targeting would place too great an administrative burden on small firms and that such firms would be uninterested in hiring the categories of disadvantaged workers specified in the legislation. Business interests were not involved in creating either the home mortgage interest deduction or the EITC.

The one case in which business influence mattered was employer pensions, and there the evidence is circumstantial. Conservative Republicans wanted to lower the tax burdens on capital in the 1920s in order to solidify business support and spur economic growth. Republicans did not need to be told in every instance which taxes to lower, and the major business organizations concentrated on larger issues such as lowering tax rates and repealing the World War I surtax. There is no evidence that businesses actively lobbied for this specific tax break.

After eliminating all the usual suspects, who's left? Part of the answer, oddly enough, is that moderate and conservative members of Congress have been instrumental in creating the hidden welfare state. These legislators have been depicted either as antagonistic to new social programs or as passive agents of powerful interest groups.[6] One would not expect them to have a constructive or independent effect on new social programs. Southern Democrats and progressive Republicans helped enact the individual income tax in 1913, which contained the home mortgage interest deduction. A coalition of southern Democrats and moderate Republicans influenced the structure of the Targeted Jobs Tax Credit and its forerunner, the New Jobs Tax Credit. Senator Russell Long (D-La.), architect of the Earned Income Tax Credit, was a vocal critic of AFDC and other welfare programs. His workfare package, including a 10 percent work bonus that eventually became the EITC, was designed to boost the work incentives of the poor and eliminate many of them from the welfare rolls. Senator George McLean (R-Conn.), who sponsored the key amendment creating the tax expenditure for employer pensions, was, of all things, a conservative Republican.

The other "actors" worth mentioning are political parties, which are usually considered peripheral to policy making in the United States. Party discipline is low, and party members are more oriented toward patronage and constituency service than broad-based policy platforms. In at least two cases discussed here—home mortgage interest and employer pensions—parties were instrumental. During the early twentieth century Democrats and Republicans fought often and hard over tax policy, and especially over income taxation. Out of these struggles emerged two of the largest tax expenditures in the late twentieth century.

The final distinctive aspect of the origins of these tax expenditures is the narrow scope of conflict. Although the process of creating new tax expenditures has become more visible and contentious over time, the scope of conflict has never reached the level of the Social Security Act or the Medicare bill. All four tax expenditures were appended to larger revenue or tax reform bills. All four were dwarfed by other parts of these bills, both in terms of dollars and the time and energy required to pass them. No separate floor votes were taken on any of these tax expenditures. Hardly anyone at the time trumpeted their passage or predicted that dire consequences would result. Hardly anyone noticed at all. Public officials and interest groups focused instead on the larger questions of tax policy, such as how heavily to rely on income taxes versus excise taxes and how progressive income tax rates should be.

CHAPTER 2

Home Mortgage Interest and Employer Pensions

ENACTMENT of the first permanent income taxes on corporations (1909) and individuals (1913) ranks among the most important legislative achievements of the twentieth century.[1] Their introduction made possible a fundamental shift in U.S. government finances away from a consumption-based system of excise taxes and tariffs to one based primarily on income taxes. This transition took decades to occur, however, and was not completed until income taxes were raised dramatically during World War II. Passage of the Social Security Act in 1935 initiated the second great shift in government finances, as social insurance taxes became the fastest growing source of revenue during the latter half of the century. Despite this growth, income taxes remained the most important source of revenues to the national government through 1995.

Few people in the early twentieth century could have confidently predicted the eventual magnitude of income taxes. After all, the first income taxes affected very few individuals and accounted for a tiny fraction of government revenues. What was obvious at the time were the distributive consequences. Because the first income taxes were more progressive than excise taxes or tariffs, they shifted the tax burden to more affluent individuals and corporations. Income taxes shifted the regional burden as well, away from the South and West and to the more affluent residents of the North and East. Given the regional nature of political parties during this era, debates over taxation typically pitted southern and western Democrats against northeastern Republicans, the former very much in favor of income taxes and the latter strongly opposed.

Deciding how to foster home ownership and retirement pensions through the tax code was literally the last thing on anyone's mind in the early twentieth century. The central debates over taxes and tariffs concerned how the national government should raise revenues and who should pay. Nevertheless, in the process of answering these questions, policy makers unwittingly created two of the largest social programs of the late twentieth century—the home mortgage interest deduction and favorable tax treatment of employer-provided retirement pensions. Knowing how and why these two accidents occurred requires further exploration of the sectional and partisan struggles over tax policy. In the case of home mortgage interest, we also need to recognize the formidable task of building the administrative capacity needed to implement a new form of taxation.

HOME MORTGAGE INTEREST

The home mortgage interest deduction originated in 1913 as part of the bill creating individual income taxes. It is by definition one of the earliest building blocks of the hidden welfare state. Students of the tax code find no evidence that this deduction was deliberately created to promote home ownership.[2] Examination of the *Congressional Record* for 1913 indicates one brief complaint about the lack of comparable treatment for renters; otherwise the connections between housing policy and tax policy were not discussed. This silence is not surprising considering that housing policy was a state and local responsibility during this era. The main function of those governments was to regulate the quality of housing construction, such as the adequacy of bathrooms and windows.[3] The core provisions of the 1913 tax bill up for debate were the progressive rate structure and the income level below which citizens would be exempt from taxation. These debates were in turn overshadowed by debates over tariff reductions and revisions that were part of the same omnibus bill.

Lacking signs of political struggle over the home mortgage interest deduction, we need to search for more circumstantial evidence. Because its origins coincided with enactment of permanent income taxes, it makes sense to start by reviewing the decades-long struggle over income taxation around the turn of the century. As we shall see, this history also helps us to understand the subsequent creation of the tax expenditure for employer pensions.

Scholars have cited a number of reasons for the origins of corporate and individual income taxes. Virtually all of them point to "geoeconomic divisions that pitted the industrialized North and Northeast against the rest of the nation" as a constant feature of tax politics throughout the late nineteenth and early twentieth centuries.[4] These cleavages help to explain which interests aligned around which tax and tariff policies. They do not help us understand why proponents of income taxation triumphed in 1909 and 1913. To explain the timing of legislation, scholars have cited growing demands for revenue in the wake of the Spanish-American War and increased peacetime spending for the navy and veterans' pensions; the spread of progressive ideology, especially growing opposition to concentrated wealth; and the shifting balance of power among political parties.[5] Of these factors I call attention to the role of parties and party competition. Demands for additional revenue could have been met with higher tariffs and excise taxes, and progressive ideology spread gradually. In contrast, the balance of power among political parties shifted precisely at the moment in which the two tax laws were passed. The combination of constant geoeconomic divisions and the fluctuating fortunes of political parties created the context needed to understand the creation of a new tax expenditure for home mortgage interest.

Overlapping regional and economic divisions were the fundamental cleavages in American politics between 1865 and 1932. The Northeast featured an increasingly industrial economy and was a stronghold of the Republican Party. The South and West were more agricultural and their citizens more likely to be Democrats, Populists, or Greenbacks. Taxation highlighted these divisions like no other issue, and the chief protagonists regularly accused one another of fostering class warfare through their choice of tax and tariff policies. Northern Republicans favored tariffs on imports, which were mostly manufactured and finished goods, as a way of deflecting the tax burden and protecting their own industries. The costs of these tariffs were borne disproportionately by the South and West. Representatives from these regions regularly introduced income tax bills in Congress during the 1870s and 1880s, to no avail. Common sense and past experience during the Civil War indicated that income taxes would fall heavily on northern wealth.[6]

The Democratic Party officially endorsed income taxes in the 1890s, in part to slow the defection of voters and politicians to the Populist camp. They succeeded in passing an individual income tax in 1894, the first national income tax in more than two decades.[7] Like the income taxes used to finance the Civil War, it imposed a 2 percent tax on income higher than $4,000. Reaction against the tax was swift and passionate: the *New York Tribune* called it "class legislation on a tremendous scale," and the *New York Sun* envisioned "a system of inquisition and espionage repugnant to American ideals and abhorrent to the free citizen."[8]

The Supreme Court sided with opponents of income taxation and declared the law unconstitutional in 1895 by a 5–4 vote (*Pollock v. Farmers Loan and Trust Company*). According to the majority, the income tax was a "direct tax," and Article I, Section 9 of the Constitution only allowed Congress to levy direct taxes in proportion to population. The national government might tax New York more than Tennessee, but only to the extent that New York had more residents and not to the extent that its residents had more income. The reasoning behind *Pollock* has been repeatedly criticized, largely because it rested on a dubious claim of original intent.[9] Somehow the majority justices ignored the existence of at least five distinct definitions of direct taxation at the time of the nation's founding. Somehow they failed to note the rarity of anything like income taxes during this era, thus making their explicit inclusion or exclusion in the Constitution unlikely. Moreover, James Madison's notes from the Constitutional Convention indicate that when Rufus King of Massachusetts asked for a precise definition of direct tax, none was offered. It seems much more reasonable to conclude that the founders left the exact meaning of direct tax unclear in order to produce a constitution that every state could support. The majority in *Pollock*, however, behaved as if the founders had always meant to equate income taxes with direct taxes.

Reaction to *Pollock* was as intense as reaction to passage of the income tax a year earlier. The *St. Louis Post Dispatch* editorialized that "today's decision shows that corporations and plutocrats are as securely entrenched in the Supreme Court as in the lower courts which they take such pains to control."[10] The *New York Tribune* and other northeastern papers countered by praising the Court's willingness to stem the tide of class hatred and communist revolution. One did not have to read between the lines of the *Pollock* decision to find evidence that economic divisions mattered. Wrote Justice Field for the majority: "The present assault upon capital is but the beginning. It will be but the stepping stone to others, larger and more sweeping, till our political contests will become a war of the poor against the rich."[11]

The *Pollock* decision initially slowed the drive for income taxation, as did the subsequent demise of the People's Party. The Democratic Party, which absorbed many former Populists, renewed its efforts during the 1900s. Democrats, however, were the minority party in Washington from 1896 to 1912. They could never have passed the corporate income tax in 1909 without the support of progressive politicians. Progressives made inroads in the Republican Party at the national, state, and local levels, particularly in the West. As part of their general attack on concentrated wealth, progressives succeeded Populists as the leading advocates of income taxation. They scored a partial victory by committing the Republican Party to lower tariffs in their 1908 platform. President Theodore Roosevelt, officially a Republican but the embodiment of the progressive movement, called for an income tax *and* an inheritance tax that same year, much to the consternation of conservative Republican politicians and Northern industrialists.

By 1909 the coalition of progressive Republicans and Democrats in Congress had grown powerful enough to pass some kind of income tax. They intended initially to tax the income of wealthy individuals and fashioned legislation to address the Supreme Court's objections in the *Pollock* case (they also hoped for a different verdict after the retirement of one of the five judges who formed the majority in *Pollock*). They attached an income tax provision drafted by Rep. Cordell Hull (D-Tenn.)

to a tariff bill working its way through Congress. This amendment created a dilemma for conservative Republicans. On the one hand, they could continue to resist any income tax whatsoever. The problem with this strategy was that Republicans' effective control of government had diminished significantly by 1909. They simply lacked the votes needed to defeat the amendment. Unyielding opposition might also have compromised other parts of the tariff bill, especially upward revisions, that Republicans supported. Their other alternative was to accept the inevitability of an income tax and try to minimize its impact on their constituents. Republicans chose what they thought was the lesser of two evils and endorsed an excise tax on corporate profits. To many members of the business community, corporate taxes were preferable to individual income taxes because their costs could more easily be shifted to consumers.[12]

Conservative Republican support for the measure was clearly strategic; they hoped that the corporate excise tax would raise sufficient revenue to make any individual income tax unnecessary. They also doubted that the states would ever pass an income tax amendment. Senate Finance chairman Nelson Aldrich (R-R.I.), a millionaire himself and a long-time proponent of high tariffs, declared, "I shall vote for a corporation tax as a means to defeat the income tax."[13] Congress enacted the corporate excise tax in 1909 as part of the Payne-Aldrich Tariff Act.

The Republican strategy backfired as soon as Democrats gained control of Congress and the White House in 1912, an achievement made possible by the defection of many moderate Republicans to the newly formed Progressive Party.[14] The Democratic Party platform of 1912 identified the tax system as the main source of growing inequality in the United States and promised to reform it. Congress passed and President Wilson signed into law the first permanent individual income tax in 1913, only months after the Sixteenth Amendment had been ratified. The income tax was part of a much larger bill revising, and in many cases reducing, tariffs, and those tariffs were the focal point of debate (this bill also transformed the corporate excise tax into a corporate income tax). According to John Witte: "No separate vote was taken on the income tax provisions. At the time the tax was accepted as a natural and inevitable culmination of the constitutional amendment. It was not deemed as important as the tariff bill itself. The income tax section occupied only 8 pages of an 814-page report."[15]

The original income tax clearly targeted the rich, primarily by exempting the first $4,000 in income at a time when the average worker earned around $600 a year.[16] The rate structure was progressive, ranging from 1 percent on incomes between $4,000 and $20,000 to 7 percent on all income above $500,000. During the first few years only about 2 percent of taxpayers filed returns. By 1916, more than 80 percent of individuals paying income taxes were "bankers, brokers, capitalists, manufacturers, merchants, or corporate officials. . . . It would be hard to find a single issue that more tightly united the nation's most wealthy citizens."[17] Early tax returns also indicated that, as expected, the burden fell disproportionately on urban, industrial states. New York, with 10 percent of the nation's population, accounted for 45 percent of total individual income tax revenues. Twelve southern states, with 27 percent of the nation's population, accounted for only 4 percent of revenues.[18]

The individual income tax was designed on the ability to pay principle. Proponents wanted to tax only those individuals who had more than enough income to buy the basic necessities of life. They believed that the combination of tariffs and excise taxes had unfairly burdened many middle-class and working-class citizens. The $4,000 exemption was the most important means of achieving this objective; some Republicans tried unsuccessfully to lower the exemption to $1,000 in order to generate opposition among more taxpayers.[19] Income taxes passed during the Civil War and in 1894 included similar exemptions. In addition, the final bill created a distinction between total income and taxable income: individuals could deduct from their total income specific sources of income (e.g., gifts and inheritances and interest on state and local bonds) and specific expenses in order to generate a lower level of taxable income. Included in these expenses was interest paid on *all* indebtedness, including but not limited to home mortgages. Thus, from the very beginning, individuals who went into debt to buy a home shared with all indebted consumers a special place in the tax code. This design effectively broadened the potential base of support for the home mortgage interest deduction.

The other reason for exempting interest on consumer debt from taxation was administrative simplicity.[20] Past experiences with income taxes indicated that implementation would be difficult. Most individuals who owed income taxes during the Civil War era did not pay them once the war ended (1866–72). States that introduced income taxes after the Civil War found that collection practices varied widely within their borders and that the monies raised were far less than expected. Although national officials had considerable experience collecting taxes on imported goods, they had no experience collecting on individual income. It made sense, then, to design a tax system that was as simple as possible to administer and did not require tax officials to make fine distinctions.

These considerations were particularly important for interest on consumer debt because of its potential overlap with interest on business debt. A basic principle of public finance was that interest on business debt should be exempt from corporate income taxation because that money was spent to produce income, as when a company took out a loan to buy a new piece of machinery. Conversely, interest on loans used to purchase everyday items like food and clothing should be taxed. The problem for tax officials was in distinguishing between the two forms of debt in an era in which business expenses and personal expenses were often commingled. Agricultural workers comprised nearly one-third of the labor force and frequently incurred heavy debts: Would interest on loans used to buy a farm be considered a business expense because farmers worked there or a personal expense because farmers lived there? Many others workers—especially self-employed tradesmen, shop owners, and restaurant owners—were in a similar position of living in the same building where they worked. Likewise, how would tax officials decide whether the interest paid on a sewing machine bought on credit should be exempt when the owner made clothes for her family and for sale? Rather than try to establish which specific rooms were dedicated to business and which to home life (a distinction created later that produces considerable confusion today), and rather than distinguish between goods purchased for business or home use, officials decided to allow deductions for interest on all debt. This approach was also simpler in the sense that it replicated the treatment of interest on indebtedness from the Civil War tax codes.

One could argue that this treatment of indebtedness favored the same agricultural interests in the South and West that championed income taxes in the first place. Opposition to the high cost of credit was a common rallying point for insurgent third parties like the Populists, which attracted much of their support from farmers.[21] In that case, the sectional and partisan struggles over taxation might be the sole factor accounting for the timing and content of the home mortgage interest deduction. Without specific evidence of legislative intent, it is probably safer to attribute the origins of this deduction to a combination of sectional and partisan struggles over taxation and the need to reduce the complexity of levying and collecting income taxes nationwide. As the next case demonstrates, these partisan struggles continued to shape tax policy and the creation of tax expenditures for many years.

EMPLOYER PENSIONS

The creation of income taxes on individuals and corporations represented a milestone in partisan struggles over taxation, not an end point. Conservative Republicans realized that even though they may have lost the battle over enactment, they might still win the war of implementation if they could reduce income taxes in the future. This they accomplished first by creating and expanding tax expenditures and then by lowering tax rates. Allowing employers to deduct contributions to their workers' retirement pensions was part of this larger struggle over income taxation.

The preferential tax treatment of employer pensions evolved incrementally, first in administrative rulings and later in congressional statutes, between 1914 and 1926. The Treasury Department ruled in 1914 that "amounts paid for pensions to retired employees or to their families or others dependent on them, or on account of injuries received by employees, are proper deductions as ordinary and necessary business expenses."[22] Subsequent Treasury rulings in 1918 and later years allowed employers to deduct their contributions as long as either a pension trust or employee were taxed that year. These rulings allowed companies to shift the burden of paying taxes on pensions in any given year but not to defer taxation to a later time, which is currently considered to be a defining feature of this tax expenditure. Its formal starting point might therefore be the Revenue Act of 1926, which included a minor amendment exempting employer contributions from taxation. In practice, however, Treasury officials allowed employers to deduct these contributions beginning in 1921. Any year one chooses is well before the Social Security Act.

At no point did this program generate much interest or debate. The exemption of pension payments in 1914 was one small part of an omnibus Treasury decision that covered everything from the deductibility of costumes purchased by actors to the tax treatment of alimony payments. The Treasury Department offered no explanation for the vast majority of these individual provisions, including pensions. Other likely clues to the Treasury's thinking are no more helpful. The annual report of the Secretary of the Treasury often included broad policy statements and specific legislative proposals during this era. Yet nowhere in these reports was there any discussion of private pensions or their tax treatment between 1913 and 1921. There is no mention of this ruling in the biography and autobiography of then Secretary of the Treasury William McAdoo; both sources devote more attention to the creation of the Federal Reserve System and the financing of World War I than to specific details of the tax code.[23] It is doubtful that Treasury officials were somehow signaled by the White House on this matter since "President Wilson had only a passing interest in tax matters and leaned heavily on his Secretary of the Treasury William G. McAdoo."[24] A review of the index to the *Congressional Record* for the Sixty-Third Congress (1913–15) suggests that signals from the Hill, in the form of bills introduced, were similarly nonexistent. Cordell Hull, the architect of the 1909 and 1913 tax laws, does not refer at all to pensions or their taxation in his seventeen-hundred-page memoirs.[25]

Nor did the Treasury's ruling cause much of a ripple outside Washington. The *Wall Street Journal*, which followed tax matters closely and regularly answered detailed questions about the tax code, mentioned this ruling briefly but focused on the section governing alimony. The article did not imply that the decision was a significant one, nor did it provide any insight into who might have pushed for more favorable tax treatment of pensions.[26] The *New York Times* made no mention of the ruling at all.

This pattern continued into the 1920s. According to a review of the legislative record by the Congressional Budget Office:

> The Revenue Acts of 1921 and 1926 were major, controversial tax bills, but the Congress paid scant attention to the sections granting tax exemptions to employer benefit trusts. The 1921 provision was inserted by the Senate Finance Committee and accepted as uncontroversial on the floor. The 1926 extension to pensions was offered as a floor amendment in the Senate only hours before passage and was also accepted without debate. Clearly, the Congress did not foresee how costly and influential the exemption would later become. In fact, the absence of floor debate or discussion in committee reports makes it unclear whether the exemption was intended as assistance to employers' nascent benefit plans or purely as a technical resolution of the difficult problem of assigning trust income to a taxable entity.[27]

Lacking much evidence, most scholars familiar with this program have declined to explain its enactment, offering instead a description of statutory changes.[28] The rest of this chapter reviews the prevailing explanation for this program's origins and then offers an alternative explanation rooted in partisan struggles over taxation.[29]

The few scholars who have tried to explain the origins of this program have assumed that policy makers were motivated by technical rationality. Altman, for example, argues that the Treasury's rulings "can be understood simply as an attempt to apply general income tax principles to employee compensation in as neutral and administratively feasible a manner as possible."[30] Reasoning by analogy and using common sense, Treasury officials decided to count pension plans as an "ordinary and necessary" business expense, and therefore excluded employers' payments or contributions from their taxable income. The soundness of the Treasury's reasoning was later accepted by Congress, and by extension the general public. Had policy makers not been acting in the public interest, a great hue and cry would surely have ensued. The politics of creating this program were more about problem solving than power.

In light of the previous discussion of home mortgage interest and administrative complexity, this explanation is plausible. Treasury officials had to implement a new system of corporate income taxation and in the process made adjustments to simplify their task. Nevertheless, this explanation strikes me as inadequate. The "problem" to be solved here affected far fewer taxpayers than did the problem of interest on personal indebtedness. It is unclear how technically rational policy makers could have considered ordinary or necessary a business expense that only a tiny fraction of employers incurred. Though American Express initiated the first corporate pension plan in 1875, decades before the first Treasury ruling, pensions spread quite slowly. Korczyk, for example, estimates that one-third of all employees covered in the mid-1920s worked for one of only four companies (U.S. Steel, the Pennsylvania Railroad, the New York Central Railroad, and American Telephone & Telegraph). According to Latimer, approximately four hundred plans were in operation and 10 percent of the nonfarm labor force was employed in firms offering pensions by 1929. Only a fraction of those workers, however, were covered, and most of them never qualified for benefits because of stringent eligibility requirements. Since fewer than two hundred of these plans had been established by 1915, we can infer that less than 5 percent of the nonfarm labor force was employed in firms offering pensions at the time of the Treasury's ruling.[31] Moreover, the majority of covered employees had no legal right to pension benefits. Pensions were "a reward for merit, a gift of the benefactor," and could be revoked by the employer for any perceived instance of employee "misconduct."[32] Benefits were contingent as well on the profitability of the corporation. All things considered, business expenses for retirement pensions were anything but ordinary and necessary for the vast majority of employers.[33]

In addition to technical rationality, it is important to note the ongoing partisan struggles over taxation, and in particular how the results of these struggles changed around World War I. Before the war, a coalition of Democrats and progressive Republicans succeeded in enacting the first permanent income taxes on corporations and individuals. That same coalition increased income taxes during the war, raising them so high that businesses and wealthy individuals started to push vigorously for selective tax relief. After the war, a pro-business coalition led by conservative Republicans returned to power and succeeded in muting some of the redistributive effects of income taxes, first through selective tax breaks and then through major reductions in tax rates. Concessions to business were seen as an essential stimulus to investment and economic growth.[34] The tax expenditure for employer pensions was thus one of several measures designed to lower the tax burdens on business.

Both the Civil War tax codes and the 1909 corporate income tax allowed businesses to deduct "ordinary and necessary" expenses before computing taxable income. In both instances Congress failed to specify which expenses qualified, relying instead on the judgment of Treasury officials. The Treasury's decision in 1914 to include retirement pensions among these expenses is puzzling. As indicated earlier, fewer than one in twenty workers would have been covered by corporate pensions at the time, and only a fraction of those workers would ever have actually received a pension. Treasury officials may have had specific firms and industries in mind when they made their rulings in 1914 and subsequent years. Though few in number, pensions were relatively common in capital-intensive industries dominated by a few large companies operating on a regional or national scale. These pensions were one of several benefits offered by corporations in order to discourage unionization and promote worker loyalty, a practice known as welfare capitalism.[35] Many railroads established pensions in the 1880s and 1890s, and more than half of all railroad employees were in a company offering pensions by 1914. Other industries soon followed suit:

> By 1920, most of the major railroads, utility companies, banks, mining companies, and petroleum companies had set up formal pension plans, and parallel pension plan growth was recorded for manufacturers of machinery, agricultural implements, chemicals, paints and varnishes, rubber, paper and printing products, and electrical apparatus.[36]

These were the giants of industry, companies like Standard Oil of New Jersey, DuPont, and U.S. Steel. The Treasury Department seems to have been favorably disposed toward big business during this same period. In 1916, for instance, the Treasury ruled that intangible drilling costs incurred by mining and petroleum companies were deductible from their taxable net income. That same year, Treasury Secretary McAdoo proposed financing the war through a combination of income and consumption taxes that spread the tax burden as widely as possible, and away from large corporations.

Many southern Democrats and progressive Republicans, as well as agricultural and labor interests, felt that McAdoo's proposal failed to place the costs of the war on those most likely to benefit from it: "There was still considerable feeling in the country that this was a rich man's war, entered into for imperialist gain and material profit."[37] They succeeded in passing a more progressive bill (the Revenue Act of 1916) that increased income tax rates and imposed a new excess profits tax on corporations. Treasury officials then recommended in 1917 and 1918 that Congress expand the category of allowable business deductions in order to offset recent increases in corporate taxation. Immediately after the war, the Treasury recommended that Congress repeal the excess profits tax levied on corporations.

Evidence of this pattern becomes clearer after World War I. The Republican Party capitalized on voters' frustrations with the conduct of the war and subsequent economic recession to regain control of Congress in 1918 and the White House in 1920. The recapture of Congress was particularly significant because it meant that southern Democrats—notably Ways and Means chairman Claude Kitchin (D-N.C.), Ways and Means Subcommittee on Internal Taxation chairman Cordell Hull (D-Tenn.), and Finance Subcommittee on Income and Estate Taxes chairman John Sharp Williams (D-Miss.)—no longer controlled tax policy. Kitchin was "a proponent of taxing the rich," Hull "had a strong populist heritage and a distinct distrust of large corporate interests," and Williams "had a genuine dislike for urban-oriented business interests."[38] After the war, although agreeing that taxes had to come down, the two major parties disagreed over the size and distribution of any tax cut. Not surprisingly, Republicans favored larger reductions in the taxes of corporations and wealthy individuals. Much like their brethren of the 1980s and 1990s, Republicans claimed that lower taxes were needed to foster investment and economic growth.

This theme struck a responsive chord among business organizations such as the National Industrial Conference Board, Business Men's National Tax Committee, and the Tax League of America. Ironically, the very successes of those favoring redistributive taxation triggered a backlash in the business community that contributed to their undoing. The rapid increases in corporate taxation during the war prompted business interests to shift their lobbying efforts away from tariffs and focus more on lowering corporate income taxes. Not wanting to seem unpatriotic, they said nothing at first about higher taxes. As soon as the war ended, they launched a "crusade" against the excess profits tax.[39] Conservative Republicans and big business accepted as settled the question of whether the United States would have income taxes. They realized that equally fundamental questions remained, particularly over tax rates and the definition of taxable income.

Once in the majority, Republicans began to deliver on their promise of tax reduction. Wholesale reductions in tax rates were initially precluded, as there were sufficient numbers of Democrats and Progressives to block radical change, so Republicans concentrated on winning tax breaks for specific constituencies. Recent changes within Congress, decentralizing power away from the Speaker and to committee chairmen, facilitated this strategy. Individual legislators were better able to attach tax breaks to revenue bills, either by striking a deal with the Ways and Means or Finance chairmen, or by offering an amendment on the floor.[40] With the demise of the Progressive challenge in 1924, Republicans were able to achieve both rate reductions and favorable tax treatment for special interests.

The most important of these tax measures with respect to employer pensions were the Revenue Acts of 1921 and 1926. Both Acts recognized the growing tendency of companies to establish trusts for the purpose of accumulating and distributing fringe benefits to their employees. The 1921 Act, the first legislation to build on the aforementioned Treasury rulings, exempted employer contributions to trusts that were part of a stock-bonus or profit-sharing plan. Revenue officials at the Treasury interpreted this legislation to apply as well to pension trusts, making 1921 the effective starting point of this tax expenditure.[41] Five years later Congress legitimated this practice when, as part of the Revenue Act of 1926, it "exempted from taxation employer contributions to pension trusts and postponed taxes on the benefits of those trusts until they had been received by the employees."[42]

Who supported these specific provisions and why is unclear. As mentioned earlier, they were enacted with little debate or justification. Still, the overall thrust of these acts is clear. Conservative Republicans were determined after the war to lower the excess profits tax on corporations and surtaxes on wealthy individuals.[43] They proposed a quid pro quo: Republicans had acquiesced in raising taxes to pay for the war, so Democrats should unite behind their plans to cut taxes after the war. The farm bloc, comprising southern Democrats and progressive Republicans, just as strenuously objected to providing tax relief to big business and the rich. They still viewed the tax code as a tool of redistribution. The lines were drawn exactly as they had been during the battles over instituting corporate and individual income taxes. This time, conservative Republicans had sufficient leverage in Congress and the White House to make some tax reduction inevitable; the only question was how much. The farm bloc was strong enough to prevent conservatives from getting everything they wanted but too weak to prevent outright repeal of the excess profits tax and substantial reductions in the surtax.[44] In the end, both sides compromised by leaving tax rates basically intact but creating many new preferences, including one for corporate stock-bonuses or profit-sharing plans in 1921.

Such compromises were unnecessary after 1924, and the Revenue Act of 1926 was the first tax bill to reflect the new balance of power in Washington. Treasury Secretary Mellon opened the bidding by proposing lower excise taxes on expensive consumer goods, further reductions in the surtax, and repeal of the estate and gift taxes. He also proposed changing the graduated rates on lower-income taxpayers from 2, 4, and 6 percent to a flat 5 percent, thereby increasing taxes for many individuals. House Democrats were at a loss over what to do. Although Mellon's proposal blatantly favored the wealthy, earlier Republican tax cuts had been associated with economic recovery and budget surpluses, making this one politically difficult to oppose. And Democrats lacked the numbers in Congress necessary to mount a serious challenge. House Democrats saved face by cutting the estate tax instead of eliminating it. Otherwise, Mellon scored a total victory. The Senate succeeded in making few changes to the House bill, mostly in the realm of corporate taxation. It clarified the depletion allowance for oil and gas properties and, at the last minute, allowed corporations to deduct their contributions to pension trusts.

This latter provision was inserted on February 12 by Sen. George McLean (R-Conn.). Most of the debate in the Senate that evening concerned estate and inheritance taxes. After this debate concluded, several senators introduced minor amendments that were accepted without debate. In introducing his amendment, McLean stated rather cryptically that "it has come to my attention that the funds which are created for the purpose of providing pensions for employees are precisely on the same basis as those which provide stock bonuses or profit-sharing plans. That is all there is to the amendment."[45] And that was all there was to the congressional debate over the taxation of employer pensions. How pensions came to McLean's attention is unclear. What is known is that McLean was a pro-business northeastern Republican who, like Mellon, believed that tax cuts for wealthy individuals and corporations were the key to economic growth.[46] It is also clear that companies gave up nothing in order to receive these tax benefits. The law only required that pensions be for "the exclusive benefit of some or all of the employees." Employers did not have to provide pensions to a specified fraction of their employees, take steps to safeguard the financial health of their pension plans, or provide employees with information about their pensions. Employers were free to limit pensions to officers and better-paid employees, and many appear to have done just that.

DISCUSSION

The timing of these two programs suggests a couple of revisions to the conventional wisdom. The first is that the national government started to subsidize what we now call social welfare years before the New Deal. The other is that social policy did not proceed along two separate tracks, one public and the other private, during the early twentieth century.[47] On the public track we find most state governments enacting mothers' pensions and workman's compensation legislation, and a few states enacting old-age pensions. Despite breakthroughs in Europe, nationwide social programs were politically infeasible in the United States. On the private track we find "welfare capitalism," which refers to a wide variety of practices pioneered by large corporations interested in exchanging fringe benefits and better work conditions for labor peace and improved productivity.[48] The only link between the two tracks, according to the conventional wisdom, is the Depression, which overwhelmed the capacity of state governments and private corporations to meet the needs of their citizens or employees. But the tracks remained separate as the Social Security Act strengthened and expanded state-level programs and as welfare capitalism temporarily collapsed. The tax expenditure for employer pensions indicates early overlap between public and private systems of social provision. Through it the national government helped in effect to underwrite welfare capitalism.[49] The forging of these links is significant if only because the current cost of underwriting fringe benefits through the tax code exceeds $100 billion (including medical and other benefits).

Along with timing, the scope of conflict was unusual. One would be hard-pressed to name another major component of the contemporary American welfare state that began as quietly as the tax expenditures for home mortgage interest and corporate pensions. Nothing approaching a public debate ever occurred. No counterpart to the Townsend Clubs of the 1930s agitated for reform. Unions, which grew considerably during the early twentieth century and were strongest in the industries most likely to offer pensions, would have been the last to push for this tax expenditure. Unions viewed company pensions "as a cheap means of getting rid of superannuated employees, an invisible chain by which workers were attached to a particular company through the promise of a pension and the threat of its loss if they quit or were fired."[50] They preferred instead to establish their own pension plans, which were ineligible for the same tax benefits accorded corporate plans.[51] Business elites were not instrumental in creating the tax expenditure for employer pensions, but policy makers were attentive to business interests in the 1920s.[52] In contrast, business played no role in creating the home mortgage interest deduction.

Nor did anything extraordinary happen within the government. No president established a blue-ribbon Committee on Housing or Retirement Security analogous to Roosevelt's Committee on Economic Security. No southern Democrats extracted concessions in exchange for their votes. Instead of unified Democratic control of Congress and the White House during the New Deal, we have unified Republican control during the 1920s when Congress formalized the tax treatment of employer pensions. Presidents Harding and Coolidge hardly compare with FDR as advocates of an activist government role in social welfare. President

Wilson is a closer match to FDR, but his domestic priorities were business regulation and civil service reform.

These tax expenditures emerged as by-products of protracted struggles over taxation among Democrats, Progressives, and conservative Republicans. When the balance of power tipped in favor of Democrats and Progressives, income taxes were created. These politicians designed individual income taxes in such a way that they would not affect their constituencies, and part of this effort included exempting all consumer debt. As conservative Republicans regained control of government, specific provisions favoring business were added to the tax code, and tax rates were lowered. The goal of tax policy changed from redistribution to investment, and part of that change involved the taxation of employer pensions.

CHAPTER 3

Earned Income Tax Credit

THE Earned Income Tax Credit (EITC) has been hailed in recent years as the policy equivalent of penicillin. The *New York Times*, for example, has described the EITC as "a wonderful but little-known anti-poverty weapon . . . the best means available for lifting the working poor out of poverty."[1] Many Republicans have embraced the program as a superior alternative to welfare (meaning AFDC), to a higher minimum wage, and to government-run day care centers. President Clinton and fellow Democrats have made an expanded EITC central to their plans for reforming welfare, increasing the progressivity of the tax system, and improving the economic security of low-wage workers. It is hard to think of another government program that has received such universal acclaim among political elites. Considering the prevailing skepticism, if not hostility, toward public assistance programs, the popularity of the EITC is remarkable.

One might expect to find a fairly extensive literature explaining the origin and development of such a promising program. Not so. We know relatively little about the politics of the Earned Income Tax Credit. This chapter begins to close that gap. The purpose is to analyze the creation of the EITC. Chapter 7 explains its subsequent development. As we shall see, on almost every count the Earned Income Tax Credit constitutes a clear exception to prevailing beliefs about the origins of means-tested social programs in the United States. Aside from the unusual timing of the EITC, perhaps the most striking difference was the role of conservatives and moderates in Congress. Southern Democrats, who have repeatedly blocked or reduced social welfare benefits for the poor (including Aid to Dependent Children [ADC] and its successor AFDC), paved the way for the EITC.

To date, Senator Russell Long (D-La.) has been given exclusive credit for passage of the Earned Income Tax Credit.[2] Although Long has rightly been cited as the program's chief architect, no one has yet explained why Long's version triumphed over a much different version originating in the House of Representatives. Nor has anyone pointed out the ways in which President Nixon, another odd pioneer in social policy, influenced the program's enactment. This chapter attempts to situate Long's actions in a larger historical and institutional context that makes this case more interesting and more instructive. Particular emphasis is placed on certain institutional reforms occurring in Congress just before the EITC was enacted.

The roots of the EITC can be traced to the explosive growth in AFDC during the 1960s and subsequent attempts at welfare reform.[3] As a result of northern migration, public protest, and a series of favorable court decisions, the number of AFDC recipients more than tripled between 1962 and 1967, reaching five million. This expansion, combined with a more conservative Congress and fears that the nation's cities were about to erupt from below, prompted many policy makers to search for ways of restructuring welfare in order to promote self-sufficiency.

The first attempt to move people off the AFDC rolls failed miserably. Under the Work Incentive Program (nicknamed WIN, rather than the more ominous WIP), AFDC recipients who worked for wages could keep $30 per month and one-third of all earnings above that. Previously each dollar of earnings brought a corresponding dollar decrease in AFDC benefits, a clear disincentive to work. Participants also received greater assistance in job counseling, training, and referrals. WIN was hampered from the beginning by inadequate funding, bureaucratic infighting, wide variations among states in eligibility rules, and lack of coordination between the job services offered and the actual needs of local labor markets. "Even when WIN managed to place women, it was usually in sex-segregated training and job slots with wages below the poverty line. Indeed, WIN participants could be required to work in jobs that paid as little as 75 percent of the minimum wage."[4] The AFDC rolls continued to swell, and by 1970 the total hit eight million.

The growing belief among conservatives that AFDC was a disaster was one reason Richard Nixon declared welfare reform a top priority of his new administration. Nixon recognized the importance of establishing his administration's identity as soon as possible after the 1968 election. The choice of welfare reform might enable Republicans to loosen the Democratic Party's grip on social policy without compromising their own party's image of fiscal prudence. Such a move was welcomed by those business leaders and moderate Republicans who had been convinced by the urban riots of 1965–68 that their party had to do more to address social issues.

In 1969 President Nixon proposed legislation to overhaul the nation's public assistance programs. The administration's Family Assistance Plan (FAP) would have replaced all means-tested cash assistance programs with a single cash transfer. That part of FAP was essentially a negative income tax: it guaranteed every family in the nation a minimum annual income, whether or not any member of that family worked for wages. In order to discourage voluntary unemployment, the minimum was set at $1,600 for a family of four, which was greater than AFDC benefits in some states but still less than one-half the poverty line. The plan included work requirements, and unemployed parents who refused "suitable" employment and training could have their benefits reduced.[5]

As a work incentive, FAP extended additional benefits to low-wage workers. When introducing FAP, Nixon declared that "for the first time the government would recognize that it has no less of an obligation to the working poor than to the nonworking poor; and for the first time, benefits would be scaled in such a way that it would always pay to work."[6] The proposed family assistance supplement equaled $1,600 for a family of four earning up to $720. The supplement was then reduced by fifty cents for every additional dollar earned. A family of four earning $2,000, for instance, would be eligible for a supplement of $960.[7] The income ceiling for this family was $3,920, roughly the equivalent of the poverty line and of one full-time, minimum-wage job.

As others have remarked, FAP embodied a curious mixture of conservative and liberal principles of welfare reform.[8] On the one hand, income transfers allowed recipients more freedom of choice as consumers than in-kind assistance. A single income transfer was more efficient than several overlapping assistance programs. Those who worked would always receive more money than those who did not. FAP also rendered obsolete the social service bureaucrats whom Nixon despised. On the other hand, by legitimating the right of the working poor to public assistance, Nixon proposed tripling the public assistance rolls at the same time that conservatives from both parties were condemning the growth of AFDC. Another feature of the plan likely to appeal to liberals were standardized welfare benefits among the states.

Had Nixon gone soft? Hardly. His motivation was less compassion than hard-boiled political realism. By 1969 means-tested social programs were becoming inextricably linked with race. Many citizens were identifying Great Society programs as black programs, an association tainted by images of urban riots and much-publicized accounts of welfare fraud. The feeling was deepening among less affluent whites that they were subsidizing blacks to engage in any number of socially undesirable behaviors. By extending benefits to the working poor, most of whom were white, Nixon hoped to mitigate any racial antagonisms that FAP might generate. He simultaneously provided tangible economic benefits to a group of voters whose allegiance to the Democratic Party, as evidenced by the success of George Wallace in the 1968 presidential election, had started to wane.[9]

Though FAP passed quickly in the House, it ran into considerable opposition in the Senate Finance Committee. Finance was dominated by conservatives from the South and West who were either indifferent to FAP or believed that it promised too much. Only Abraham Ribicoff of Connecticut could be said to have represented urban and liberal interests, and he felt that FAP's income threshold was too low. Administration officials did a poor job initially of explaining the proposal to skeptical committee members. By the time they had straightened out their argument, interest groups from the Right and Left had begun to criticize FAP. Business interests argued that it represented too large an expansion. Liberals and welfare rights groups argued that the income threshold was too low and frankly distrusted any social welfare initiative backed by President Nixon. FAP consequently stalled in Finance through 1971, despite efforts by Nixon officials to redesign the program.

Russell Long led opposition to the plan in the Senate. While conceding the need for comprehensive reform, Long was concerned about FAP's cost and work disincentives. He believed that the current welfare system was already too generous. A guaranteed income would simply make matters worse. And the promise of generally higher benefits in the South would encourage the "wrong" sorts of behaviors. It was Long, after all, who allegedly referred to the National Welfare Rights Organization as "Black Brood Mares, Inc." The welfare population, in Long's view, should be divided into two groups, the employable and the truly needy. The government should target aid to the truly needy and weed out those who could be working but found it easier not to. When FAP was reconsidered in 1972, Long proposed an alternative. His workfare bill declared all employable persons ineligible for cash assistance.[10] They would instead have to find work or accept a government job paying 60 percent of the minimum wage.

By setting the wage scale so low, Long clearly intended to minimize the need for public jobs. As an added incentive, Long stipulated that workers earning low wages in the private sector would be eligible for a wage supplement and, more important, a 10 percent work bonus.[11] Heads of households with children would be eligible for a cash rebate equivalent to 10 percent of their income as long as family income was less than $4,000. Long had essentially jettisoned FAP's guaranteed income but kept the plan's work incentives and benefits for the working poor. Long's work bonus, typically viewed as the earliest version of the EITC, actually owed much in spirit and structure to Nixon's family assistance supplement.

Some conservatives argue that Ronald Reagan and not Russell Long should be credited with inventing the EITC.[12] The case for Reagan, then the conservative governor of California, hinges on the timing and supposed novelty of his testimony before the Finance Committee. Most of his comments were devoted to criticizing FAP and touting recent welfare reforms in California.[13] In one brief passage, however, Reagan tacitly admitted that employment did not always guarantee self-sufficiency. He suggested that the national government should "exempt low-income families from the federal and state income tax (including withholding) and provide them a rebate for their social security taxes, including the employer's contribution thereto."[14] Long was present when Reagan testified, and he strongly endorsed the governor's comments. Several months later Long proposed the work bonus, which would have given him and his staff enough time to incorporate Reagan's ideas into his own welfare reform package. That, in a nutshell, is the rather circumstantial case for Reagan as the inventor of the EITC.

Clearly the idea of assisting the working poor through the tax system antedated Reagan's testimony.[15] Nixon's family assistance supplement provided Long with a far more concrete model for his work bonus than did Reagan's brief, general suggestion. Moreover, Long was no stranger to the uses of tax policy as social policy. His committee had worked on the Revenue Act of 1971, which included a tax credit for employers who hired participants in the WIN program. For much of his career, "Long saw the tax code as his tool for changing society."[16]

The one original contribution Reagan may have made was in linking payroll taxes and the plight of the working poor. Nixon never fully specified the reasons why the working poor needed a family assistance supplement. Reagan attributed their plight to high taxes, as did Long later that year. The work bonus, according to Long, was a "dignified way" to "prevent the taxing of people onto the welfare rolls." One of its purposes was to "prevent the social security tax from taking away from the poor and low-income earners the money they need for support of their families."[17] On the other hand, Reagan's testimony may have been irrelevant here, too. His suggestions for tax relief were buried in his written testimony and omitted from his spoken comments to Long and the Finance Committee.[18] As a general rule, senators do not read the full written statements submitted by witnesses, though members of their staff sometimes do. Long may never have known about Reagan's call for tax relief.

The Senate Finance Committee replaced FAP with Long's workfare proposal in September 1972. The full Senate voted to test FAP, Long's workfare proposal, and a more generous version of FAP backed by Ribicoff. When the House and Senate could not agree on a compromise bill, FAP died in conference, and with it Long's work bonus. Long reintroduced the work bonus idea in 1973 when the Finance Committee considered a series of amendments to the Social Security Act. The most important of these amendments were substantial increases in Social Security benefits and payroll taxes. Long repeated his concerns about the effect of payroll taxes on the working poor: "It is just not fair that these poor people should be taxed so heavily . . . especially when you recognize the fact that in many instances we are actually taxing these people into poverty."[19] The work bonus encountered resistance on the Senate floor when some members mistook it for a negative income tax. Senator Sam Ervin (D-N.C.) charged that it "uses the Social Security system as an excuse for paying a guaranteed annual income out of the Treasury" and demanded that it be dropped.[20] Still, the full Senate upheld Long's work bonus by a vote of 57 to 21. Even staunch liberals such as Hubert Humphrey and Ted Kennedy cast their vote for Long, a traditional antagonist on social issues.[21] But the measure failed to emerge out of conference committee, apparently because liberal House members still associated it with Long's workfare package from the year before. The same fate befell Long's attempt to attach the tax credit to a bill revising guidelines for state social service programs in 1974.[22]

Persistence finally paid off for Long. Buried deep in the Tax Reduction Act of 1975 was a new, refundable 10 percent tax credit for poor families—the Earned Income Tax Credit.[23] Like the work bonus, it was available only to wage-earning families with at least one dependent child. It equaled 10 percent of the first $4,000 in income and $400 minus ten cents for every dollar earned between $4,000 and $8,000. The only major modification was a longer phase-out range (from $5,600 in 1973 to $8,000 in 1975), and hence a slower phase-out rate. This change was important for it meant that more families above the poverty line were eligible.[24] The credit was estimated to cost $1.5 billion in lost revenue in 1975, a fraction of the Act's $22.8 billion total price tag.

The obvious question to ask is why legislation that had been defeated in 1972, 1973, and 1974 passed in 1975. More specifically, why did the House no longer object to Long's work bonus. Here we must speculate a bit about what happened. The basic problem is that the EITC was a footnote to a rather unremarkable tax bill. No separate hearings were held regarding the EITC, and no separate floor votes were taken. The most contentious issue surrounding the Tax Reduction Act was the oil depletion allowance, which pitted northern Democrats against representatives of oil-producing states (including Russell Long) and Republicans. Other features of the bill receiving careful scrutiny included taxation of foreign earnings by multinational corporations and the size of a one-time rebate on 1974 income taxes.

It seems likely that several events facilitated passage of the EITC. The first was the decision to append the EITC to tax legislation rather than to social welfare legislation. As a tax measure, the EITC was less likely to evoke images of workfare among House liberals. Tax legislation was also more likely to receive prompt attention by policy makers in 1975. In the wake of the OPEC oil shock and subsequent recession, stimulating the economy with tax cuts rose quickly to the top of the domestic agenda.[25] Legislators would have wanted to avoid blame for delaying tax relief and prolonging the recession just because they objected to some small provision like the EITC. Some EITC advocates even argued that given the poor's higher marginal propensity to consume, the EITC would boost the economy faster than an equivalent tax reduction for more affluent taxpayers.

The combination of recession and recent increases in payroll taxes bolstered Long's argument that low-income families needed tax relief. A report issued by the Joint Economic Committee showed that although food, housing, and transportation costs had fueled inflation, the cost of income taxes and payroll taxes had risen even faster.[26] The report also demonstrated that the combined burden of these tax increases fell disproportionately on low-income families. These findings resonated in the House. House Democrats openly criticized Ford's initial tax reduction proposal for doing too little for low-income families. They put forward their own version of the EITC, pushed for a larger standard deduction, and targeted Ford's one-time tax rebate at families earning less than $30,000.[27]

Finally, the new chairman of the House Ways and Means Committee was more attracted to the EITC than was his predecessor. Al Ullman (D-Oreg.) replaced Wilbur Mills (D-Ark.) as chairman in 1974. Though not as conservative as Long, Ullman objected on principle to the notion of a guaranteed income, considered the government to be the employer of last resort, and strongly advocated private sector employment for welfare recipients.[28] He was also concerned with the growing tax burdens of low-income workers. The EITC thus enabled him to address two problems at one time.

Ullman, not Long, was the first to attach the EITC to the administration's tax package. Although Ullman clearly used Long's work bonus as a model, he changed its structure in one crucial respect. If, as Long and others argued, the problems of the working poor were primarily the result of payroll taxes, then the EITC should be available to *all* low-income individuals, regardless of marital status or children. Accordingly, the House version of the EITC covered twenty-eight million taxpayers, several times the population eligible under Long's work bonus. In order to keep costs down, the House cut the tax credit from 10 to 5 percent of earned income. Even so, it was expected to cost $3 billion in its first year.

Despite portraying the EITC as an antidote to higher payroll taxes,[29] Finance members insisted on targeting the EITC at those most likely to land on the AFDC rolls, namely, low-income workers with dependent children: "The most significant objective of the provision should be to assist in encouraging people to obtain employment, reducing the unemployment rate and reducing the welfare rolls. Thus, the provision should be similar in structure and objective to the work bonus credit the committee has reported out previously."[30] The Senate version set the tax credit at 10 percent and increased the size of the phase-out range. The combined effect of these changes was to reduce the eligible population to seven million and to cut the projected cost of the EITC in half.

These two versions created distinctly different social programs. The House version served a population larger than that of any other means-tested program, larger even than Medicare. By defining eligibility strictly according to income—rather than according to some combination of income, family structure, age, or disability—it had the potential to promote a kind of class politics seldom found in the American welfare state. Though the benefits were small, they might grow over time, particularly considering the size of the program's constituency; witness the development of Social Security. The Senate version, in contrast, created a more typical means-tested program. Like AFDC, it served a small clientele, grouped according to income and family structure, that had few political resources, and its prospects for generating broad support were similarly dim. Whereas the House version depicted the EITC as tax relief, the Senate version portrayed it as welfare reform.[31]

The Senate version of the EITC triumphed in conference committee for reasons that are not entirely clear. One possibility is that the EITC was simply traded for some other tax reduction favoring low-income workers. For instance, the Senate won on the EITC and the House managed to target the one-time tax rebate toward the less affluent. House members may have accepted such a trade because the Senate version of the EITC still allowed them to claim they had done something for low-income workers or because they were more intent on hammering out an agreement on the oil depletion allowance, the main bone of contention between the two chambers.

A more institutional explanation would highlight the diminished influence of Ways and Means in tax politics. During the late 1960s and early 1970s, a series of reforms redefined the internal structure of

Congress. The underlying motive was to wrest control of the committee system out of the hands of a few senior chairmen who were, on average, more conservative than Congress as a whole:

> The end result of these reforms was to distribute political influence more evenly throughout the two chambers, but especially in the House, which was the more rule bound of the two. More than most committees, the House Ways and Means Committee, the key tax committee in Congress, was buffeted by several waves of reform . . .
>
> Formal reforms that most affected the Ways and Means Committee during the 1960s and 1970s included the following: the committee's size was increased by approximately fifty percent; the Democratic members of the committee ceased to function as the party's "committee on committees"; Ways and Means was required to create subcommittees with staff and agendas controlled by the subcommittee, not the committee chair; and the use of the "closed rule" was severely restricted and brought under the oversight of the Democratic caucus.[32]

In the process of ousting incumbent chairmen, the House also lost Wilbur Mills's considerable expertise in tax policy and his bargaining clout with Finance.

The sum total of these reforms initially produced disorder and confusion within Ways and Means: "The [Ways and Means] committee's struggles left the Senate—particularly Senate Finance Committee Chairman Russell B. Long (D-La.)—to dominate 1975 tax legislation."[33] For a variety of reasons, the Finance Committee was relatively impervious to the reforms sweeping Congress and remained Russell Long's "fiefdom."[34] Long was thus better able to influence the final structure of the Tax Reduction Act than was Ullman. It seems reasonable to assume that Long took particular care to ensure that his work bonus became the EITC.

The truth may lie somewhere in between. Perhaps Long was in a position to dictate terms with the House, demanded that he prevail on the EITC, and allowed the House to declare victory on other parts of the Act about which he was indifferent. Regardless of the precise explanation, the important points to note are that the EITC was a small part of a larger revenue bill; that no hearings were held or votes taken specifically concerning the EITC; that it generated little debate and reflected little input from interest groups; that moderate to conservative members of the revenue committees were instrumental to its passage; that it appealed simultaneously to proponents of welfare reform and tax relief for the working poor; and that the impact of institutional reforms on the two revenue committees helped determine the final structure of the EITC.

DISCUSSION

In trying to account for the origins of the EITC, an exclusive focus on societal pressures does not get us very far. By the early 1970s, the civil rights movement had lost whatever power it had in the 1960s to influence national social welfare legislation. Subsequent movements for black power, women's rights, and an end to the Vietnam War did not include tax relief for low-income families on their political agendas. Because the structure of the EITC differentiates more along class lines than racial or gender lines, one might expect that business and labor interests were influential. As a wage subsidy, the EITC might have appealed particularly to business interests seeking to reduce demands for higher wages. There is no evidence, however, that representatives of business or labor played any part in proposing or passing the EITC. Nor did those responsible for passing the EITC ever claim to be acting on behalf of these interests. The absence of business influence makes the EITC an exception to corporate liberal models of social policy and to standard explanations of the origins of tax expenditures found in the tax policy literature.

One *can* argue that a variety of societal pressures compelled political elites to debate welfare reform during the late 1960s and early 1970s and that out of these debates came the initial model of the EITC. The most important of these pressures were growth in the AFDC program and urban riots. Still, no welfare rights organization or representative of the poor advocated anything like the EITC, and none lobbied for the tax credit once it had been proposed. They tried instead to increase benefit levels and expand eligibility for the existing AFDC program. Borrowing from Kingdon's model of the policy process, we might say that societal actors helped set the agenda but had little impact on either the range of policy alternatives considered or the decision to enact the EITC.[35]

The origin of the EITC poses problems for traditional state-centered explanations as well. Liberal Democrats had less influence in national politics during the early 1970s than they did in the mid-1930s. Although the Watergate scandal did cost a number of congressional Republicans their jobs in 1974, their replacements did not behave like classic liberal Democrats. Their districts were still moderate to conservative on matters of social policy, and far from safe.[36] Moreover, Republicans controlled the White House throughout the period in which the EITC was debated and enacted. Presidential leadership, so crucial to passage of the Social Security Act and Great Society programs, was not decisive. True, the Nixon administration did legitimate the principle of cash assistance to the working poor, and its Family Assistance Plan did contain the earliest version of the EITC. However, once FAP was defeated in 1972, Nixon lost interest in comprehensive welfare reform and, more important, in the family assistance supplement. His administration subsequently defined welfare reform more narrowly to mean administrative changes in AFDC.[37] President Ford played no part whatsoever in enacting the EITC.

Although all the traditional explanations for new social programs stress the rare and the extraordinary, what sets the EITC apart is how mundane and ordinary were its origins. Politicians who were moderate to conservative on social policy—Richard Nixon, Russell Long, and Al Ullman—were responsible for the timing and structure of the EITC. The key figure was Long, a strategically located member of the Senate Finance Committee and a conservative Democrat. Long transformed the family assistance supplement into the work bonus, kept the work bonus idea alive between 1972 and 1975, and successfully portrayed the EITC as an amalgam of welfare reform and tax relief for low-income workers. He did not have to publicize the merits of his proposal or engineer any groundswell of popular support. He did not have to win the president's endorsement, knit together a coalition of support in Congress, or even engage in explicit log-rolling. Instead, Long had to find the right legislative vehicle to essentially hide the EITC and the right language to portray its objectives to anyone who noticed. He then used his power as Senate Finance chairman, which happened to reach a high water mark in 1975, to guarantee passage of this tax credit.

CHAPTER 4

Targeted Jobs Tax Credit

AT LEAST since Franklin Roosevelt, presidents have introduced signature pieces of legislation soon after their election; Reagan's 1981 tax and spending cuts come immediately to mind. During these moments presidents try to set the agenda for their entire term with reference to some electoral mandate from the people. The New Jobs Tax Credit (NJTC), forerunner of the Targeted Jobs Tax Credit, originated during one of these moments.[1] President Carter's ambitions were not nearly as grand as Roosevelt's or Reagan's, but he too tried to seize the initiative immediately after his election. The most pressing problem facing Carter was the economy, a decisive issue in the 1976 campaign. The year 1975 had been the worst single year since the end of the Depression: real GNP declined by 1.1 percent, and inflation and unemployment reached what were then postwar highs of 9.3 and 8.5 percent, respectively. Although inflation declined to 5.2 percent in 1976, unemployment only dropped slightly, to 7.7 percent. The unemployment figure was still one and one-half times the average rate of the 1960s. Many economists predicted continued sluggishness in 1977 and perhaps even into 1978.

In the two months following his election, Carter and his advisers hammered out an economic stimulus package. The initial proposal, made public before Carter's inauguration, was a two-year, $30 billion combination of tax cuts and spending increases that offered something for just about everyone. Approximately one-third of the package consisted of major increases in direct spending for public service employment (PSE), public works, targeted job-training programs, and counter-cyclical revenue sharing. This approach was preferred by governors, mayors, organized labor, and various groups representing minorities and the poor.[2] The rest of Carter's proposal consisted of tax cuts for individuals and corporations, the route favored by business interests and most economists. Individual taxpayers were slated to receive the majority of these tax cuts because studies indicated that they "spend more of any tax cut they receive and spend it faster than do businesses,"[3] and because Carter wanted to cement ties with as many voters as possible. The major benefits for individual taxpayers were a one-time, $50 income tax rebate and a larger standard deduction.

Of the $3 billion or so earmarked for corporate tax relief, the main component was a 5 percent tax credit against payroll taxes designed to

increase employment. Missing was any increase in the existing investment tax credit (ITC), which was favored by manufacturers but opposed
by core Carter supporters—blacks and organized labor—who believed it
would encourage employers to substitute capital for labor. The lack of
an ITC expansion was singled out as a "notable exception" in a package
that otherwise "embodie[d] some part of every plan that ha[d] ever
been offered" to Carter.[4] Carter officials indicated at the time, however,
that they had not ruled out such an expansion.

By the time Carter submitted his final proposal to Congress, the mix
of business tax cuts had changed. Corporations could now choose between "a credit against income taxes of 4 percent of social security payroll taxes paid by the employer or an increase in the investment tax credit
for machinery and equipment from 10 to 12 percent."[5] The latter option encouraged capital-intensive industries to improve their capital
stock and hence their productivity. The former option, acclaimed as
"the only new thing"[6] in Carter's economic stimulus package, rewarded
labor-intensive industries for increasing employment. After considerable
congressional input, the payroll tax credit became the New Jobs Tax
Credit.

That Carter chose to promote employment through the tax code was
not surprising. As the most conservative Democrat to occupy the White
House in the twentieth century, Carter was favorably disposed toward
market-like remedies to public problems. Much of his energy policy, for
example, hinged on a variety of market incentives. In addition, Carter
named Charles Schultze, a prominent critic of overregulation, to head
his Council of Economic Advisers. Schultze's influential book, *The Public Use of Private Interest*, was originally delivered as the Godkin Lec-
tures at Harvard University in November and December of 1976, the
same period in which Carter was drafting his economic recovery package. An interesting note is that Schultze repeatedly cited employment
and training programs as prime candidates for greater use of market incentives, though he mentioned vouchers rather than tax credits.[7]

Neither Carter nor Schultze was the first to propose employment tax
credits. Similar measures had been suggested as early as 1936 by the
economist Nicholas Kaldor, and in the 1960s some Republicans, business leaders, and the Kerner Commission on urban riots had floated the
idea of offering businesses tax incentives to hire and train disadvantaged
workers.[8] Several contemporary economists—among them John Bishop
(University of Wisconsin), Robert Eisner (Northwestern University),
Gary Fethke (University of Iowa), and John Palmer (Brookings Institution)—pushed variants of this idea during the mid-1970s.[9] In early
1975, the Labor Department estimated that a general employment tax
credit would cost a fraction of that spent on public service employment

jobs.[10] In March of that same year, the National Small Business Association proposed a Job Creation Tax Credit geared toward small business. Legislators from both parties introduced several bills in 1976 that would have given employers tax credits for hiring or training workers.[11] A study prepared for the Joint Economic Committee predicted in 1976 that even a 1 percent wage subsidy would have an almost magical effect on the economy: it would "increase employment by 0.9 percent, increase real GNP by 0.5 percent, reduce consumer prices by 0.5 percent, raise real wages by 0.6 percent, while leaving the budget deficit unchanged or slightly lower."[12] The idea of using the tax code to combat unemployment, then, was definitely "in the air."

Few in Congress dared oppose the $50 rebate, and most agreed on the need to promote investment in plants and equipment. As a result, Carter's employment tax credit quickly took center stage. Most members of Congress considered it inadequate. A 4 percent reduction in employers' 5.85 percent Social Security tax rate reduced labor costs by less than one-quarter of 1 percent, hardly enough to affect hiring and production decisions. More fundamental was congressional opposition to any tax credit that benefited all employers whether or not they hired new workers. Many felt that Carter's proposal would produce windfall gains for employers.

Congress soon began to develop tax credit alternatives that rewarded only those firms hiring additional workers. Ways and Means chairman Al Ullman (D-Oreg.), for example, proposed giving firms a 25 percent tax credit on the first $4,200 of wages for new employees. Barber Conable (R-N.Y.), the ranking minority member of Ways and Means, proposed a $1 per hour tax credit for all incremental employment, and an additional fifty cents per hour for firms that hired the long-term unemployed (meaning more than twenty-six weeks). Rep. Butler Derrick (D-S.C.) also proposed a larger tax credit targeted at the long-term unemployed. Altogether, eleven separate proposals were introduced in the House and Senate, primarily from members of the two tax committees and the Senate Select Committee on Small Business. Most were introduced by conservative southern Democrats or moderate Republicans. Individual proposals differed primarily over providing additional tax benefits to economically distressed regions, to particular categories of hard-to-employ individuals, or to small versus large businesses.[13]

The subsequent congressional debates over these proposals were notable in two respects. First, legislators and expert witnesses delved more deeply into questions of program structure and implementation than had been typical of previous tax expenditures. Second, employment tax credits generated as much interest outside Washington as any previously proposed tax expenditure with social welfare objectives. Interest group support developed along predictable lines. The National Small Business Association and the National Federation of Independent Business, both of which represented small businesses and labor-intensive industries, were enthusiastic. The Chamber of Commerce, comprising diverse business interests, offered lukewarm support and expressed a preference for general cuts in corporate and individual taxes. Organized labor led opposition to the employment tax cut. The AFL-CIO called for greater spending on public works, housing, and job training rather than tax cuts, which it felt were likely to produce windfall benefits for many employers. It also worried that such a tax credit gave firms an incentive to substitute lower-skilled for higher-skilled workers and part-time for full-time workers, both of which would adversely affect its members. Capital-intensive firms such as U.S. Steel and General Electric favored greater emphasis on the investment tax credit for machinery, as did the National Association of Manufacturers. Among government officials, the most notable dissenters were liberal Democrats allied with organized labor (e.g., Sen. Ted Kennedy of Massachusetts) and the Treasury Department. Treasury officials argued that tax credits for incremental gains in employment were procyclical instead of countercyclical and thus bad economic policy. They also doubted the tax credit's impact on the economy and declared that incremental tax credits were no more immune from employer windfall than was the administration's more universal tax credit.[14]

None of these objections dented legislators' enthusiasm for an incremental employment tax credit. When Treasury officials pointed to the potential for employer windfalls, proponents in Congress politely replied that they were counting on the Treasury's considerable expertise in tax matters to minimize their occurrence. Capital-intensive industries might complain about the mix of tax credits, but the overall tax package certainly did not ignore their interests. Organized labor's demands were politically infeasible given the growing disillusionment in Congress and the White House with direct spending programs. Its political clout was further compromised by declining membership.

The differences among the various congressional proposals were small enough to permit the House and Senate to fashion a compromise bill fairly quickly. By the end of April, Carter's 4 percent payroll tax credit had been transformed into the New Jobs Tax Credit and incorporated, against the administration's wishes, into the Tax Reduction and Simplification Act of 1977. Under the NJTC program, firms that increased employment more than 2 percent (the expected rate of job growth in the economy) were eligible for a tax credit equal to 50 percent of the first $4,200 in wages for those additional employees. The size of the credit was limited to $100,000 per employer per year to prevent large companies from dominating the program. The Treasury estimated that the NJTC would reduce revenues by almost $700 million in fiscal year 1977, $2.5 billion the next year, and $1.9 billion in 1979.

Though billed as a general employment tax credit, the NJTC did single out the disabled for special treatment. Employers who hired the disabled could claim an additional 10 percent tax credit.[15] Special provisions added in the House for distressed regions, Vietnam veterans, welfare recipients, and the unemployed were later deleted. Implicitly, however, the New Jobs Tax Credit favored a variety of interests. As an employment rather than equipment tax credit, the NJTC was effectively targeted at labor-intensive industries. The dollar cap favored small- and medium-sized firms. And because the NJTC rewarded increases in employment above a certain threshold, it favored regions of the country, industries, and firms that were growing faster than the national average.

FROM NEW JOBS TO TARGETED JOBS

Congress allowed the New Jobs Tax Credit to expire and replaced it with the Targeted Jobs Tax Credit (TJTC) the following year.[16] To understand this transformation, we first need to consider President Carter's modest foray into urban policy. Greater aid to distressed cities was very much in demand after a series of fiscal crises rocked some of the nation's largest cities in the early 1970s. Carter had won the support of many big-city mayors during his 1976 presidential campaign by pledging to make urban policy a top domestic priority. Little of anything came of his pledges until March 1978 when Carter announced his "New Partnership to Conserve America's Communities." The Partnership was a somewhat uninspired mixture of old and new remedies. In addition to increasing funding for CETA (Comprehensive Employment and Training Act), Urban Development Action Grants, and housing rehabilitation, the proposal called for a new National Development Bank and a new tax credit for companies investing in distressed urban areas.

The New Partnership also proposed replacing the New Jobs Tax Credit with a Targeted Employment Tax Credit for companies that hired economically disadvantaged youths aged eighteen to twenty-four or disabled persons of any age. Though economic recovery was well under way, thus reducing the need for the more universal New Jobs Tax Credit, unemployment rates for disadvantaged youths hovered around 30 percent, five times the national average. Employers who hired such workers, most of whom lived in urban areas, would be eligible for a 33 percent tax credit (based on the first $6,000 of wages) in the first year of employment and a 25 percent tax credit in the second: "The proposed employment credit would give a direct incentive for taxpaying businesses to make more jobs available for young people from low-income families. It will also provide employers an incentive to retain eligible workers during the critical first two years in which their work habits and skills are developed."[17] Special consideration for the disabled was a carryover from the New Jobs Tax Credit. Administration spokesmen predicted that the Targeted Employment Tax Credit would be more efficient, less complex to administer, and more effective than the New Jobs Tax Credit, whose initial impact fell short of expectations.[18]

Business interests were split over the Targeted Employment Tax Credit. Representatives of the Business Roundtable, National Alliance of Business, and Smaller Manufacturers Council supported the administration's proposal. The chief naysayer was the National Federation of Independent Business (NFIB), which argued that targeting the credit would add yet another layer of bureaucracy to an already complex tax credit and that many small businesses would be reluctant to hire the types of workers targeted. It recommended continuing the New Jobs Tax Credit with minor administrative changes. No other interest group opposed the targeted tax credit, and a number of academic economists testified in favor of it. For all the concern expressed about the plight of the structurally unemployed, no group claiming to represent the interests of economically disadvantaged youths or the disabled testified before Congress.

While some legislators felt that Carter's proposal did too little to move workers into the private sector, the real undoing of the Targeted Employment Tax Credit was that the New Partnership cost too much. In light of the public's apparent opposition to more government, reflected most clearly by the passage of Proposition 13 in California, many members of Congress were unwilling to spend the necessary monies.[19] Carter's initiative died in Congress, though its less ambitious features were later incorporated in appropriations for various agencies.

Congress could defer action on new spending programs if legislators detected the slightest hint of resistance in the electorate. The one measure legislators absolutely had to pass was the annual budget, and the employment tax credit idea was resurrected later that year during deliberations over the Revenue Act of 1978. The administration's original proposal targeted tax relief to lower-income families hit hard by inflation. The centerpiece was a proposed 2 percent reduction in tax rates, which was a proportionally larger benefit for those in the lowest bracket (14 percent) than those at the upper end (70 percent). The package also included restrictions on a host of tax expenditures, including business entertainment expenses, fringe benefits, export earnings, and capital gains. House Democrats were badly split over this bill. Although most liberal Democrats supported it, many moderate and conservative Democrats believed that voters had reached their limit of progressive taxation and that more attention had to be given to stimulating investment. They allied with Republicans to completely overhaul Carter's proposal. Congress voted to lower tax rates on capital gains, reduce corporate income tax rates for firms with $100,000 or less in income, make permanent the 10 percent investment tax credit, and create a once-in-a-lifetime exclusion of $100,000 in capital gains from home sales for those aged fifty-five and older. Congress preserved some of Carter's individual tax cuts, but the overall distribution of benefits was hardly progressive.[20]

Given the growing resistance to new spending initiatives, some legislators seized the opportunity to enact their pet proposals surreptitiously, as amendments to the revenue bill. As we will see in chapter 7, members of the revenue committees used the 1978 Revenue Act to expand and make permanent the EITC. In a similar fashion, members of the Ways and Means Committee attached a tax incentive for hiring disadvantaged workers that strongly resembled Carter's Targeted Employment Tax Credit. The original version of this Targeted Jobs Tax Credit was proposed by Rep. Charles Rangel, a liberal Democrat and member of the Ways and Means Committee. As a representative from New York City, Rangel was understandably concerned with welfare and urban policy.[21] The recent failure of Carter's New Partnership, which Rangel had strongly supported, had hurt his constituents. Furthermore, Rangel, like other liberal Democrats, wanted to ensure that the final Revenue Act did not promote business investment to the exclusion of less affluent citizens. The other key architect of the program was Ways and Means chairman Ullman, who viewed the TJTC more as welfare reform. Ullman had been interested in employment alternatives to welfare since the FAP debates and had been influential in creating the New Jobs and Earned Income Tax Credits.[22]

The Ways and Means bill replaced the New Jobs Tax Credit with a tax credit that was both more generous per employee and more narrowly targeted. Employers who hired welfare recipients, youths from cooperative educational programs, and Vietnam veterans (all of whom tended to live in large cities) were eligible for a tax credit equal to one-half of the first $6,000 in wages in the first year and one-sixth of the first $6,000 in wages in the second. According to Bill Signer, then a member of Rangel's staff who helped draft the TJTC legislation, these tax benefits were intended to offset the additional training costs that were thought to deter employers from hiring these workers.[23] Subsequent Senate amendments added categories for economically disadvantaged youths aged eighteen to twenty-four, physically and mentally disabled individuals undergoing vocational rehabilitation, and ex-convicts from economically disadvantaged families. The Senate also refined the category of welfare recipients to include only SSI and General Assistance recipients; the WIN tax credit for AFDC recipients remained a separate incentive and increased in value. The final version of the Revenue Act also increased the value of the tax credit in the second year from one-sixth to one-fourth of the first $6,000 in wages. Unlike the NJTC, the TJTC legislation did not set an absolute dollar cap per employer in order to favor small- and medium-sized firms.

During months of hearings on the Revenue Act of 1978, only one interest group, the Council of Vietnam Veterans, testified in favor of the TJTC. No one testified against it.[24] Business interests that might have benefited from hiring these workers were otherwise occupied. Restaurant and hotel industry lobbyists, for instance, were busy fighting Carter's proposed reductions in the deductibility of business entertainment expenses (the legendary "three-martini lunches"). Legislators spent the vast majority of their time on the bill debating the tax treatment of capital gains, domestic international sales corporations, and itemized deductions. No separate hearings were held or floor votes taken concerning the TJTC.

Sustained debate was probably unnecessary. Because a variety of tax credits had been discussed the year before, many policy makers already knew the strengths and weaknesses of the proposed TJTC. Several business organizations had expressed support for Carter's failed Targeted Employment Tax Credit earlier in the year. Liberal Democrats were anxious to find a politically feasible approach to urban policy or employment policy. Conservative Democrats and Republicans could support the use of market mechanisms generally and jobs programs in particular in light of evidence of abuse in the CETA program. A number of prominent Republicans sponsored legislation in 1977 similar to the New Jobs Tax Credit, thereby demonstrating an interest in using the tax code to foster employment. Furthermore, three Republican members of the Senate Finance Committee sponsored an alternative to Carter's Targeted Employment Tax Credit in 1978 that obviously resembled the TJTC. In short, support for the TJTC was clearly bipartisan, and the revenue committees were unquestionably the most important architects of the legislation.

DISCUSSION

Enactment of the New Jobs and Targeted Jobs Tax Credits was more public and more contested than the other three tax expenditures in this study. Representatives of big business, small business, organized labor, academia, Congress, and the Carter administration debated the relative merits of general versus incremental employment tax credits, as well as alternative designs for an incremental tax credit. These debates were substantive, and the extent of disagreement was considerable. The number and variety of tax credit proposals, and their emergence from committees other than the revenue committees, sets this case apart. Nevertheless, important points of continuity with previous tax expenditures were evident. The jobs tax credits were again attached to annual revenue bills rather than new spending initiatives; they were a small part of the overall bill; and, again, no specific votes were taken.

The degree of contrast with direct spending programs for employment and training is likewise not as sharp as in previous chapters. Timing remains a key difference: the major periods of innovation in the visible welfare state were the 1930s, when the Roosevelt administration initiated a variety of temporary jobs programs, and the 1960s, when the Kennedy and Johnson administrations inaugurated the first of a series of programs providing skills and jobs to the unemployed. This second burst of innovation is typically dated by the passage of the Manpower Development and Training Act (MDTA) and the Economic Opportunity Act.[25] The New Jobs and Targeted Jobs Tax Credits appeared more than a decade later.

The circumstances surrounding enactment are somewhat similar, primarily because the MDTA is a bit of an anomoly in the visible welfare state.[26] It was enacted in 1962, before the historic 1964 elections and before the civil rights movement had a major impact on national politics. Groups representing business and labor were conspicuously absent from the entire legislative process. If anything, union officials feared that government-sponsored employment and training programs might interfere with their own apprenticeship programs and subsidize nonunion shops.[27] The main advocates in Congress were northern and midwestern Democrats, led by Sen. Joseph Clark of Pennsylvania, who were worried about structural unemployment in their districts. These legislators were influenced by a small group of academic economists and labor specialists who attributed structural unemployment to technological change and who proposed retraining workers adversely affected by automation, most of whom were skilled or semiskilled. Clark introduced legislation in 1962 modeled closely after a proposal made by the American Vocational Association (AVA), a recognized authority on employment and training issues in the early 1960s. The AVA was more of a collection of policy experts than an interest group representing business, labor, program beneficiaries, or state governments. The bill passed in Congress with little fanfare. Kennedy signed the bill but continued to stress more general tools of macroeconomic management. There was, in short, nothing terribly extraordinary about the enactment of the MDTA.

The Economic Opportunity Act of 1964 is a more typical example of extraordinary circumstances producing new social welfare legislation. This Act, the foundation of Johnson's so-called war on poverty, created a variety of employment and training programs (e.g., Neighborhood Youth Corps and Jobs Corps) targeted at blacks, youths, and cities. Though scholars agree that the Act was a highly visible, much debated piece of legislation—and that groups representing business and labor were peripheral—they disagree about which extraordinary circumstances were decisive. The most likely candidates include the civil rights movement and President Johnson's ability to turn Kennedy's assassination into a mandate for government action. These events contributed to passage of not only the Economic Opportunity Act but also the Civil Rights Act of 1964 and the Voting Rights Act of 1965.[28] In terms of the scope of conflict, the jobs tax credits fall somewhere between the MDTA and the Economic Opportunity Act. They differed primarily to the extent that business and labor cared much more about tax credits than about comparable direct spending programs.

Created just a few years after the Earned Income Tax Credit, the Targeted Jobs Tax Credit nevertheless indicates real change in the politics of enacting tax expenditures. Many of these changes were the result of the congressional reforms mentioned in the last chapter, which had just begun to take effect when the EITC passed. These developments are elaborated on in the concluding chapter, which highlights important milestones in the politics of the hidden welfare state. Despite these changes, congressional revenue committees and tax politics continued to exert a major influence on the creation of new tax expenditures with social welfare objectives.

PART THREE

Development

THE FOLLOWING chapters analyze the development of four tax expenditures from the time of their enactment to the mid-1990s. The level of detail in each chapter varies, as two of the programs have existed for almost eighty years and two for only twenty years. The main message in all four cases is the same: the development of the hidden welfare state has been quite different from that of the visible welfare state. To appreciate these differences, one needs to know how scholars have characterized the development of traditional social programs.[1]

According to the social policy literature, the most important feature of U.S. social programs is the extent to which they are inclusive or targeted.[2] Inclusive social programs like Social Security and Medicare develop broad bases of political support that enable them to grow faster and resist retrenchment longer than targeted social programs like AFDC. One obvious reason is the sheer number of people with a material stake in these programs. The broad scope of inclusive programs makes it difficult for elected officials, regardless of ideology or party affiliation, to initiate cutbacks. Although interest groups representing beneficiaries (e.g., the American Association of Retired Persons [AARP]) do lobby to preserve and expand benefits, their efforts are sometimes superfluous. Politicians know all too well how sacred these programs are to many voters and may act in anticipation of interest group demands.[3] A second reason for the strength of inclusive programs is their financing. Inclusive programs are typically funded according to social insurance principles in which individuals contribute a portion of their wages to a common fund and, in return, are entitled to a certain level of benefits if they retire, fall ill, or are disabled. Recipients earn their benefits through paid work. Such programs carry considerable moral weight in a nation that glorifies the individual and the work ethic.

Broad-based support for inclusive programs does not always develop naturally or automatically. Martha Derthick describes how politically savvy bureaucrats at the Social Security Administration nurtured Social Security during its formative years until its expansion became a priority to many voters. Program administrators consciously cultivated support for Social Security among key members of Congress, and they portrayed the program to the public in such a way that would tap into classic liberal values. Their actions paved the way for incremental expansion of eligibility; Social Security covered roughly half of all workers in the private sector in 1935 and almost all of them by 1960. Their actions made it more likely that elected officials would feel compelled to increase benefits substantially, as they did in the late 1960s and early 1970s. By that point, organized groups like the AARP had become a powerful constituency, and policy makers had become aware of the elderly's propensity to vote on specific issues. Thus inclusive programs may require an initial boost from advocates within the government before they develop mass appeal.[4]

Retrenchment of inclusive programs is politically difficult but not impossible. The key is how the issue is framed. If critics claim that cutbacks are needed to fight the deficit or to shrink the size of the government, they will usually fail. Whatever support deficit reduction may generate in the abstract starts to melt away once voters are asked to give up some of their retirement or medical benefits. The more promising approach is to frame any cuts as a remedy to a trust fund crisis in a specific program. That way, voters have the sense that policy makers are trying to "save" the program rather than undermine it; voters believe that cutting back now will assure benefits in the future. Policy makers used the trust fund approach when passing major reforms to Social Security in 1983, including an increase in the retirement age and taxation of some benefits. More recently, congressional Republicans have used this strategy to justify substantial cuts to Medicare.[5]

If these insights apply to the hidden welfare state, then we would expect eligibility for the tax expenditures for home mortgage interest and employer pensions to start small and expand gradually. We would expect officials at the Treasury Department, which administers the program, to take the lead in pushing for expansion. Once these programs covered a large portion of home owners and workers, we should see widespread consensus concerning the program's basic objectives and steady growth. Groups representing home owners and retirees should become vocal advocates. Proposed cuts should be politically contentious and justified as a way of saving the program.

Targeted social programs are supposed to follow a rockier path. By definition they benefit a minority of voters. Being few in number might not be a problem if beneficiaries could persuade elected officials that they cared intensely about the program and would punish anyone who threatened their interests. This threat is simply not credible for AFDC, public housing, and other programs aimed at low-income citizens. The poor are less likely to vote, participate in campaigns, contribute money to candidates, join interest groups, and even protest than are more affluent citizens.[6] Beneficiaries are disproportionately black, Hispanic, female, and quite young—hardly anyone's notion of the power elite.

Nor does the method of financing targeted programs help. These programs are funded out of general revenues rather than contributory taxes, making it easier for citizens to believe that their money is going to someone who has not earned it. When programs are repeatedly referred to as "handouts" and "the dole," it is a pretty good indication that they lack legitimacy.

Whatever political support these targeted programs can muster is cobbled together from congressional committees and administrative agencies with jurisdiction over the programs, as well as liberal antipoverty groups, academic policy experts, and, in some cases, third-party service providers. Although this arrangement resembles the classic iron triangle or policy subgovernment in which advocates insulate themselves from oversight and cutbacks, in practice targeted social programs are quite vulnerable. Some members of the relevant congressional committees are openly hostile to these programs; some agency heads are indifferent; and some prominent analysts favor abolishing targeted programs and relying more on private charity and self-reliance. Cutbacks are common and occasionally drastic, as during the first years of the Reagan administration. Even during favorable periods of economic growth or Democratic Party rule, their expansion can elicit significant opposition. The experience of targeted social programs leads us to expect a far different story for the Earned Income Tax Credit and Targeted Jobs Tax Credit than for home mortgage interest and employer pensions. The first two programs should generate less support and more controversy. Their rate of growth should be slower and may even be negative during the 1980s.

A second distinction commonly made in the literature is between the development of cash transfers versus in-kind benefits.[7] Though less important than the inclusive/targeted distinction, cash/in-kind helps explain differences among inclusive programs and particularly among targeted programs. In-kind benefits are supposedly advantaged because third-party providers acquire a direct stake in the program. Medicaid recipients may lack political clout, but the doctors, hospitals, and nursing homes that Medicaid reimburses for medical care are politically powerful. One can extend this argument to Medicare to help account for its rapid growth in recent years, expanding even faster than Social Security. Moreover, in-kind benefits are advantaged because citizens know better where their tax dollars are being spent. Citizens are more likely to worry about cash transfers like AFDC—which can be used to buy anything, no matter how unwise or illegal—than they are in-kind benefits like job training. If this distinction holds true, then the tax expenditure for home mortgage interest should develop differently from employer pensions because the former is an incentive for purchasing a specific good, and the latter is an open-ended cash transfer to retirees. The Targeted Jobs Tax Credit (in-kind) should develop a broader base of support than the Earned Income Tax Credit (cash) for similar reasons, and that support should translate into faster growth.

The tax policy literature suggests that the inclusive/targeted and cash/in-kind distinctions are unimportant.[8] What matters instead are the institutional advantages enjoyed by all tax expenditures relative to all direct expenditure programs. Once enacted, tax expenditures are allegedly removed from politics. They become permanent fixtures of the tax code and are never required to go through the rigors of the annual appropriations process. Few tax expenditures are evaluated against any standard of performance, and fewer still contain sunset provisions mandating their termination unless explicitly reauthorized by Congress. Their continuation and expansion does not require any understanding between politicians and voters nor any coalition of interest group advocates. If this literature is correct, then all four cases should experience roughly the same pattern of development. None of them should be politicized to the extent that direct expenditure programs are.

As the following chapters demonstrate, few of these expectations are borne out by the evidence. The basic distinction between inclusive and targeted programs does not capture important differences in program growth. The Earned Income Tax Credit, a targeted tax expenditure, has grown faster than comparable programs for home mortgage interest and employer pensions since 1980. Policy makers greatly expanded the EITC's eligibility criteria and benefit levels at the same time they were reducing the number of taxpayers eligible for the home mortgage interest deduction. Cash assistance through the EITC grew more rapidly than in-kind employment and training benefits financed by the TJTC, again contrary to expectations.

Patterns of political support were likewise distinctive. In no case did home owners or retirees or the working poor create an organization of beneficiaries comparable to the American Association of Retired Persons. The major interest groups for each tax expenditure represented third-party providers, even in the case of retirement pensions, a cash transfer program. Interest group support, however, sometimes took decades to materialize.

In no case were program administrators important advocates of tax expenditures. On the contrary, the Treasury Department has been one of their harshest and most consistent critics. During the late 1930s, Treasury officials identified the tax expenditure for employer pensions as an unwanted loophole favoring the rich. Although Treasury officials have since come to accept this program as a political fact of life, they proposed major restrictions to it as part of comprehensive tax reform proposals prepared in 1977 and 1984. Some Treasury officials considered eliminating the home mortgage interest deduction in the mid-1980s. Treasury officials were peripheral to the EITC program for all but 1984–86, and even then offered qualified support. The TJTC is the most striking case, for the Treasury publicized its shortcomings and repeatedly asked Congress to terminate the program. Such behavior is almost unheard of from the Department of Health and Human Services. Chapter 9 suggests some reasons for Treasury officials' seemingly perverse behavior.

Nevertheless, all evidence indicates that the absence of bureaucratic and at times interest group support did not necessarily translate into slow growth or retrenchment. Some tax expenditures experienced periods of what I call *growth without advocacy*, largely owing to the peculiar properties of tax expenditures as policy tools. These properties are discussed in the following chapters and in the conclusion. Such growth is consistent with predictions derived from the tax policy literature, and yet it is easy to overstate the extent to which these programs are removed from politics.[9] The Targeted Jobs Tax Credit, a temporary tax expenditure, has been formally extended approximately once every other year since its enactment. Congressional hearings, some of them quite critical of the program, have been common. The Earned Income Tax Credit has been substantially altered on several occasions and its expansion debated regularly since the latter half of the 1980s. The tax expenditure for employer pensions has been subject to constant legislative tinkering for almost two decades, and home mortgage interest for the last ten years.

By the 1980s growth without advocacy had ended: all four tax expenditures had developed support among interest groups and elected officials; all four had experienced statutory changes in eligibility or benefit levels. Several of these changes involved retrenchment, and here again the politics differed from those of the visible welfare state. Tax expenditures for employer pensions and home mortgage interest were reduced *not* to preserve their long-run fiscal viability but to help reduce the deficit and promote a fairer, simpler tax code. This is the exact opposite of what scholars have found with respect to Social Security and other inclusive social programs. Beneficiaries of tax expenditures discovered that just as a broader tax base and higher rates can indirectly promote growth, reducing that base and cutting tax rates can indirectly lead to retrenchment. The smaller the tax bite, the lower the value of tax expenditures. They discovered, too, that a program's impressive size and reliance on general revenues (rather than dedicated trust funds) could be liabilities if enough policy makers were looking for ways to reduce the budget deficit. As always, the fate of these programs depended heavily on the outcome of struggles over tax policy and budget policy. In this sense, the development of tax expenditures has closely resembled their origins.

CHAPTER 5

Home Mortgage Interest

IF ONE had to name a Holy Trinity of U.S. social programs in the late twentieth century, it would consist of Social Security, Medicare, and the home mortgage interest deduction. All three programs are budgetary entitlements, protected from the annual appropriations process. All three are among the largest programs in the entire budget, and the fastest growing. All three have millions of middle- and upper-middle-class beneficiaries and millions more who count on becoming beneficiaries. These people make campaign contributions; these people vote.

Of the three programs, the home mortgage interest deduction has arguably the strongest base of political support. It has existed longer than Social Security or Medicare, thus appearing even more firmly a part of the "natural" political landscape. Like Medicare (and unlike Social Security), it can depend on third-party providers for support. Home builders, building material suppliers, developers, realtors, lenders, and construction unions consider the program essential to their livelihoods; national organizations representing these trades are among the most powerful in Washington and cut across party lines. Their support helps account for the program's impressive growth: between 1967 and 1995, the total cost of the home mortgage interest deduction increased by an average of almost 7 percent per year, adjusted for inflation. Like Social Security (and unlike Medicare), the home mortgage interest deduction has been effectively declared off-limits by Republican members of Congress intent on balancing the budget in the 1990s. At an estimated cost of more than $50 billion in 1995, this is a major omission. If power consists of the ability not only to resist change but also to discourage serious debate over change, then the home mortgage interest deduction is truly powerful.

The puzzle here is how a small wrinkle in the original tax code became, many decades later, a huge and sacrosanct social program. The answer cannot be found in the deliberate actions of program administrators intent on expanding the home mortgage interest deduction. At times Treasury officials have posed one of the few threats to the program. The chairmen of important congressional committees did not develop a special sense of ownership early in the program's history. Interest group lobbying took decades to materialize, and home owners never formed an organization equivalent to the AARP. No conscious effort was made to expand the program or even to prevent cutbacks until the early 1960s. For most of its history the home mortgage interest deduction experienced growth without advocacy. The program has become somewhat more visible and politicized since then, but advocates still do not have to alter its structure in order to produce growth.

The main solution to this puzzle is that the structure of tax expenditures as a policy tool makes growth without advocacy possible. As more people pay income taxes and marginal tax rates increase, the value of not paying taxes goes up. The cost of tax expenditures increases. In this case, the transformation of the individual income tax from an elite tax to a mass tax around World War II had a profound impact on the home mortgage interest deduction, for it meant that many more home owners were paying income taxes and therefore potentially eligible to take the deduction. Second, the behaviors rewarded by tax expenditures may become more common, for reasons unrelated to the tax code, causing the size of tax expenditures to increase. Home ownership grew rapidly between 1940 and 1960, in part because of tax incentives but also in part because of greater affluence, the availability of long-term, low down-payment loans, and a host of demographic changes. These developments were as much by-products of other policy initiatives, designed to ease the pain of the Depression and foster economic recovery after World War II, as they were of any tax incentive. Home mortgage interest thus became a more substantial expense for more taxpayers in the immediate postwar era.[1]

By the time policy makers became aware of the home mortgage interest deduction, their options were limited. The program provided too many benefits to too many voters and donors. Home ownership had become the norm and a basic part of the American dream. Individuals had started to factor the deduction into their calculations of how much home they could afford, and to count on the future availability of the deduction to anyone who wanted to buy their home. Groups representing third-party providers had organized, grown powerful, and grasped the significance of the home mortgage interest deduction for their members. Anyone who suggested cutting or eliminating the home mortgage interest deduction risked being labeled an enemy of the nation's housing industry and a threat to home values everywhere. Policy makers were, in short, "locked in" by past decisions that substantially increased the political costs of opposing the home mortgage interest deduction. This program offers further proof of Paul Pierson's claim that "lock-in effects are likely to be important when public policies encourage individuals to make significant investments that are not easily reversed."[2]

Advocates appeared to be in an ideal position: they did not have to lobby for the program's expansion; its structure fostered growth as long as the economy was relatively healthy and people were buying homes. Their main policy objective was to preserve the status quo and prevent cutbacks, and for the most part they succeeded.[3] The home mortgage interest deduction is by far the largest housing program in the United States and one of the largest tax expenditures. Nevertheless, the program suffered some setbacks beginning in the mid-1980s. Although some of these setbacks were deliberate, the most important one was an unintended by-product of efforts to reform the tax code. Of the deliberate cuts, the main motive was deficit reduction and not some effort to save the program's long-run viability. As with its origins, the development of the home mortgage interest deduction depended heavily on larger debates over taxing and spending.

This chapter identifies critical moments in the development of the home mortgage interest deduction, noting how few of them were deliberate attempts to modify the program. Its history during the twentieth century is largely the product of successive ripple effects from other programs and policies.

THE IMPACT OF THE NEW DEAL AND WORLD WAR II

We cannot know precisely when or how fast the home mortgage interest deduction grew during its first half century. The Treasury Department did not start estimating the cost of individual tax expenditures until the late 1960s. Before that, the government did report the annual dollar value of itemized deductions, but that category combined several sizable deductions (charitable contributions, real estate taxes, state and local income taxes) along with home mortgage interest. The absence of precise numbers reflected the invisibility of the program. When the U.S. Housing and Home Finance Agency published a summary of government housing programs in 1950, it never mentioned the home mortgage interest deduction.[4]

The best numbers I have found come from a 1960 study sponsored by the National Bureau of Economic Research.[5] Using a variety of government documents (primarily the *Statistics of Income*) and secondary studies, Kahn estimates the annual size of most individual income tax deductions between the mid-1920s and mid-1950s, as well as the distribution of tax benefits by income levels. Chapter 6 of that study covers personal interest payments. Home mortgage interest is likely the largest component, but how large is unknown. By looping home mortgages in with all other forms of consumer indebtedness, the original architects of the income tax made precise figures concerning this program difficult to derive. Kahn's figures therefore represent an upper bound on the home mortgage interest deduction and are probably most useful in charting general trends over time. His figures make sense in light of several developments in housing and taxation discussed below.

The home mortgage interest deduction must have started small and stayed that way until World War II. Kahn estimates that all personal interest deductions cost the national treasury $827 million in 1927, rose above $900 million by 1929, and then declined rapidly during the Depression. By 1939 the figure stood at $383 million.[6] Part of the story here is clearly the negative impact of the Depression on home building and buying. The relatively small sums, even in good economic times, reflected the relatively small size of home mortgage interest in the early twentieth century. Lenders during this era typically required a large down payment equal to 40 to 50 percent of the home's assessed value and extended loans for three to five years (and occasionally up to ten years).[7] More important, the vast majority of individuals during this era avoided income taxation, principally by earning less than the personal exemption. By 1939, barely one worker in twenty paid income taxes.[8] Those individuals who took advantage of this deduction were by definition fairly affluent.

There were, of course, major national initiatives in housing policy during this era, largely in response to the Great Depression.[9] One set of initiatives acknowledged the close links among housing, financial institutions, and unemployment. The Federal Home Loan Bank System created a series of district banks that purchased loans from private lenders (mostly savings and loans) in order to foster greater lending activity, and thus greater building activity. The Home Owners Loan Corporation helped families facing default or foreclosure to refinance their mortgages; in effect, it substituted long-term government loans for shorter-term private loans. Between 1933 and 1935, it issued loans totaling $3 billion to approximately one million families. The most important initiative was the Housing Act of 1934. It created mortgage insurance for private loans on one- to four-unit dwellings, administered by the Federal Housing Administration (FHA). If borrowers defaulted on their loans, lenders could now collect the outstanding balance from the government. The 1934 Act created the Federal Savings and Loan Insurance Corporation, a counterpart to the Federal Deposit Insurance Corporation for banks, to ensure that the main institutions making home loans would not go bankrupt. In the process of shoring up housing and credit markets, the Act also created jobs. According to one administration official, testifying before Congress in 1934, "The building trades in America represent by all odds the largest single unit of our unemployment. Probably more than one-third of all the unemployed are identified, directly or indirectly with the building trades. . . . a fundamental purpose of this bill, is an effort to get the people back to work."[10]

The other set of initiatives involved construction of low-income housing. The National Industrial Recovery Act (1933) authorized funds for slum clearance and the Public Works Administration to build low-income housing. The Supreme Court ruled in 1936 (*United States v. Butler*) that the Act illegally intruded on the states' power of eminent domain. Thereafter the national government worked with state governments to clear slums and build public housing. The Housing Act of 1937 codified this arrangement and marked the beginning of a long-term commitment to housing (some of) the poor.

The cumulative effect of these policies is well known: they established a two-tiered approach to housing that remains today. The national government fosters home ownership among the middle classes by making the terms of private loans more attractive, and it houses the poor by working with state governments to build and administer low-cost dwellings. While serving far more people, the top tier is less visible and less stigmatizing than the bottom tier of public housing projects. What is less well known are the unanticipated effects of New Deal housing policies on the home mortgage interest deduction. For example, with FHA insurance private lenders were able to offer much longer-term loans (up to twenty years) and lower the down payment to 20 percent and later 10 percent of assessed value. FHA mortgage insurance covered 40 percent of all new housing starts by 1940. Seeing the viability of FHA-backed loans, private lenders started to offer twenty- and thirty-year mortgages without the government guarantee. Interest payments consequently became a larger expense for many home owners, and their potential value as a tax deduction increased.

The other ripple effect worth noting concerns the political behavior of builders, lenders, and realtors.[11] Before the 1930s, these trade groups had little reason to lobby the national government concerning housing programs because there were so few. At times trade groups even fought one another over policies such as interest rates. The introduction of so many housing programs in the thirties caused them to put aside their differences and work together to ensure that the national government was working with the private sector and not against it. Organizations like the National Association of Real Estate Boards (now the National Association of Realtors), the National Retail Lumber Dealers Association, and the U.S. Savings and Loan League were wary of government efforts to subsidize private borrowers and lenders and were openly hostile to public housing. They worked together to influence the 1934 and 1937 Housing Acts. The National Association of House Builders joined the coalition several years later. Organized labor, on the other hand, was interested in construction jobs and generally supported government housing initiatives in the 1930s. These organizations, rather than any group representing home owners or renters, became the most influential interest groups with respect to U.S. housing policy—including the home mortgage interest deduction—for the rest of the century. Although it took decades for the provider coalition to focus on this program, what is noteworthy is that trade groups became accustomed to working with one another to influence housing policies in the 1930s, and later extended that practice to the home mortgage interest deduction.

Neither the changes in mortgage practices nor the formation of a housing provider coalition would have been significant without subsequent changes in tax policy. It is impossible to overstate the impact of World War II on taxation, and especially individual income taxes.[12] Lowering the personal exemption for individuals and couples added five million taxpayers in 1941. That same year policy makers raised the tax rate on the lowest bracket from 4 to 10 percent. The Revenue Act of 1942 lowered the personal exemption again and raised the tax rate on the lowest bracket to 19 percent. It also imposed a 5 percent Victory Tax on all incomes above $624. These changes more than doubled the size of the tax base and brought many working- and middle-class individuals into the tax system for the first time. The 1942 Act represented the single most important change to the individual income tax since its creation. To put these changes in perspective, consider that in 1932 the Bureau of Internal Revenue (forerunner of the Internal Revenue Service) processed fewer than two million individual tax returns; by 1943 it processed more than forty million. By 1945, 70 percent of all workers paid income taxes, compared with only 6 percent in 1939. The income tax was now a mass tax. Given the growing length of home mortgages and the greatly expanded tax base, it stands to reason that many more people should have been deducting mortgage interest after the war than before it. Kahn estimates that the cost of personal deductions tripled between 1939 and 1943.[13] The program's beneficiaries should have been, on average, less affluent than before.

Not all changes to the tax code pointed in the direction of expansion. Along with several largely administrative changes to the tax code, Congress enacted the standard deduction in 1944. If taxpayers' itemized deductions were greater than the new standard deduction, they would continue to itemize; if they were less, taxpayers would claim the standard deduction. Either way, their taxes would be reduced. This change to the tax code had complicated ramifications for housing and the home mortgage interest deduction. On the one hand, because home mortgage interest was an itemized deduction, the standard deduction meant that home owners with relatively small interest payments or with few other itemized deductions would no longer claim the home mortgage interest deduction. The program would shrink. But no home owner would pay more taxes and most would pay less, so cutting the program in this way did not seem to penalize home owners. On the other hand, those who financed and built homes could be hurt since the standard deduction reduced the relative tax benefits of owning versus renting a home. This would be particularly true at the lower end of the market, houses with smaller mortgages requiring smaller interest payments. Owners of such homes might also be hurt in the future when they tried to resell and found fewer interested buyers.

Policy makers appear to have been unaware of, or at most unconcerned about, the possible ripple effects of the standard deduction on housing. They created the standard deduction to address two more pressing problems. The first was that revenue officials were quickly overwhelmed with the growing mountain of tax returns during the war. Adding the standard deduction would reduce the number of returns with itemized deductions to verify and would simplify their administrative tasks. In addition, "The business community was very supportive of these efforts because its members had been inundated by their employees with requests to aid in calculating and filing returns."[14] The deduction was set high enough that over 80 percent of all taxpayers used it in 1944. The second problem was growing resentment of rapidly escalating income taxes. Several states passed resolutions calling for repeal of the Sixteenth Amendment, and administration officials worried that prosecuting the war would be compromised if citizens mounted a serious challenge to the income tax. They responded by passing a measure that would reduce the tax burden for many individuals who had recently been added into the tax system. The standard deduction was not large enough to eliminate many people from the tax rolls but enough to stem the tide of taxpayer revolt.

Although tax rates declined a bit and the personal exemption went up a bit after the war ended, the income tax remained a mass tax. Its base was far broader and the amount of revenues generated far larger than before the war. Changes in tax policy designed to finance a massive military operation thus constituted one of the key turning points in the history of the home mortgage interest deduction. Although the new standard deduction probably lowered the size of the home mortgage interest deduction, this drop must have been offset by the unprecedented increase in the number of people paying income taxes. It was also a very temporary drop. After the war, policy makers allowed the value of the standard deduction to lag income growth, thereby increasing the number of taxpayers itemizing their deductions. According to Kahn, deductions for personal interest payments dropped considerably in 1944, but were still almost twice the level of 1939, and steadily returned to their wartime peak by 1949.[15] Changes in the value of the standard deduction thus became another determinant of the size of the home mortgage interest deduction.

Housing policy in the immediate postwar era continued patterns established during the 1930s.[16] Policy makers focused less on housing the poor and more on promoting residential construction and home ownership for middle-class citizens. New housing starts dropped substantially during the war years, and policy makers feared a major housing shortage. Their immediate policy objective was to lower the cost of credit. The Federal National Mortgage Association (FNMA, or "Fannie Mae"), created in 1938 as an amendment to the 1934 Housing Act, became an important player in the secondary mortgage market after the war. The GI Bill, passed in 1944, created a new loan insurance program for veterans and was administered by the Veterans Administration (VA). This program closely resembled FHA loan insurance (except that veterans often needed no down payment instead of a low FHA down payment), and soon millions of prospective home buyers were qualifying for VA or FHA loans. Approximately 40 percent of all World War II veterans ultimately received a VA-insured home loan.

More widely available credit worked to the advantage of the housing and lending industries, and they became increasingly supportive of FHA and VA loans. They also continued pressing the government for low interest rates. Over time, housing providers learned to think of housing policy strictly in terms of these policies—a fact that helps account for their belated support for the home mortgage interest deduction. Finally, the provider coalition continued working to limit the scope of government involvement in housing beyond loan insurance. In 1945 the U.S. Savings and Loan League, National Association of Real Estate Boards, and National Association of House Builders opposed a bill expanding the powers of the FHA and requiring builders to guarantee the structural soundness of FHA-insured homes. The following year these same groups joined the Mortgage Bankers Association and the National Retail Lumber Dealers Association to prevent creation of a National Housing Agency to coordinate all the nation's various housing programs.[17]

The connections between housing policy and macroeconomic policy grew tighter. Many policy makers in the 1930s viewed housing programs partly as public works programs, a temporary remedy for record-high unemployment. This view remained important during and immediately after the war, as policy makers worried about the potential for massive unemployment once soldiers started to return. Cheap credit meant jobs, thousands and thousands of jobs, for tradesmen, developers, and realtors. At the same time, as Keynesian ideas started to take hold, policy makers began to see housing as integral to the long-run

health of the economy. According to Alvin Hansen, a Harvard economist and one-time adviser to the Roosevelt administration, government
housing programs were one of several automatic stabilizers capable of
smoothing out fluctuations in the business cycle. Government could
make home mortgages cheaper in times of recession, thereby increasing
consumer demand for housing and large durable goods like appliances.
This was a powerful tool of fiscal policy. Writing in 1957, Hansen argued that "a highly important ingredient in our postwar prosperity has
been the high level of housing construction. This, again, is no accident.
Today housing rests largely on government programs. Over two-fifths
of the entire home-mortgage debt is represented by loans insured by the
Federal government."[18] Even policy makers who did not embrace
Keynesian fiscal policy could agree that residential construction was a
leading barometer of the economy's overall health and that boosting
construction was needed to bring the economy out of recession. Anything that hurt residential construction hurt the economy—a powerful
belief for anyone interested in promoting home ownership.

Cheaper credit and tax incentives were one reason why home ownership grew faster between 1940 and 1960 than in any other comparable
period this century. Before 1930, owner-occupied homes comprised 45
to 50 percent of all residential units, and that figure dipped slightly during the Depression. Between 1940 and 1960 the rate increased from 44
to 62 percent, making home ownership a legitimate expectation among
middle-class citizens.[19] Housing policies, much less the home mortgage
interest deduction, were not the only engine of growth.[20] Substantial
real growth in income and wages right after World War II enabled more
individuals to buy a home for the first time. Population shifts from big
cities to suburbs enabled more people to build and own their own
homes. Longer life spans mattered because home ownership is strongly
and positively correlated with age. The combination of more home
owners, more taxpayers, higher tax rates, and the declining value of the
standard deduction means that the home mortgage interest deduction
must have grown substantially between 1940 and 1960. Kahn's figures
for all interest deductions show a tenfold increase for the period from
1940 to 1956.[21]

Initial Skirmishes

In theory, this growth might have spurred builders, realtors, and developers to recognize the importance of the home mortgage interest deduction and lobby for expansion. Scholars have found many examples in
the United States in which public programs triggered interest group activity rather than vice versa.[22] In practice, the first people to pay much

attention to the tax treatment of housing were experts in taxation, and they were quite critical of the status quo. In the late 1940s and 1950s Randolph Paul (a senior tax official in the Treasury Department), Joseph Pechman (Brookings Institution economist), Stanley Surrey (professor of tax law at Harvard), and others started to point out problems with tax preferences or loopholes, as they were then called. First, the myriad exceptions distorted the price system by subsidizing the purchase of specific goods and services. Taxpayers would therefore buy too many of these goods and services and not enough of others. Second, these exceptions tended to benefit more affluent taxpayers because they could more easily afford the goods and services subsidized by the tax code (e.g., homes), and because a progressive rate structure made tax breaks more valuable to those with higher incomes. Offering benefits to these individuals was wasteful; they were not "needy" by any reasonable definition of the term. Finally, these exceptions violated the principle of horizontal equity, that is, that individuals with the same income should pay the same taxes, regardless of how they spent their money. One of their main targets was the home mortgage interest deduction, which unfairly favored home owners over renters. To be fair, they argued, home owners should count as income the imputed rent they effectively paid themselves to live in their house. This added income would offset the value of the interest deduction, leaving home owners no better off than renters.[23]

Critics gained some visibility when Ways and Means chairman Wilbur Mills (D-Ark.) commissioned a series of academic studies detailing options for broadening the tax base in 1959. Though Congress took no immediate action, the three-volume *Tax Revision Compendium* became a source of numerous reform proposals during the 1960s.[24] More significant was the appointment of Stanley Surrey, the most prominent critic of tax preferences, as Assistant Secretary of the Treasury for Tax Policy under Kennedy and Johnson.[25] Surrey used his official position to increase awareness of tax preferences among policy makers and push for a "cleaner," fairer tax code. The opening volley occurred in April 1961 when President Kennedy delivered a special message to Congress on taxation, which Surrey helped draft, calling for a broader tax base and lower tax rates. The administration was not declaring war on all tax preferences—it later initiated the individual deduction for moving expenses and the corporate tax credit for new plants and equipment—but it did want to limit their overall number and size.[26] This issue was ideally suited to Kennedy, for it combined his interests in promoting equity and economic growth. A tax code with fewer exceptions would enable Kennedy to lower tax rates and alter a system that, in Surrey's words, "places a premium on tax planning and tax avoidance," neither of which were economically productive.[27] A tax code with fewer exceptions would also enhance horizontal equity; for those individuals who might not appreciate this goal in the abstract, Kennedy would play up cutting tax breaks for expensive business lunches and entertainment.

The major tax initiative of the Kennedy administration began in 1963 and emerged the following year as the Revenue Act of 1964.[28] In its initial form, the proposal featured new loopholes for business investment and substantial tax cuts—what Republicans later termed a classic supply-side approach to generating economic growth. The central debate concerned the administration's unwillingness to cut spending in order to pay for its tax cuts. Many members in Congress agreed on the need for tax cuts but not at the expense of adding to the deficit. Kennedy officials, on the other hand, thought more in terms of balancing the economy than balancing the budget. A secondary debate hinged on the proper timing of any tax cut. These tax cuts were, along with civil rights, the major domestic policy struggle of 1963–64.

A much smaller debate concerned proposed limits on itemized deductions that Kennedy officials included to partially offset the revenue losses from tax cuts. The administration proposed allowing taxpayers to deduct only those itemized expenses that exceeded 5 percent of their income. This change would reduce the value of itemized deductions for many affluent taxpayers, making the tax code more equitable. It would have the added benefit of making the tax system easier to administer by forcing more taxpayers to use the standard deduction. Between the introduction of the standard deduction in 1944 and 1962, itemizers rose from less than 20 to almost 50 percent of all individual taxpayers, and the number of itemized returns increased from eight to twenty-five million.[29] By allowing the standard deduction to lag income growth, policy makers had complicated tax administration and, more important, increased the number of individuals benefiting from specific itemized deductions.

This proposal may have been good policy but it was terrible politics. The administration was potentially cutting every single itemized deduction, and a variety of third-party providers quickly voiced their opposition.[30] The American Medical Association protested the implicit cuts in the deduction for extraordinary medical expenses. Several educational and charitable organizations claimed that their organizations would suffer if wealthy individuals could deduct fewer of their gifts. State and local governments warned that they would have to raise taxes or cut services if their residents could not deduct what they paid in state and local taxes from their federal tax obligations. And, for the first time, home builders and realtors lobbied on behalf of itemized deductions for home mortgage interest and property taxes. They were not, however, the most important opponents to the administration's proposal; according to Surrey, college presidents and charity officials were.[31] The combination of nonprofits, doctors, state and local governments, home builders, and developers proved overwhelming, especially when the administration could find no major interest group that supported these limits, and this part of the tax proposal soon died. Instead, the Revenue Act of 1964 eliminated deductions for state and local excise taxes and motor vehicle license fees, producing a much smaller increase in revenues that affected rich and poor alike.

This episode could have triggered a major shift in the politics of the home mortgage interest deduction. Before 1963, builders, realtors, and lenders had lobbied primarily for cheap credit through a combination of low interest rates and government-insured loans. The only taxes that mattered affected them as small businesses.[32] Having recognized the potential vulnerability of the home mortgage interest deduction, they might have expanded the range of programs on which they lobbied. But they did not. The relevant trade associations had spent a couple of decades developing close contacts with FHA officials and with legislators on the relevant congressional committees with jurisdiction over government loan programs. They had acquired considerable expertise in the technical details of loan programs and educated their members about the need to press constantly for cheaper credit. They had hired former officials at FHA and HUD (Housing and Urban Development), not the Treasury, to head up their Washington offices.[33] They simply had too much political capital invested in a certain kind of housing program to change quickly.[34] Moreover, providers could do little directly to make the deduction any larger, for it already covered all mortgage interest. The other main avenues for expanding the program—raising tax rates and lowering the standard deduction—were political nonstarters. Their role in the future, as in 1963, was to block any and all efforts to curb the home mortgage interest deduction. The next serious efforts would not materialize until the mid-1980s.

Despite failing to limit itemized deductions, Assistant Secretary Surrey continued to push for greater attention to the assorted costs of tax preferences.[35] It was he who coined the phrase "tax expenditures," thus highlighting their equivalence with direct expenditures. It was he who worked tirelessly to persuade officials in the White House, public finance experts, and members of the financial community that tax expenditures represented a sizable drain on the public treasury and a threat to basic principles of equity and efficiency. President Kennedy was more receptive to these arguments than was Johnson, who associated tax reform with limits on the oil depletion allowance, a key benefit to his home state of Texas and to major campaign contributors. Surrey spent much of the

Johnson years out of the limelight, compiling studies about the true size and scope of tax expenditures. Perhaps most important, Surrey supervised the creation of the first tax expenditure budget, which interim Secretary of the Treasury Joseph Barr presented to Congress in January 1969. Barr's main objective was to force the incoming Nixon administration to tackle tax reform by dramatizing how many wealthy individuals were avoiding taxes altogether: he revealed that in 1967, 155 taxpayers with incomes over $200,000 and twenty-one millionaires had paid no income taxes, numbers that generated considerable media attention.[36] One reason was the availability of so many loopholes, and here Surrey's studies took center stage.

For the first time in U.S. history, policy makers could see a complete list of major holes in the tax code and identify the cost of individual items. Although policy makers had been aware of some of these programs, advocates were free to claim that their tax break produced sizable benefits without worrying that opponents might highlight the costs. The Treasury Department under Nixon balked at publishing an annual tax expenditure budget, doing so only in 1972 and 1973 and only then after the budget had been passed. Congress then required, as part of the historic Budget Act of 1974, that these estimates be incorporated in the annual budget process. If, as the old saying goes, we measure what we treasure, then the publication of annual cost estimates represented a major turning point in the development of the hidden welfare state. Henceforth, the idea of deliberately creating new tax expenditures and modifying existing ones would occur to more and more people. The distributive consequences would also become more apparent, as government documents started to indicate which income groups were receiving which tax benefits. Tax expenditures never gained the prominence of direct expenditures, but overt efforts to create, expand, and retrench tax expenditures were more common after 1969 than before.

Knowing exactly how large and how upwardly skewed the benefits were made it easier for critics to single out the home mortgage interest deduction for reform. Numbers alone, however, were not enough to trigger an immediate change in the politics of the program. By 1970, home builders, realtors, and lenders had developed sophisticated national organizations with dedicated members in every district of the country.[37] The National Association of Home Builders, in particular, enjoyed a reputation of being among the most influential lobbies in Washington and routinely held informational and strategy meetings with representatives of the realty, mortgage banking, savings and loan, and building products industries.[38] Home ownership had been well established as the normal residence pattern by 1970, and home owners factored the mortgage interest deduction into their decisions to buy and sell. Even though many home owners did not take the deduction, perhaps because they had paid off their mortgage or had too few deductions to itemize, the resale value of all homes hinged on the future availability of the deduction. The approximately 120 million people who lived in owner-occupied housing had a direct stake in the program. Absent some major crisis, little was to be gained politically by suggesting cuts to this program.[39] In the interim, the program continued to expand without conscious effort, driven by inflation in housing prices, interest rates, "bracket creep" in tax rates, the steady erosion of the standard deduction and personal exemption, and demographic changes.[40]

MANY CHALLENGES, SMALL SETBACKS, CONTINUED GROWTH

President Reagan achieved significant cuts in social spending in 1981, and traditional housing programs were a prime target. New budget authority for public housing and Section 8 housing vouchers was barely half that of President Carter's final budget ($17.5 billion versus $30 billion), and Reagan succeeded in cutting an additional $4 billion that had been previously appropriated but not spent.[41] Advocates for low-income housing initially tried to restore funds for these programs, but Republican control of the White House and the Senate made it impossible to do much beyond preventing deeper cuts. To make matters worse, their traditional allies at HUD had been fired, replaced with weak leaders (e.g., Secretary Samuel Pierce), or circumvented by budget knife-wielding analysts at the Office of Management and Budget (OMB).[42] To dramatize budget cuts, some advocates started to highlight the growing disparities between tax subsidies for middle-class home owners and direct subsidies for the poor. In one study, Cushing Dolbeare found that housing subsidies for individuals earning more than $50,000 per year were seven times those for individuals earning less than $10,000 per year. To make government aid more equitable, Dolbeare suggested limiting the deduction to principal residences, imposing some fixed dollar cap, and using the monies saved to revive housing programs for the poor.[43] Without substantial infusions of public monies, he claimed, the nation faced an affordable housing crisis.

Advocates for low-income housing have always been among the weakest pressure groups in the American welfare state, and studies like Dolbeare's generally fell on deaf ears. On the other hand, policy makers became more inclined to cut the home mortgage interest deduction in the context of tax reform and deficit reduction. The largest cutbacks in the history of the program were contained in the Tax Reform Act (TRA) of 1986, "the most significant piece of tax legislation since the income tax was converted to a mass tax during World War II."[44] In the name of producing a simpler, fairer tax code, this Act reduced the marginal rates (lowering the top rate from 50 to 33 percent), reduced the number of tax brackets from fourteen to three, and made deliberate cuts to many tax expenditures. Although the TRA did nothing to reduce the deficit, it effectively lowered income taxes for 80 percent of individuals and raised taxes on the affluent and many corporations.[45] In addition, it removed six million of the working poor from the tax rolls altogether, primarily by increasing the value of the standard deduction, personal exemption, and the Earned Income Tax Credit. The main question was not how to raise more revenue but who should pay the taxes.

In the words of Joseph Pechman, economist and noted tax expert, the TRA constituted a "frontal assault on major loopholes and special benefits."[46] Tax expenditures for home owners and real estate development were prime targets. Housing programs were inviting because of their sheer size and well-established bias in favor of more affluent taxpayers. Real estate came under attack because of numerous stories in the media highlighting the ability of wealthy investors to shelter their income by registering paper losses, sometimes far larger than their original investment, that lowered their overall tax bill. These tax provisions benefited similar coalitions of builders, developers, realtors, and financial institutions. In a preemptive move, some members of this coalition tried to portray the home mortgage interest deduction as politically untouchable and suggested that policy makers intent on comprehensive tax reform replace or at least supplement the income tax with a consumption tax.[47]

Their lobbying efforts escalated after President Reagan announced in his 1984 State of the Union address that he was directing the Treasury Department to conduct a comprehensive study of the nation's tax system. Given recent tax reform proposals in Congress, housing providers had reason to worry. In particular, a bill co-sponsored by Sen. Bill Bradley (D-N.J.) and Rep. Richard Gephardt (D-Mo.) in 1982 and 1983, dubbed the Fair Tax Act, would have lowered tax rates and then allowed taxpayers to deduct home mortgage interest only at the lowest rate, 14 percent. Such changes not only would have reduced the program substantially but also would have dampened the upward skew of benefits. Before Treasury Department officials had time to finish a first draft of their study, real estate lobbyists were pressuring the White House for assurance that the home mortgage interest deduction would be spared. "With the election approaching, the president and his advisers decided to ease the realtors' minds. 'In case there's still any doubt,' he said [to several thousand members of the National Association of Realtors], 'I want you to know we will preserve the part of the American dream which the home mortgage interest deduction symbolizes.'"[48] Unbeknownst to Reagan, some Treasury officials had indeed been considering major changes to the deduction, including the possibility of eliminating it entirely. His speech forced them to temper their desire for an ideal tax system—low rates, few brackets, and no loopholes—and make a few concessions to powerful interest groups.

Nevertheless, when Treasury released its final study (Treasury I), shortly after the fall elections, it unleashed a torrent of criticism. Treasury I targeted virtually every tax expenditure for reduction or elimination, including such sacred cows as state and local taxes and charitable contributions. Home mortgage interest would be limited to principal residences; no longer would individuals be able to deduct interest on their second homes or vacation homes. The plan also placed a dollar ceiling on personal interest deductions exclusive of interest on investments (e.g., housing). By curbing tax expenditures such as these, Treasury I would lower marginal rates and make the entire package deficit neutral. Housing providers were less interested in these goals than in preserving their tax benefits and soon tried every possible tactic to preserve the status quo: urging members at the state and local level to contact their local representative; rating legislators based on their votes on housing-related issues and publicizing their scores; circulating figures showing the importance of second homes and vacation homes in each legislative district; conducting opinion polls that (not surprisingly) showed strong support for the home mortgage interest deduction; recruiting members to run for Congress; and, of course, donating thousands and thousands of dollars to key politicians.

Their efforts produced mixed results. Despite industry warnings of "a virtual shutdown on construction of new office buildings, motels, and apartments, and widespread loan defaults in weak markets such as Texas and Colorado,"[49] Congress enacted substantial restrictions on passive losses and longer depreciation schedules for real estate investments. To counter the potentially negative impact of these changes on construction of affordable housing, Congress created a new tax credit for owners of low-income rental properties. The final bill also replaced the old deduction for consumer interest with a "qualified residence" interest deduction. This change meant the end of deductions for most consumer debt besides mortgage interest—a definite blow to financial institutions—and somewhat tighter restrictions on the kinds of structures that counted as residences. But the earlier restrictions on second homes had been dropped, a major victory. Compared with other groups and industries, home owners and residential construction fared as well or better in preserving their tax benefits.

Builders, realtors, and lenders were less successful at preventing a series of indirect cuts to the home mortgage interest deduction that were
just as large as those contained in Treasury I. One consequence of lowering tax rates was a substantial decrease in the cost of all tax expenditures, including the home mortgage interest deduction. The smaller the
initial tax obligation, the smaller the value of provisions that reduced
that obligation. The TRA also increased the standard deduction to
$3,000 for individuals and $5,000 for married couples by 1990, nearly
doubled the value of the personal exemption, and then indexed both to
inflation in an effort to provide low- and middle-income individuals with
some tax relief. The effect, as with the creation of the standard deduction in 1944, was to reduce the number of taxpayers eligible to itemize
deductions, including home mortgage interest.[50] The Congressional
Budget Office estimated that lower rates and higher standard deductions were the main reasons why the home mortgage interest deduction
would cost almost 20 percent less in 1991 than under previous law.[51]
Finally, by eliminating the deductability of most consumer interest besides home mortgage interest, the TRA made it harder for some taxpayers to amass enough deductions to itemize. This, too, cut into the overall size of the home mortgage interest deduction.

It was no surprise that housing providers found it politically difficult
to oppose lower tax rates, higher personal exemptions, or a larger standard deduction. David Seiders, chief economist of the National Association of Home Builders, conceded that "home owners will not be worse
off overall, because the drop in the value of the home mortgage interest
deduction will be offset by lower tax rates on income, but it does mean
that the cost of home ownership will be higher."[52] He predicted that the
main long-term effect would be a switch to less expensive homes—and
by implication lower profit margins for builders, smaller commissions
for realtors, and smaller mortgages and interest payments for lenders.
For years the provider coalition had worked to equate their interests
with those of home owners; now they faced proposals that disrupted
that equation. It was in fact possible to make changes in the tax code
that reduced the cost of the home mortgage interest deduction without
making home owners noticeably worse off financially. The secret was in
targeting the same features of the tax code that indirectly fostered this
program's growth. Just as adding taxpayers and increasing tax rates
could increase the home mortgage interest deduction, reducing the tax
rolls and lowering tax rates could decrease it.

Two subsequent cuts to the home mortgage interest deduction attracted little attention until they became law. As part of the 1987 budget
reconciliation bill, Congress placed a dollar cap on the value of home
mortgage debt eligible for the interest deduction.[53] Individuals could

not claim interest paid on any mortgages of more than $1 million or on any second mortgages of more than $100,000. These changes affected only the most affluent taxpayers and, even so, allowed them to deduct interest on two homes provided both met the "qualified residence" test established in 1986 and their combined mortgage debt was less than $1 million. Who initiated this measure and why are unclear: "No one in Congress is willing to claim authorship of the provisions—making it, as Hill staffers like to joke, an 'immaculate conception' provision."[54] It seems reasonable to assume that one motivation was deficit reduction, a primary objective of the overall bill. Another was shifting some of the tax burden to the rich via a "mansion tax"; Democrats had retaken the Senate in 1986 and were eager to roll back some of the tax benefits conferred on the rich during the first Reagan administration. The evidence suggests that this cut had less to do with housing policy than with larger questions of fiscal policy.[55]

Housing providers were disturbed less by the size of the cut than by the precedent it set. The $1 million cap still made it possible for taxpayers to deduct up to $100,000 each year (assuming a 10 percent interest rate); the cap thus harmed few people and raised little revenue. The danger was that once policy makers thought a cap was politically feasible, some might start lowering it. The president of the National Association of Realtors warned that certain Democrats in the Ways and Means Committee (e.g., Tom Downey and Sam Gibbons) were considering limiting the annual interest deduction to $20,000 or less. Such a move would "'devastate the market for second homes' and financially squeeze many potential home buyers in areas with high housing costs."[56] Moreover, the Congressional Budget Office had started listing cuts to the home mortgage interest deduction among its options for deficit reduction, and it was one of the single largest items on that list. Realtors quickly joined with builders, bankers, and savings and loan officials to monitor and influence legislators' views toward further caps on the home mortgage interest deduction. Besides the usual arguments about making the American dream harder to attain and destroying jobs, housing providers stressed the distributive consequences of a lower cap for certain regions of the country. In parts of New Jersey, New York, and Connecticut, in much of California, and in urban areas like Boston and Washington, housing was so expensive that many home owners carried mortgages in excess of $250,000. Were legislators from these districts about to harm many of their middle- and upper-middle-class constituents? A lower cap also posed a threat to vacation homes around the country, especially in Florida and many beach communities. Did legislators from these districts want to kill off tourism? Evidently the answer was no. Under substantial pressure from trade lobbies, including the local Long Island Board of Realtors, Representative Downey of New York disavowed any intent to curb the program. Representative Gibbons of Florida faced similar pressures and also backed down.[57]

As pressures to lower the deficit mounted, housing providers continued working to head off proposals to limit the home mortgage interest deduction. The National Association of Realtors reminded President Bush in July 1990 that he had pledged a year earlier to support deductions for home mortgage interest and property taxes. The National Association of Home Builders urged its members to send a similar message to Congress when their local representatives returned home during the August recess.[58] Yet despite all their efforts, these trade groups were outflanked by a rather anonymous member of the House Ways and Means Committee, Rep. Donald Pease (D-Ohio).[59] The Pease amendment to the 1990 budget reconciliation bill reduced the value of itemized deductions by 3 percent for every dollar of adjusted gross income over $100,000. "This limit was, Pease admitted, a backdoor way to increase taxes on high incomes."[60] He initially toyed with the idea of phasing out all itemized deductions for taxpayers earning more than $125,000 but decided that a more modest proposal stood a better chance of passage.

One might wonder how Pease succeeded when President Kennedy failed with a similar proposal in 1963. The short answer is better strategy. Pease portrayed his amendment as a deficit reduction measure; Kennedy, in contrast, promoted a plan that ultimately added to the deficit. Once Pease obtained figures from the staff of the Joint Committee on Taxation showing that his provision would raise almost $18 billion over a five-year period, fellow legislators became very interested.[61] A limit on itemizing had the advantage of raising taxes on more affluent individuals without being so blatant as the surtax on millionaires and higher marginal tax rates, the options favored by many Democrats. Under Pease's plan, Democrats could still claim they targeted the rich, and Republicans could not be blamed as easily for raising taxes. The other part of Pease's strategy was *not* to introduce his idea in committee or on the floor of the House, where it might attract attention from opponents. Instead, he worked through the conference committee hammering out differences between the House and Senate budgets. Compared with other steps in the budget process, conference committees are relatively insulated from interest group pressure and media scrutiny, and this was especially true in 1990. Faced with growing pressure to do something about the deficit, conferees accepted the Pease amendment but did little to draw attention to it. The main stories coming out of the conference committee were that Congress had passed the largest deficit reduction package in years and that President Bush had reneged on his campaign promise never to raise taxes.

That year Congress also passed the Budget Enforcement Act (BEA) to institute procedural controls on government spending and the deficit. The BEA imposed fixed dollar caps on discretionary spending for the next five years and required that any new entitlement spending be fully paid for out of tax increases or spending cuts elsewhere in the budget (existing entitlements, however, could continue growing as long as no statutory changes to eligibility or benefits were made). The 1993 budget agreement under Clinton extended these controls for another five years. The BEA formalized the zero-sum nature of government spending that had emerged in the 1980s and forced claimants to be more critical of competing programs. For example, advocates of low-income housing programs stepped up their attacks on the home mortgage interest deduction.[62] One of the more creative proposals involves converting the current tax deduction to a tax credit so that more working-class home owners can take advantage of it (thus working around the standard deduction) and phasing that credit out for more affluent home owners. This approach avoids the political problems associated with cutting home owners' subsidies to help poor public housing tenants, as well as the stigma of spending monies through traditional housing bureaucracies. It also has the advantage of preserving existing tax benefits for the majority of home owners.[63]

The main attacks, however, continued to come from those worried about the deficit and about tax policy. The Concord Coalition, a leading group of deficit hawks from both parties, has listed reductions in the home mortgage interest deduction, especially for the affluent, among its list of options to produce a balanced budget. Ross Perot, erstwhile presidential candidate, has expressed similar views. These challenges are dangerous because they emanate from the political center and not, as with low-income housing advocates, from the Left. The Congressional Budget Office continues to list cuts among its options for reducing the deficit, and the bipartisan Kerrey-Danforth Commission on Entitlement and Tax Reform did likewise in its final report to the president. The most recent attack has come in the form of various flat tax proposals. Best known as the centerpiece of millionaire Steve Forbes's campaign for the Republican presidential nomination in 1996, the flat tax has circulated in conservative policy circles for years. In some versions of the flat tax, deductions for home mortgage interest and property taxes on owner-occupied homes are completely eliminated.

In response, the affected industries have repeated old arguments with new data. The National Association of Home Builders estimates that capping the dollar value of the deduction would devastate California, which accounts for more than half the nation's mortgages in excess of $250,000. California, New York, New Jersey, Florida, Connecticut, and Maryland account for more than three-quarters of these large mortgages.[64] These are also states with large numbers of electoral college votes, which may be one reason why President Clinton made it clear to industry representatives that he would not touch the home mortgage interest deduction when looking for ways to lower the deficit.[65] In the short term a flat tax would allegedly produce a huge drop in new housing construction and sales of existing homes and huge increases in unemployment. A study conducted by DRI-McGraw Hill for the National Association of Realtors found that sixty-two million home owners would lose a combined $1.6 trillion in equity the first year of a flat tax, as they could no longer factor the tax subsidy into the sale price of their home.[66] Such dire warnings are too much for most politicians to bear, and the majority of flat tax proposals now preserve a select number of deductions, including home mortgage interest. Housing providers are, in short, trying very hard to persuade policy makers and voters that they are too heavily invested in (i.e., "locked into") the status quo to contemplate further limits to the home mortgage interest deduction.

All these recent cuts and criticisms make it easy to overlook one simple fact: the home mortgage interest deduction has continued to grow faster than the economy and faster than the rest of the budget. Between 1980 and 1995, the most vulnerable period in its history, the program still experienced real (inflation-adjusted) growth at a rate of 5.7 percent per year. By the year 2000, the OMB estimates that the home mortgage interest deduction will cost the outlay equivalent of $67.5 billion.[67] However many statutory changes critics may propose and enact, they appear to have had little effect compared with interest rates, inflation, income growth, marginal tax rates on the rich, and other factors that foster the growth of the home mortgage interest deduction.

DISCUSSION

Although it is impossible to tell the story of U.S. housing policy without reference to the home mortgage interest deduction, the reverse is not necessarily true. The home mortgage interest deduction is the oldest and largest housing subsidy, costing far more than everything the national government does to house the poor. Readers should rightly be suspicious of any discussion of housing policy that omits it or similar tax breaks for home owners (e.g., deductability of local property taxes, limits on taxation of capital gains for sellers over the age of fifty-five). Nevertheless, one can understand the development of the home mortgage

interest deduction without knowing much about the rest of U.S. housing policy, simply by focusing on certain milestones in fiscal policy. The
expansion of the income tax during World War II, the introduction of
the standard deduction in 1944 and its subsequent erosion, President
Kennedy's proposed limits on itemized deductions, the Tax Reform Act
of 1986, and the ongoing quest for deficit reduction in the 1980s and
1990s—these were the key events in the history of the home mortgage
interest deduction. Add in the effects of FHA and VA loan insurance on
the length and size of private mortgages and you have a fairly complete
picture of which policies affected this program over the last half century.

What did not happen to this program is in some ways more important
than what did. The lead agency, the Treasury Department, did not become a staunch advocate; instead, Treasury officials proposed cuts in
1963 and 1984. The ostensible beneficiaries, home owners, did not
form any organization to lobby on behalf of the program, as the AARP
does for Social Security and Medicare.[68] The entire burden of lobbying
was borne by third-party providers like the National Association of
Home Builders and the National Association of Realtors. Their main
role was to block cutbacks rather than foster expansion, a luxury resulting in part from the initial design of the program (allowing all mortgage
interest to be deducted from the start) and in part from the porous nature of tax expenditures as a policy tool. Despite a few setbacks, housing
providers managed to ensure that the home mortgage interest deduction grew substantially for the second half of the twentieth century. The
most important sources of expansion were not deliberate changes to the
program's eligibility or benefits but often unintended ripple effects from
decisions concerning taxation, inflation, and interest rates. Finally,
whatever cuts did occur had nothing to do with any perceived crisis in
housing or the financing of this program and everything to do with tax
reform and the deficit.

CHAPTER 6

Employer Pensions

IMPORTANT parallels can be drawn between the development of the home mortgage interest deduction and the tax expenditure for employer pensions. Both programs were political nonissues for many years after their enactment. Over time, ripple effects from elsewhere in the polity made both programs larger as well as more difficult to control. World War II was again the first turning point; in the case of employer pensions, significant increases in corporate tax rates and changes in collective bargaining during and immediately after the war fostered a considerable period of expansion. The Tax Reform Act of 1986 had a considerable impact on the overall size of the program. The politics of employer pensions was also influenced by the deficits of the 1980s and 1990s. For the last twenty years this tax expenditure has been a frequent subject of congressional hearings and legislative changes. As one of the largest of all tax expenditures, it stands as a massive exception to the claim that tax expenditures are removed from politics once enacted.

This program has experienced three separate phases of development. Although continuities can be found among these phases, each featured a distinct combination of actors working for and against the program, important changes to program structure, and distinct changes in program size. This chapter analyzes the politics of each phase of development and offers explanations for each transformation.[1] Despite these changes, the politics of employer pensions remain distinctly different from Social Security, the other major income support program for retirees. The core interest group advocates are not organizations representing retirees (like the AARP) but a whole host of third-party providers, including large corporations, actuaries, tax lawyers, and the financial institutions that manage billions of dollars in pension assets. Just as striking, the tax expenditure for employer pensions has been targeted for cutbacks in order to lower the deficit and reform the tax code, not to preserve its long-run viability. Cuts to Social Security, in contrast, have been possible only to the extent that policy makers believed them necessary to avert a trust fund crisis (e.g., cuts in benefits and increases to the retirement age made in 1983).

PHASE I: 1920s–1942

After Congress rewrote the provisions of the tax code governing pensions in 1942—including the introduction of the first nondiscrimination regulations—one pension trust officer lamented the end of a "Golden Age" of pensions, meaning an age of minimal government intervention.[2] He was right. The regulations governing pensions were insignificant to begin with and remained that way between 1921 and 1942. Unlike Social Security, which remained a prominent political issue following its enactment, the tax treatment of employer pensions dropped out of view. While bureaucrats at the Social Security Administration worked diligently to entrench and expand old age insurance, Treasury officials, to the extent they paid any attention at all to this tax expenditure, tried to make benefits more difficult to obtain. Social Security was expanded by Congress in 1939, 1950, and 1954. Between 1940 and 1955, the number of persons insured under Social Security increased from 23 million to 70 million, the number of beneficiaries grew from 200,000 to 8 million, and cash benefits increased from $35 million to $5 billion.[3] Though tax expenditure data are unavailable before 1967,[4] it seems reasonable to assume that this program grew slowly if at all between 1921 and the onset of World War II, partly because the Depression retarded the spread of corporate pensions.[5] The other reason, as with home mortgage interest, is that income tax rates were not yet high enough to create much of an incentive to avoid taxation. According to the Congressional Budget Office:

> As broad as the tax exemption became in the 1920s, it had little influence on the development of employer pensions before World War II. In the 1920s, only 1 percent of the population paid any income tax, and rates were 8 percent or less for many of those who paid. Corporate rates were only 12 percent to 13 percent . . . With rates so low, employees gained little, as compared with private saving, from employer contributions to trusts. Moreover, employers saved little on their contributions as compared with the taxes due on higher profits.[6]

Nevertheless, it would be wrong to infer from the lack of legislative or administrative activity that employer pensions were completely ignored. What is interesting about this period is what almost happened but did not. The defining event of the period was of course the Depression, which wreaked havoc on pension plans and every other source of economic security. Union plans, never on sound financial ground to begin with, were almost totally wiped out. Corporate plans were either terminated or retrenched. The most spectacular failures occurred in the railroad industry, prompting the national government to establish a separate, quasi-public retirement system for railroad employees in 1934.[7] Overall, the number of corporate plans appears to have dropped below four hundred at the onset of the Depression and then increased slowly to around five hundred by 1938. The number of workers covered, however, dropped by half, to around 5 percent of the nonfarm labor force. Ironically, the Social Security Act also contributed to the contraction of corporate pensions. One study conducted in 1940 estimated that the Act reduced pension benefits by one-third as employers factored in anticipated (but not actual) Social Security benefits.[8] Beth Stevens argues that the Act also gave employers an incentive to limit pensions to employees making more than $3,000 "since this was the salary limit for employer payroll contributions to the Social Security trust fund."[9] These outcomes were unexpected; the architects of the Act intended to bolster and not supplant private sources of retirement income.

Striking the right balance between public and private pensions was one of two developments that almost changed the politics of this tax expenditure before World War II. One of the most contentious debates during passage of the Social Security Act, and literally the last one to be resolved, was over the Clark amendment. This amendment would have allowed companies to opt out of the new Old Age Insurance (OAI) program—the core of what we now call Social Security—if they offered retirement benefits equal to or greater than those offered by the government. The Clark amendment was the brainchild of an insurance industry executive; as someone who managed pension trusts, he feared losing business to the government. The House deleted the amendment from its version of the Act, partly because members were concerned about the administrative headaches of coordinating public and private pensions so closely and partly because they favored a truly universal program of old age security. In response, insurance industry representatives mobilized many of the large corporations still offering retirement benefits to lobby the Senate. They succeeded in attaching the Clark amendment to the Senate version of the Act. In the ensuing conference committee, both sides staunchly refused to compromise. The logjam was broken only after Senate conferees agreed to delete the amendment if House conferees agreed to have a special committee propose a similar measure in the next session of Congress. The final version of the Social Security Act thus made no provision for coordinating or integrating public and private retirement pensions. Curiously, nothing ever came of the special committee, and the insurance industry stopped pushing for separate retirement systems. Insurance executives probably switched tactics because business had not fallen off as expected, because Social Security benefits remained low, and because they did not want to become too involved in national politics for fear of triggering an investigation into insurance practices.

Had the Clark amendment passed, the American welfare state would likely have developed much differently. Retirement pensions would have bifurcated, with many workers covered by employer plans and the rest covered by a residual public program. Social Security would have resembled Medicaid, and political support for Social Security would have been undercut. Initially many employers might have been unable to offer pensions as large as those provided by OAI and therefore unable to opt out of the public system. But as economic conditions improved, companies would have exited Social Security, beginning with large firms and unionized industries. Social Security would have served those firms that could not afford or were not compelled to provide pensions for their workers. It might well have merged with Old Age Assistance, the means-tested program of income support for the poor elderly, that has since been refashioned as Supplemental Security Income. The tax treatment of employer pensions would have loomed larger as a political issue sooner. All of this is admittedly speculative, though plausible. What is certain is that the absence of any language defining the relationship between OAI and private pensions in 1935 opened the door for business and labor to define this relationship in later years.[10]

The other development of note concerns President Roosevelt's attack on "economic royalists" during the Second New Deal.[11] The suddenness and intensity of these attacks caught many by surprise, in part because the president was friends with many of the nation's wealthiest families and was himself a man of means. Roosevelt had shown little interest as recently as 1934 in a Treasury proposal to tax the wealthy and close tax loopholes. The president seems to have experienced a change of heart after sensing what the historian Charles Beard termed the *thunder on the Left*—the populist appeal of Robert LaFollette, Jr., Father Coughlin, and especially Huey Long. Eager to prevent these challenges (Long's Share the Wealth Plan in particular) from harming his chances at reelection, Roosevelt proposed a series of tax increases on corporations and wealthy individuals beginning in 1935 and made tax fairness an important theme of the 1936 election.

The Treasury continued the attack in 1937 by recommending the elimination or reduction of various tax loopholes favoring large corporations and the wealthy. "Tax avoidance," according to Randolph Paul, a leading expert on taxation, "had developed into a fine art," one that conflicted with the Treasury's need to raise revenue and balance the budget.[12] Treasury Secretary Morgenthau singled out pension trusts as a prime example of abuse:

> Recently this exemption has been twisted into a means of tax avoidance by the creation of pension trusts which include as beneficiaries only small groups of officers and directors who are in the high income brackets. In this fashion, high-salaried officers seek to provide themselves with generous retiring allowances, while at the same time the corporation claims a deduction therefor, in the hope that the fund may accumulate income free from tax.[13]

One might think that Roosevelt's overwhelming victory in 1936 would have enabled him to dictate the terms of tax policy to Congress. Yet, by 1937 the administration's campaign against privilege, combined with its court-packing plan, had so antagonized conservative Democrats and Republicans that they began to unite in opposition to Roosevelt's tax proposals. Roosevelt succeeded in closing some of the loopholes on his list, but a number of key provisions, including pension trusts, emerged unscathed. Conservatives then blamed the ensuing recession of 1937–38 on the administration's tax policies, and Roosevelt stopped trying to use the tax code to redistribute wealth.

Treasury officials did manage to insert a nondiversion rule into the Revenue Act of 1938 that prohibited companies from claiming deductions for pension contributions in good times and then terminating their pension plans in bad times. This rule effectively recognized employees' legal right to pension benefits. But it did nothing to prevent companies from offering pensions solely to senior executives and highly paid employees. The Treasury's subsequent attempt to broaden pension coverage via administrative ruling was quickly declared unconstitutional by the Supreme Court in 1939.[14] I mention these episodes to document the Treasury's repeated efforts to curb this tax expenditure and to suggest why the Roosevelt administration was eager to introduce nondiscrimination rules during World War II.

PHASE II: 1942–1974

Between 1942 and 1949 the national government promoted the spread of employer pensions through an ad hoc series of laws, administrative rulings, and court decisions. Few if any of these decisions were intended to promote the retirement security of workers. Their main objectives were financing the war and securing labor peace. The resulting policies had two principal effects: they gave employers substantial incentives to establish pension plans, and they shifted the site of conflict from Washington to the shop floor. Business and labor, working within the framework of collective bargaining, had the most direct influence on the subsequent spread of corporate pensions and growth of this tax expenditure. The only changes to the pension laws between 1950 and 1974 were two relatively modest efforts to prevent fraud by pension fund administrators.

Scholars have well described the impact of World War II and its immediate aftermath on employer pensions. I will therefore devote more attention to the 1960s and early 1970s, the period when the "system" of pension laws and regulations created during the 1940s broke down and was reconstituted. That system consisted of the following pieces, presented in roughly chronological order.

The foundation was the Revenue Act of 1942.[15] As mentioned in the previous chapter, this historic Act transformed the income tax into a mass tax in order to finance the war effort. The middle class bore the brunt of this increase as policy makers, especially in Congress, concluded that higher taxes on corporations and the wealthy could not raise the necessary funds. Some feared that too much corporate taxation might even compromise business's willingness to cooperate in prosecuting the war. Nevertheless, business interests did not emerge totally unscathed. Corporate tax rates increased slightly and, more important, Congress raised the tax rate on excess profits (i.e., profits above prewar levels). Designed to prevent wartime profiteering, this latter provision had the unintended effect of "encouraging employers to lower their pretax profits by depositing earnings in exempt pension trusts rather than have them taxed."[16]

In addition, a small section of this Act created the first nondiscrimination rules for employer pensions. Companies now had to offer pensions to 70 percent of all full-time workers employed with them for five or more years in order to deduct their contributions as ordinary and necessary business expenses. The Act also contained language prohibiting companies from skewing benefits in favor of officers and senior employees. This language was fairly complex and left the IRS with considerable discretion in determining eligibility. However, the Act did allow employers to factor in their employees' expected Social Security benefits when calculating the extent of discrimination in their plans—thereby legalizing a practice initiated by employers in the late 1930s.

The specific formula for integration depended on two largely unstated assumptions. First, policy makers assumed that Social Security and employer pensions were interchangeable sources of retirement income. Just as important, they assumed that the goal of retirement policy was to produce approximately the same distribution of income postretirement as preretirement. Because Social Security benefits were somewhat progressive, employer pension benefits could be regressive and still qualify for favorable tax treatment. This Act therefore marked the first point at which Social Security and employer pensions were formally integrated.

Although these provisions "constituted a complete revision and rewriting of the code dealing with pension plans," they generated little debate and reflected little societal input.[17] Business and labor were more interested in basic questions of tax rates and the overall mix of corporate and individual tax increases than they were in nondiscrimination regulations. The impetus for nondiscrimination rules came from the Treasury Department, whose primary objective in creating these rules was to reduce tax avoidance among upper-income taxpayers, the same objective as in 1937. Secondarily, Treasury officials wanted to show ordinary citizens (and to some extent soldiers) that the rich would pay their fair share of the war's costs.[18] Business interests did, however, manage to block two other Treasury initiatives concerning pensions, immediate vesting and maximum limits on contributions and benefits. Both initiatives were designed to extend pensions faster to ordinary workers.

The second key piece of the postwar system was a 1943 ruling by the National War Labor Board (NWLB) exempting employer contributions to pension plans from existing wage and price controls.[19] This ruling enabled the NWLB to satisfy labor's demands for higher compensation without triggering a corresponding rise in wages and inflation. The combination of this ruling and higher excess profits taxes prompted a surge in employer pensions. The IRS approved three times as many new pension plans between September 1942 and December 1944 as it had between 1930 and 1942.[20]

Immediately after the war, the national government failed to expand the visible welfare state as many European nations did.[21] This failure consisted of programs such as full employment and national health insurance that were proposed but never enacted, and of existing programs such as Social Security that expanded rather slowly. The average old age insurance benefit in 1940, for example, was $22.71 per month, the equivalent of 27 percent of average monthly earnings. The average benefit rose to $29.03 per month by 1950 but, because of wage growth, had dropped to 15 percent of average monthly earnings. The most vocal proponent of welfare state expansion, and retirement pensions in particular, was organized labor. The chief barrier to such expansion were business interests and congressional conservatives, and the size of this barrier grew when Republicans retook Congress in 1946. Realizing that new social spending initiatives were politically infeasible, labor began to press management to provide greater fringe benefits.[22]

Labor's strategy received support from the executive branch and the Supreme Court.[23] The Truman administration helped to broker a deal in 1946 between striking mine workers and mine owners that included welfare and retirement benefits. Two years later the National Labor Relations Board (NLRB) ruled in a landmark case that employers could not exclude retirement benefits from collective bargaining agreements (*Inland Steel Company v. United Steel Workers of America*). The Board even suggested that employers had "a social obligation to provide workers with pensions . . . [considering] the obvious inadequacy of social security benefits" at the time.[24] The Supreme Court upheld the NLRB ruling in 1949. In general, according to Stevens:

> The federal government supported the negotiation over employee benefits in order to dampen the raging labor disputes of the postwar years and as part of a move by the Democratic executive branch to contest conservative congressional efforts to restrict the scope of collective bargaining and to block further development of public social-welfare programs. . . .
>
> Throughout the concentrated campaign of bargaining for employee benefits in 1946 and 1947, federal experts from the Social Security Administration and the Department of Labor met with labor-policy planners to give advice and even design exploratory surveys.[25]

Perhaps it is more accurate to say that labor's strategy received qualified support.[26] As part of a larger effort to limit the power of organized labor, section 302 of the 1947 Taft-Hartley Act established certain conditions for the administration of pension plans. The most important of these conditions prevented unions from assuming majority control of pension funds and established guidelines for investment that favored management of pension funds by third parties in the financial community. These requirements were inserted to allay the fears of Republicans and southern Democrats that pension funds would strengthen organized labor.

The final piece of this system, postwar tax policy, was in some ways the most critical.[27] Even with the repeal of excess profits taxes and reductions in corporate and individual tax rates, postwar taxes remained well above prewar levels in order to finance the government's new domestic and international commitments. The lowest corporate tax rate had been around 15 percent during the 1930s, rose above 25 percent during the war, and dropped only to 23 percent by 1950. The top tax rate in 1950 was 42 percent, on all income above $25,000.[28] Higher tax rates gave both employers and employees a clear financial incentive to establish pension plans.

These decisions, as stated earlier, were motivated primarily by the exigencies of war and the desire to secure labor peace during and after the war. Retirement security was a by-product. Nevertheless, the collective impact of these decisions on corporate pensions was substantial. Organized labor, led by the United Auto Workers (UAW), made pension plans a central issue of collective bargaining in the postwar era. Employers had good reason to agree to labor's demands: the tax system exempted employer contributions to pension plans; employers were legally required to bargain over pensions; union strength was substantial, even after Taft-Hartley; employers in capital-intensive industries such as steel and automobiles, usually among the first to offer pensions, could ill afford work stoppages and strikes; and most companies were largely unfettered by international competition and could thus afford to provide benefits that competing firms in other nations might not provide to their workers. The financial incentives alone were sufficient for many employers to establish pension plans in advance of labor demands. The number of workers covered by private pension plans more than doubled between 1940 and 1950, from 4.1 to 9.8 million, and almost doubled again to 18.7 million by 1960. This increase was not solely a function of an expanding labor force. Pension coverage increased from 15 percent of all private wage and salary workers in 1940 to 41 percent in 1960. This period thus represents the real growth phase of private pensions in terms of coverage. The portion of the workforce covered by private pensions climbed to 45 percent by 1970 and has since leveled off.[29]

These decisions had an indirect effect on Social Security as well. As part of their bargaining strategy, organized labor hoped that by winning large increases in corporate pensions, it would force employers to support increases in Social Security benefits. Labor succeeded, sort of. Prominent executives such as Charles Wilson of General Motors did urge Congress to expand Social Security in the early 1950s, and Congress responded. The strategy backfired, however, when employers reacted to these increases with proportional cuts in their pension benefits. What looked like the surest path to improving workers' standard of living became an avenue for those employers who offered pensions to shed some of the costs of providing retirement security to their workers. Quadagno has found evidence that government officials accepted this trade-off as the price to pay if employers were going to support expansion of Social Security. Some unions did not accept this trade-off and managed to "dis-integrate" pension benefits and Social Security benefits in their negotiations with employers. This tactic may explain why Social Security benefits grew more slowly during the latter half of the 1950s and most of the 1960s, as employers found it more difficult to offset these increases with corporate pension decreases. That unions devoted more of their energies to winning concessions from employers and less to expanding public programs was no doubt also a factor.[30]

The particular structure of these policies, then, created incentives for business and labor to determine the size and scope of corporate pensions within the framework of collective bargaining. The nondiscrimination rules passed in 1942 were neither so onerous as to prompt employers to seek their relaxation nor so permissive as to prompt labor to push for their tightening. Both sides were able to pursue their interests with respect to retirement pensions satisfactorily at the bargaining table.

Legislative changes to the regulations governing pensions were few in number and modest in scope between 1942 and 1974.[31] The Welfare and Pension Plans Disclosure Act of 1958 required pension plans to disclose more financial information to the Labor Department, and to plan participants upon request, in order to qualify for favorable tax treatment. In theory, more information would enable participants and the government to police pension plans more carefully. In practice, "the information required was not sufficient to reveal questionable financial practices or plan operations, and audits were not provided for. Staffing by the Labor Department for examination of the required reports was never adequate."[32] This Act also modified section 302 of the Taft-Hartley Act by further limiting labor's role in administering pension funds and by augmenting the role of financial intermediaries. The Welfare Pension Plan Act of 1962 gave the Labor Department the right to prosecute fraud and other criminal activities connected with pension funds. Both these measures were initiated and written by government officials responding to evidence of "embezzlement, kickbacks, and conflict of interest" in the administration of pension funds.[33] The most significant long-run effect of these laws was to give the Labor Department a role in the regulation of employer pensions.

In short, steps taken by government actors during and immediately after World War II initiated the second phase of this program, one characterized by a rapid expansion in employer pensions. This expansion was not triggered by changes in the tax code governing the treatment of pensions. It was fueled instead by significant increases in corporate tax rates and by changes in the legal framework governing collective bargaining between labor and management. It was propelled as well by the failure to expand the visible American welfare state as fast as organized labor desired. The subsequent growth of pensions, coupled with high corporate tax rates, undoubtedly contributed to the growth of this tax expenditure. Factors outside the arena of policy making for tax expenditures thus had an important impact on the growth of this program. These factors did not, however, help to politicize the tax treatment of employer pensions in Washington. The scope of conflict remained narrow, and neither business nor labor made much of an effort to change the relevant parts of the tax code. The few changes that were made were initiated primarily by a handful of government officials concerned with fraud and abuse.

This system began to unravel in the 1960s. The cumulative effect of several developments, none of them a crisis in and of itself, convinced policy makers that comprehensive pension reform was necessary. After much pulling and hauling, Congress passed the Employee Retirement Income Security Act (ERISA), which President Ford signed into law on Labor Day, 1974. This law subsequently reshaped the basic patterns of policy making for this program and ushered in the third phase of development. The process of creating ERISA illustrates well the ambiguity of tax expenditures, as policy makers seized upon the regulation of employer pensions as a means of addressing a variety of social ills.

The basic structure of pension regulations seemed sound when President Kennedy appointed a Committee on Corporate Pension Funds and Other Private and Retirement and Welfare Programs in 1962.[34] As a member of the Senate Labor and Public Welfare Committee, Kennedy had participated in the investigation of pension fraud during the 1950s and helped draft the 1958 Act. By the early 1960s, Kennedy was worried less about fraud or retirement security than the impact of pensions on national savings, capital markets, and labor mobility.[35] Pension funds thus fit into a larger framework of macroeconomic policy. The membership of his Committee on Corporate Pension Funds reflected these concerns. It was chaired by Secretary of Labor Willard Wirtz and included the Secretary of the Treasury, Secretary of Health, Education, and Welfare, director of the Budget Bureau, and the chairmen of the Council of Economic Advisers, the Federal Reserve System, and the Securities and Exchange Commission.

Between the time the Committee was appointed and issued its recommendations in 1965, several developments heightened official concern over pensions. The first was the continuing stream of complaints to members of Congress by individual workers who had lost their pension benefits. The second was publication of Merton Bernstein's *The Future of Private Pensions* (1964), a highly critical analysis of the existing pension system. Bernstein, an Ohio State professor of law, argued that corporate pensions were so thoroughly flawed that policy makers concerned with retirement security ought to significantly expand Social Security. Perhaps the most important development was the bankruptcy of the Studebaker automobile company in 1963 and the widely publicized collapse of its pension plan. Because the plan was underfunded, thousands of employees with fully vested pension rights received only a fraction of their expected benefits. The plan's collapse prompted the United Auto Workers to become more politically active concerning pensions in general and the fiscal integrity of benefits in particular.[36]

The Committee's report, *Public Policy and Private Pension Programs* (1965), marked a "turning point" in the development of pension regulations.[37] It helped to elevate employer pensions as a policy issue and was the first official proposal for comprehensive reform. The Committee reaffirmed the importance of private pensions as one leg of the three-legged stool of retirement security, along with Social Security and individual savings. This leg, however, needed support. The Committee reasoned that because the government afforded these pensions favorable tax treatment, it had an interest in regulating them more closely. It recommended a broad series of reforms including faster vesting schedules, dollar ceilings on contributions and benefits to senior employees, and minimum funding standards. It also recommended further study of plan termination insurance and of ways to improve the portability of pension benefits as employees changed jobs.[38]

The report generated considerable controversy, especially from employers who objected to the proposed scope of government regulation. Organized labor endorsed plan termination insurance and other measures to guarantee benefits but worried that other parts of the Committee's report might impose so large a regulatory burden that employers would terminate or reduce their pension plans. As a result, President Johnson declined to follow up with any concrete legislative proposals. Instead he appointed an interagency task force to continue studying the problem.

Meanwhile, individual members of Congress began to submit proposals for reforming various parts of the private pension system. Senator Vance Hartke (D-Ind.) introduced a termination insurance bill at the insistence of the UAW (the major Studebaker plant was located in South Bend, Indiana). Sen. John McClellan (D-Ark.) introduced legislation to curb fraud by establishing tighter fiduciary standards for pension plans, an issue the president's Committee had not addressed. The most important advocate of reform was Sen. Jacob Javits of New York, the ranking minority member of the Labor and Public Welfare Subcommittee on Labor and a moderate Republican. Javits was convinced that a more comprehensive approach, along the lines of the Committee's report, was necessary. According to Gordon, Senator Javits viewed pension reform "as the opening wedge in a drive to modernize labor-management relations and reinvigorate the practices of industrial capitalism."[39] Javits hoped that if pensions were made more widely available and their benefits somehow protected, then employees would find it easier to change jobs, pressures to expand Social Security would ease, and workers would generally look more to employers for social welfare benefits. His bill, introduced in 1967, went nowhere. Though Javits tried to ensure that the proposed regulations would not burden employers, Ways and Means chairman Wilbur Mills (D-Ark.) refused to consider his bill for fear of alienating business, and President Johnson backed away from the issue for similar reasons.

The initiative of a policy entrepreneur like Javits was crucial because, as Sen. John Heinz (R-Pa.) observed years later, pension regulations have "very little sex appeal and a lot of complexity. . . . The people you help are never going to know that you helped them, and the people you have a direct and measurable impact on—employers—often find the reform unpalatable."[40] Javits continued to press for reform. During Senate investigations of fraud in union benefit plans in 1969–70, Javits managed to persuade the Senate to sponsor a broad study of pensions. That study, released in March 1971, found a huge gap between the number of workers employed in firms offering pensions and the number who actually qualified for pension benefits. Since 1950, barely one-fourth of employees covered by plans requiring up to ten years of service for pension eligibility received any pension benefits, and less than one-tenth of employees covered in plans requiring eleven or more years of service received any benefits.[41] Javits then followed up with a series of hearings featuring individuals who had lost their pension benefits. Simultaneously, the media began to highlight specific cases of lost benefits, and Ralph Nader launched an attack on pension plans, calling them consumer fraud on a grand scale.

This combination of pressures increased support for pension reform in Congress. The leading advocates of reform represented the more industrialized, more unionized states. Unlike Javits, they, and Democrats in particular, tended to view pension reform as a means of safeguarding the interests of organized labor. Chief among them was Sen. Harrison Williams (D-N.J.), chairman of the Subcommittee on Labor, who put forward his own package of comprehensive reforms. Interest in the House lagged somewhat, but Representatives Dent (D-Pa.) and Erlenborn (R-Ill.) of the House Subcommittee on Labor did establish a pension task force in November 1971. The Nixon administration, hoping to head off any major increase in business regulation, endorsed tighter fiduciary standards and greater disclosure of information, changes that business had already indicated a willingness to accept. Many members of Congress felt that these changes alone were inadequate.

Between 1972 and 1974, Congress held numerous hearings and considered a large number of bills designed to shore up employer pensions. The ensuing legislative battles were fought along two closely related fronts: which features of pension plans would be regulated, and which congressional committees and bureaucratic agencies would monitor compliance with these regulations. The major substantive issues were fiduciary standards, vesting, funding standards, plan termination insurance, reporting and disclosure requirements, portability of pension rights, and integration of employer pensions with Social Security. Some bills addressed one or two of these issues, others addressed all of them. Some bills distinguished between single-employer plans and multiemployer plans, and others treated all plans alike.[42]

The jurisdictional battles pitted the revenue committees against the labor committees. The former tended to be sympathetic to employers and favor modest changes to fiduciary standards and funding. The latter tended to represent the interests of organized labor and favor more sweeping reform. The labor committees' insistence on plan termination insurance, financed by employer contributions, was one of the most controversial topics of debate. Not surprisingly, the Nixon administration favored those changes that would prevent the labor committees from increasing their authority over employer pensions. The long-standing cleavages between the revenue and labor committees were exacerbated by the push to decentralize power within Congress. As mentioned in chapter 3, many legislators during the late 1960s and early 1970s felt that a few committees and chairmen had become too powerful, and they were especially critical of the power wielded by the House Ways and Means Committee. Thus some legislators who favored more incremental changes in pension regulations might hesitate to give the revenue committees this added responsibility. In addition, there were major disagreements within the labor committees over creating an independent agency responsible for all pension regulations (the Javits bill) or augmenting the powers of the Labor Department (the Williams bill).

At times it seemed as if the issues were so complex and the possible combinations so numerous that compromise was impossible. Calculating the impact of different accounting procedures and vesting schedules was difficult; solid numbers on the costs and benefits of alternative proposals were "almost totally lacking."[43] Complicating matters further was the lack of clear signals from major interest groups. Aside from plan termination insurance, which organized labor clearly supported, most of these proposals were top-down initiatives. "A small and disorganized band of members of Congress have sought to publicize pension problems, but they have been hampered by a lack of interest group support when legislation comes under consideration."[44] The relevant interest groups had a much better sense of what they wanted to prevent from happening than what changes were desirable. This was particularly true of business. Business interests generally lacked cohesion during this era, and pensions were no exception. Representatives of unionized and nonunionized industries, big and small business, financial institutions, and pension consultants never spoke with one voice. Consistent with other instances of business regulation during this era, "the business community's lobbying was poorly coordinated, and its credibility was undermined by its unwillingness to offer an alternative solution to what was commonly recognized as a serious problem."[45]

Two developments finally broke the legislative logjam. The first was perceived problems in Social Security. Despite major increases in benefits in 1971 and 1972, the media circulated reports in 1974 that Social Security might collapse unless payroll taxes were substantially increased.[46] Legislators could therefore support bills that expanded employer pension coverage and protected benefits to prevent Social Security from expanding further. Second, members of Congress resolved their jurisdictional battles in Solomonic fashion. The revenue and labor committees agreed to share jurisdiction over employer pensions and to split administrative responsibilities among the Treasury Department, the Labor Department, and a new government-owned corporation, the Pension Benefit Guaranty Corporation (PBGC). Treasury was responsible for regulations governing vesting, nondiscrimination, and funding standards; Labor, for fiduciary standards and reporting and disclosure requirements; and the PBGC, for plan termination insurance. The structure of the PBGC, created to insure defined benefit plans, illustrates how many interests had a stake in this issue. The Secretary of Labor chairs the three-member board of directors, which also includes the Secretaries of the Treasury and Commerce. The PBGC Advisory Committee has designated seats for representatives of employers, employees, accountants, actuaries, insurance companies, commercial and investment banks, and the general public. The ERISA law, in short, created opportunities for numerous governmental and societal actors to monitor government regulation of employer pensions and to influence the substance of these regulations.

In the process of enacting ERISA, Congress recognized "that the natural tendency is for the [Internal Revenue] Service to emphasize those areas that produce revenue rather than those areas primarily concerned with maintaining the integrity and carrying out the purposes of exemption provisions."[47] Its solution was to reorganize the IRS, creating a new office for Employee Plans and Exempt Organizations that would specialize in the tax treatment of fringe benefits and charities. This step did not, however, change the Treasury's attitude toward this program. Treasury officials later recommended substantial cuts in this tax expenditure as part of proposals for comprehensive tax reform in 1977 and 1984. Again, the contrast with Social Security is stark. The Social Security Administration has never perceived a conflict between it and Social Security; it exists because the program exists.

The substance of ERISA reflected multiple compromises as well.[48] The most obvious of these benefited organized labor, and ERISA was widely considered at the time to be a defeat for business. The Act created new vesting and minimum funding requirements. It required all employers who offered defined benefit plans to participate in a new insurance program, administered by the Pension Benefit Guaranty Corporation. Nondiscrimination rules were revised slightly to expand pension coverage within firms. The law tightened existing regulations governing the investment of pension funds and increased the reporting and disclosure requirements. On the whole, ERISA represented the largest single redefinition of pension regulations, then or since.

Nevertheless, the use of incentives to promote the voluntary expansion of employer pensions placed real limits on reform. Legislators could not impose too heavy a regulatory burden lest employers reduce or eliminate their pension plans. In introducing its version of ERISA, the House Education and Labor Committee noted:

> The primary purpose of the bill is the protection of individual pension rights, but the committee has been constrained to recognize the voluntary nature of private retirement plans. The relative improvements required by this Act have been weighed against the additional burdens to be placed on the system. While modest cost increases are to be anticipated when the Act becomes effective, the adverse impact of these increases have been minimized.[49]

This constraint was probably more decisive in limiting the scope of regulation than whatever pressures business exerted directly. Two key issues, portability and integration with Social Security, were excluded. Portability posed too great an administrative headache and potentially created an even larger role for the government, for it required some institution to keep track of employees' pensions as they changed jobs. Most of the proposals for integration with Social Security would have lessened the extent of integration, thereby forcing employers to curb benefits to higher-paid employees or increase benefits to lower-paid employees. Employers and pension consultants successfully persuaded Congress that such a move would force some employers to reduce pension benefits, so it was tabled. Postponement also enabled legislators to avoid a fundamental and potentially protracted debate over the definition of adequate retirement income. In addition, the architects of ERISA provided employers with alternative means of demonstrating compliance with several of these regulations. The new vesting requirements, for instance, contained three different schedules from which employers could choose. The law also exempted fringe benefits other than pensions (e.g., health benefits) from the minimum funding requirements and from participation in the plan termination insurance program.

One final provision deserves mention. In addition to overhauling the regulation of corporate pensions, ERISA created new tax incentives for Individual Retirement Accounts (IRAs). The Nixon administration had initially proposed IRAs in 1971 to head off more comprehensive reforms that Congress was considering. IRAs would appeal particularly to "highly-mobile professional employees . . . who were unlikely to achieve vesting even under the liberal vesting schedule in the Javits bill."[50] The ploy failed, but Nixon officials did manage to attach IRAs to the final bill. It does not appear to have generated near the controversy of other provisions of ERISA such as plan termination insurance or congressional jurisdiction, which is consistent with the "stealth" quality of new tax expenditures.

PHASE III: 1974–PRESENT

As President Ford prepared to sign ERISA into law, the executive director of the Association of Private Pension and Welfare Plans publicly "doubted whether more than a 'handful' of Congressmen 'have any good idea of what's in the bill' and that 'hundreds of experts' who have closely followed the legislation for years are uncertain about many of its provisions."[51] Whether they hailed ERISA as a breakthrough, an illusion, or a step backward, most observers were likewise unsure about what impact ERISA would have on the availability and magnitude of pensions in the future. Changes in the scope and complexity of regulation were so dramatic as to make such projections almost impossible. These same changes, however, made certain political developments fairly predictable.

The process of enacting ERISA and the enlarged scope of government regulation transformed the politics of this tax expenditure. In this third phase, changes to pension regulations became more visible and more frequent. The scope of conflict expanded well beyond its earlier bounds. Some of the most important statutory changes were incorporated in the Multi-Employer Pension Plan Amendments Act of 1980, the Tax Equity and Fiscal Responsibility Act of 1982, the Retirement Equity Act of 1984, and especially the Tax Reform Act of 1986, which included the most sweeping changes to pension regulations since ERISA. Other notable changes were made in 1976, 1978, 1981, 1987, 1989, 1990, and 1993. Groups representing business and labor became more active in lobbying for changes in the relevant tax laws, as did groups representing pension consultants, financial institutions, the elderly, and women. The revenue, labor, and government operations committees emerged as important arenas of policy making and sources of reform proposals. ERISA created a new agency (the Pension Benefit

Guaranty Corporation, discussed above) to ensure the fiscal health of defined benefit plans, and it expanded the powers of two existing agencies (the Labor and Treasury Departments) to help assure corporate compliance with pension regulations.[52]

There is no better indicator of the program's complexity than the nearly one thousand pages devoted to employer pensions in the Internal Revenue Code.[53] According to the Joint Committee on Taxation, "The Federal laws and regulations governing employer-provided retirement benefits are recognized as among the most complex set of rules applicable to any area of the tax law."[54] A recent article in the specialty journal *Tax Notes* included a flow chart for employers trying to comply with the section of the tax code dealing with nondiscrimination regulations for pensions. That chart alone, including references to the appropriate parts of the Internal Revenue Code but no discussion of their meaning, was thirteen pages long.[55] In a series of interviews, representatives of business, labor, retirees, and pension consulting firms all voiced frustration and discontent with policy making since passage of ERISA.[56] Ask these individuals to name a consistent winner or loser over the last two decades and they cannot. Ask them to identify any patterns in policy making and they roll their eyes to the ceiling. The only constants are the regularity with which pension regulations are debated and amended, and the vast array of interest groups and government officials who regularly participate in these debates.

The very incoherence of policy making has been one of the defining features of this program over the last two decades.[57] The enlarged scope of pension regulations prompted many societal interests to become involved for the first time. This was particularly true of interest groups representing employers and pension consultants. The decision to create overlapping jurisdiction in Congress among the revenue, labor, and governmental operations committees created multiple points of access, multiple arenas for legislative change. The decision to distribute administrative duties among the Treasury Department, Labor Department, and PBGC produced a similar result. Each arena favored certain kinds of interests over others, and these interests often worked at cross-purposes. The combination of multiple interests and multiple arenas is responsible for the incoherence that everyone involved correctly perceives. Without trying to account for every twist and turn, the remainder of this section traces the basic contours of policy making after ERISA.

One of the most basic changes wrought by ERISA occurred in the representation of interests. ERISA, part of a larger wave of corporate regulations passed in the late 1960s and early 1970s, helped mobilize business interests to become more unified and more involved in public affairs.[58] The Chamber of Commerce, National Association of Manufacturers, American Bankers Association, and American Council of Life Insurance all stepped up their efforts to influence pension regulations in the wake of ERISA. The National Federation of Independent Business (NFIB) grew in large part because of the passage of laws like ERISA and OSHA (Occupational Safety and Health Act), which regulated many small businesses for the first time. The NFIB in turn worked to ease the regulation of pensions offered by small business. This mobilization extended beyond business. The American Association of Retired Persons (AARP), the leading lobby of the elderly, branched out from Social Security and Medicare to corporate pensions. The National Organization of Women (NOW) began to push for expanded pension coverage on behalf of lower-paid workers, many of whom are women.

New organizations devoted specifically to pensions formed almost immediately after ERISA.[59] Those representing employers included the National Employee Benefits Institute (1977) and the ERISA Industry Committee (1977). The latter represents many of the largest companies offering pensions, and its membership overlaps substantially with the Business Roundtable. Unions covered by multiemployer plans established the National Coordinating Committee for Multiemployer Plans in 1975. Professionals responsible for designing and administering pension plans formed the Society of Professional Benefits Administrators that same year. Karen Ferguson, a former associate of Ralph Nader, helped found the Pension Rights Center in 1976, the only organization devoted solely to defending the interests of workers and pensioners. It is not, however, a broad-based membership organization like the AARP. One of the most influential organizations currently is the Employee Benefits Research Institute (EBRI), formed in 1978. Sponsored by employers, unions, banks, insurance companies, and consultants, EBRI has a full-time staff of twenty-four and an annual budget of $3 million. Aside from the U.S. government, EBRI is the single most important source of information and analysis concerning employer pensions.

Initially, these organizations worked through those channels that had historically been sympathetic to their interests. Organized labor worked through the congressional labor committees and the Labor Department; AARP, the National Organization for Women, and the Pension Rights Center worked through the labor committees and select committees on aging; large employers, financial institutions, and pension consultants worked through the congressional revenue committees; small employers worked through the revenue committees and Senate Select Committee on Small Business. Many of these organizations also established ties with the governmental operations committees, which had jurisdiction over the Pension Benefit Guaranty Corporation. Most of these committees had a vested interest in some part of the ERISA regulations, and most had a characteristic bias. The labor committees, for instance, were inclined to expand the reporting and disclosure requirements on business in order to keep workers better informed. Each committee produced fairly predictable legislation, which then had to be countered on the floor of each chamber by whatever interest was adversely affected.

The resulting volume and complexity of pension regulations created a need for two types of third-party expertise. The rules governing "prudent" management of plan assets have led to greater reliance on banks, insurance companies, and investment houses. "While prudence has never been easy to define, it is clear that the more experts who can be found to ratify the wisdom of a certain investment decision, the more it will be deemed to have been prudent."[60] This pressure, combined with companies' desire to diversify their pension investments, prompted a large employer like AT&T to hire more than seventy separate firms to help it manage $41 billion worth of pension investments in 1989. Even a relatively small company like Food Lion, a grocery store chain with $229 million in pension assets, used ten outside firms.[61] The second type of expertise is provided by actuaries, accountants, and tax lawyers. Few companies can make sense of these regulations alone, so they hire a variety of specialists to design their pension plans, keep abreast of changes in pension regulations, and redesign their plans as needed. These specialists are highly educated, white-collar workers, and their services are not cheap. The other major function of these specialists is to comment on proposed Treasury regulations, pointing out internal contradictions, vague language, and the potential for unintended consequences.

Many of these third parties require specialized (usually postgraduate) education in order to understand pension regulations and help administer pension plans. And they must track recent changes to these regulations. To do so, they consult any one of a number of specialized journals that regularly feature articles explaining changes in pension regulations and providing advice on pension design: *Benefits Law Journal, Employee Benefit Plan Review, Employee Benefits Journal, Institutional Investor, Journal of Compensation and Benefits, Journal of Pension Planning and Compliance, Pension World, Pensions & Investment.* Other, more general journals also monitor pension regulations, including *Accountancy, American Journal of Tax Policy, CPA Journal, Journal of Accounting, Journal of Tax Policy, Journal of Taxation, National Tax Journal, Tax Notes,* and *Taxes.* Those who trumpet the administrative simplicity of tax expenditures clearly do not have this program in mind.

This program exhibited the same, seemingly random pattern of policy outcomes that Terry Moe has observed in regulatory agencies.[62] For example, individual access to retirement benefits has expanded and contracted. Congress has simultaneously tightened nondiscrimination rules, forcing employers to cover more of their lower-paid employees, and made it more attractive for employers to create voluntary savings plans (known as 401k plans) that cater to better-paid employees.[63] The government has made it easier for covered workers to retire early, while raising the age of mandatory retirement from sixty-five to seventy and the normal age for receiving Social Security from sixty-five to sixty-seven. The tax advantages for workers who are covered by employer pensions and want to contribute to IRAs expanded in 1981 and contracted in 1986. At times Congress has prohibited the Internal Revenue Service from ruling on the taxation of employer pensions, thereby creating uncertainty in the pension community and frustration within the IRS.[64] At other times the IRS has taken years to incorporate new tax legislation into the tax code and then expected immediate compliance. Occasionally, legislators tried modifying pension regulations to solve problems that the architects of ERISA never envisioned. Senators Dole and Kassenbaum of Kansas, for example, once proposed taxing the capital gains of pension fund investments held less than six months in order to promote longer-term investment practices in the financial community.

Systematic reform has been almost impossible. President Carter's Commission on Pension Policy recommended sweeping changes to ERISA, including immediate vesting, full portability, and mandatory pension coverage by all employers. The Commission tried to reflect the variety of interests involved by including representatives of business, labor, government, and academia, yet its recommendations were subsequently ignored by the Reagan administration.[65] The Pension Benefit Guaranty Corporation has been on shaky financial footing for most of its lifetime and nearly collapsed in the mid-1980s when a few large firms went bankrupt. Various remedies have been tried; none of them have been satisfactory. Efforts to consolidate administrative responsibilities within an Employee Benefits Commission or similar agency have always come up short. Literally no attempt has been made to discuss employer pensions and Social Security within some larger framework of retirement policy, even after Social Security was restructured in 1983. All these outcomes are understandable in light of the fragmented structure created by ERISA in 1974.

ERISA had a greater impact on the representation of interests and frequency of overt changes to the tax expenditure for employer pensions than it did on its growth. As with home mortgage interest, the major changes to the overall size of the program resulted from efforts to reform the tax code and reduce the deficit. The Tax Reform Act of 1986 reduced the estimated size of the program in 1991 from $72 billion to $54 billion, the largest single cut in its history.[66] Because part of this tax expenditure involves the deferral of taxation on pension earnings until the individual receives the pension, the lower rates on individual income taxes indirectly produced cuts. Lower marginal tax rates on corporate income indirectly reduced the value of avoiding taxation via contributions to pension funds. There were also deliberate changes to the program's structure. The Act limited the ability of higher-paid employees to accumulate large pensions and changed the rules governing the proper ratio of pension plan assets to liabilities. Both changes worked to reduce the size of the program. Finally, the Act imposed limits on contributions to Individual Retirement Accounts which the CBO estimated would cut that program in half by 1991.

As with home mortgage interest, pressures to reduce the deficit led to several smaller cuts. Considering its enormous size, small reductions in this tax expenditure could produce considerable revenue. The first important restrictions were incorporated in the Tax Equity and Fiscal Responsibility Act of 1982. Later restrictions were included in the Omnibus Budget Reconciliation Act of 1987 and similar budget accords in 1990 and 1993. The latter two bills were notable for making substantial reductions in future deficits. Typically these changes were buried in the fine print of these large and complex bills, and they generated little debate or discussion relative to questions of how much deficit reduction was necessary, how much to increase taxes on the rich, and how many cuts to make in Medicare.

The vulnerability of employer pensions was partly the legacy of ERISA in fragmenting interests. No single organization speaks for pensioners; the AARP, NOW, labor unions, and the Pension Rights Center have overlapping but distinct concerns and constituencies. No single organization represents employers or the many third parties responsible for designing pension plans and investing pension funds. Under pressure, these actors scrambled to protect their individual interests, making it easier for those bent on raising revenue to pick off the weak or inattentive or to set one interest against another. Fragmentation among congressional committees and bureaucratic agencies likewise hindered government officials from uniting. By contrast, the American Association of Retired Persons can credibly claim to represent recipients of Social Security. The revenue committees and Social Security Administration alone have jurisdiction. Likewise, the housing provider coalition was far more unified in fighting off efforts to cap the home mortgage interest deduction in the late 1980s and early 1990s.

Despite these cuts, the tax expenditure for employer pensions has grown by an average of 6 percent annually since the late 1960s, adjusted for inflation. That rate has been virtually unchanged since 1980, the period in which tax reform and deficit reduction prompted some cuts. Such growth was not the result of changes in corporate tax rates, which declined during this era. And it is unlikely that deliberate changes to this tax expenditure had a large effect, given the lack of any clear pattern of change. Such growth was instead owing largely to a variety of factors—such as the performance of pension fund assets invested in the stock market, or inflation—beyond the direct control of public officials.

DISCUSSION

Few public officials or interest groups demonstrated any interest in the tax treatment of employer pensions until the mid-1960s, some forty years after the program had been created. Until that point, the only interested actors were more concerned with patrolling instances of fraud and abuse than with promoting expansion. During that same period, bureaucrats at the Social Security Administration and members of the revenue committees were carefully expanding old age insurance by adding in survivors' and disability benefits, extending coverage to virtually the entire workforce, and deliberately increasing benefits. After 1974 the coalition supporting this tax expenditure did bear a surface resemblance to the coalition supporting Social Security in that congressional committees, administrative agencies, and beneficiaries were all active, and support among political elites was bipartisan. But the extent of fragmentation within each branch of the coalition, the lack of consensus on basic goals, and the frequent internecine battles clearly set the tax treatment of employer pensions apart. Instead of one, relatively unified advocacy coalition, this program featured several advocacy coalitions whose interests sometimes coincided but just as often conflicted. The Treasury Department repeatedly tried to limit the revenues lost via this tax expenditure rather than lead the drive for expansion.

The usual connections between program coverage, political support, and growth did not hold either. The greatest period of expansion in pension coverage, 1940 to 1960, was not the result of advocates mobilizing to broaden the definition of eligibility. There was no advocacy coalition to speak of, and the introduction of nondiscrimination rules in 1942 tended, if anything, to deter employers from establishing pension plans. The expansion was owing instead to a combination of laws, administrative rulings, and court decisions whose primary objectives were raising revenue and assuring labor peace. These policies just happened to encourage workers to demand and employers to provide retirement pensions. Between 1940 and 1960, then, this program experienced growth without advocacy. Years later the opposite occurred—advocacy with retrenchment—some of it deliberate and some of it unintended. In short, although enactment of this tax expenditure was rather mundane, its development has been complex and unpredictable.

CHAPTER 7

Earned Income Tax Credit

THE DEVELOPMENT of the Earned Income Tax Credit (EITC) has been extraordinary. What started in 1975 as a minor amendment to a forgettable tax bill has now become one of the most popular programs in Washington. As mentioned in chapter 3, the national media and officials from both major parties have repeatedly praised the program. Little of this rhetoric amounted to cheap talk. The EITC has been expanded on four separate occasions—1978, 1986, 1990, and 1993. These changes added several million more families and several billion more dollars to the program. The most recent expansion of the EITC, as part of the 1993 budget accord, is expected to increase the program's cost by 50 percent over the next five years. This same budget accord slashed billions of dollars from such sacred cows as Medicare and federal employee pensions. Only in the spring of 1995, as policy makers sought to balance the budget within seven years, did some congressional Republicans seriously contemplate cutting this program, and they encountered stiff opposition. Assuming for the moment that no changes are made, by 1998 the EITC will provide approximately $20 billion in income support—by reducing income taxes and increasing the size of tax refunds—to sixteen million poor and near-poor households. It will become the single largest income transfer program for low-income citizens in the United States.

Expansion of the Earned Income Tax Credit coincided with some of the least favorable economic conditions imaginable: slow economic growth, but not so slow as to constitute a major crisis (as in the Depression); record budget deficits, and a widespread belief among policy makers that deficit reduction should be a top policy priority; and adoption of formal budgetary rules in 1990, designed to slow the growth of government spending. The political environment was just as inhospitable. The EITC somehow prospered during Republican administrations that favored defense over domestic spending and openly waged war on means-tested social programs. It lacked the support of a third-party service provider, such as the doctors and nursing homes that supported Medicaid. No organized or unorganized group of the working poor took to the streets demanding government action. And the program encountered divided government and heightened ideological polarization in Washington, conditions widely believed to promote gridlock. Despite these obstacles, the EITC expanded faster than every other major means-tested program between 1980 and 1992, and its growth even surpassed that of inclusive programs like Social Security and Medicare (see Table 7.1). Much as a biologist might explain how plants and animals can survive in the desert, this chapter explains how the EITC managed to flourish in a time of economic and political stress.

To proponents of the EITC, the program's success is easily explained: consistency with basic American values.[1] Because benefits go only to people who work for wages, the EITC reinforces the work ethic. AFDC, by contrast, allegedly undermines the work ethic by providing payments to those who do not work at all.[2] The same flaw is attributed to various negative income tax schemes that have been proposed over the years. The EITC also appears consistent with the value of limited government. By working through the tax code, the EITC eliminates the need for large social service bureaucracies. It requires seemingly small changes to established tax forms and existing procedures of tax collection. The program is largely self-executing: individuals determine their own eligibility and calculate their own benefits based on simple instructions accompanying the annual tax return. Though limited government might seem to appeal only to conservatives, liberals have also expressed an interest in doing away with the intrusive and often demeaning administration of traditional public assistance programs in favor of the more anonymous, arm's-length administration of the Earned Income Tax Credit.

These attributes have been cited repeatedly by policy makers wishing to expand the EITC, and one would be hard-pressed to dismiss them entirely as a rhetorical smoke screen. Based on personal interviews and analysis of the written record, I am convinced that the program's core supporters believed, as a matter of principle, that people who worked—particularly those who worked full-time and had dependent children—should not be poor. Still, there are reasons to be dissatisfied with a pure values explanation. One might expect these same liberal values to promote expansion of jobs and training programs, and yet these programs were cut dramatically in the 1980s (Table 7.1). More important, one might wonder why the EITC closely resembled traditional means-tested programs during its first decade, then sharply diverged. The real (inflation-adjusted) value of the average tax credit actually *declined* between 1975 and 1985, as did the overall size of the EITC program. Its political base was narrow; interest groups representing beneficiaries were notably absent. Only since the mid-1980s has the program been significantly expanded and widely backed in Washington. Unless the work ethic and distrust of big government somehow became much more salient in the mid-1980s—and studies indicate considerable stability in such core values[3]—then we need to identify additional forces at work.

TABLE 7.1
Growth of Major U.S. Social Programs, 1980–1992 (in billions of 1992 dollars)

	1980	1992	Average annual growth rate
Targeted programs			
Medicaid	$24.9	$67.8	8.7%
Food Stamps	15.5	23.5	3.5
Supplemental Security Income	10.9	18.7	4.6
AFDC	12.3	13.6	0.8
Earned Income Tax Credit	3.4	12.4	11.4
Jobs and training	14.8	5.0	−8.6
Title XX social services	4.8	2.8	−4.4
Head Start	1.2	2.2	5.2
Women, Infant, Children food program	1.2	2.6	6.7
Inclusive programs			
Social Security	201.8	287.6	3.0
Medicare	54.7	119.0	6.7

Sources: U.S. Bureau of the Census, *Statistical Abstract of the United States 1994* (Washington, D.C.: Government Printing Office, 1994); U.S. Bureau of the Census, *Statistical Abstract of the United States 1987* (Washington, D.C.: Government Printing Office, 1986), for 1980 data concerning jobs and training; U.S. House of Representatives, Committee on Ways and Means, *Overview of Entitlement Programs: 1994 Green Book* (Washington, D.C.: Government Printing Office, 1994).

Notes: Spending figures are adjusted using CPI-U index. Figures reflect spending by the national government only. Figures for EITC include taxes forgone and tax refunds.

To understand fully the development of the Earned Income Tax Credit, we need to recognize how certain policy attributes privileged it over comparable direct expenditures. The most important of these attributes is *ambiguity*. As an open-ended tax expenditure, not tied to consumption of any specific good or service, the EITC was easily linked to a wide variety of problems that beset the working poor. This ambiguity enabled the program to build an ever widening base of support among political elites who could defend the program on multiple and often distinct grounds.

Equally important, we need to recognize how the 1980 election changed the political calculations of Democrats and Republicans. Many observers interpreted the Republicans' capture of the White House and Senate as the end of the New Deal era and the beginning of a new Republican regime. In response, members of both parties attempted to forge a new majority coalition of voters.[4] Part of their strategy entailed mobilizing financial support from corporations and wealthy individuals. Another part involved appealing to voters whose party ties were weak.[5] One of the most volatile blocs of voters consisted of the working poor. Based on returns from presidential elections, voters earning less than $12,500 became progressively more likely to vote Democratic during the 1980s whereas voters earning more than $25,000 became more likely to vote Republican. Those earning between $12,500 and $25,000—a good approximation of the working poor—voted Democratic in 1980 (by a 46–44 margin), Republican in 1984 (57–42), and Democratic again in 1988 (50–49). Many of these voters were recent blue-collar and working-class defectors from the Democratic Party, the so-called Reagan Democrats. Numerous opinion polls, focus groups, and elections persuaded leaders of both parties that the allegiance of the working poor was up for grabs. Comprising roughly 20 percent of voters, the working poor represented a substantial target of opportunity.[6]

Based on a revealing series of interviews, pollster Stanley Greenberg found that the working poor saw themselves "as a new middle class, defined by hard work and taxes and life just above the margin. It is a class of working people that acts virtuously, yet feels it is treated as marginal or invisible."[7] Many had seen their standard of living erode in recent years. Some lived in two-earner families out of economic necessity, not choice, and even with two incomes lived close to poverty. They placed a high value on work and feared having to go on welfare. At bottom, many were frustrated about doing everything right in terms of work and family and still being unable to afford a house, child care, or health insurance, or to save for retirement. These were the people policy makers and the media had in mind when they "discovered" the working poor in the 1980s.[8] These voters tended to view Republicans as the party of the rich and Democrats as the party of special interests, especially blacks. Whichever party broadened its appeal to the working poor most convincingly might win enough votes to swing many (if not most) elections for national office.

Politicians hoping to improve their individual or party's electoral chances became more receptive to programs that benefited the working poor.[9] As John Gilmour observes, "Highly visible issues that appeal to sizable constituencies whose votes are seen as movable from one party to another can readily stimulate competitive bidding between the parties."[10] Politicians varied in the extent to which they used the EITC as a campaign issue. For some it was primarily an efficient means of improving the distribution of costs and benefits in large budget bills. They used the EITC to improve the lot of the working poor and trumpeted those gains in rather general terms. Other politicians referred to the program by name. No one, however, wanted to appear insensitive to the working poor. Thus party competition over the EITC often had a defensive quality to it, as politicians tried to prevent their opponents from "capturing" this issue. The remainder of this chapter presents evidence for this argument by chronicling the transformation of the EITC program from its creation in 1975 to the present.

WELFARE REFORM (PART 1)

President Carter was the first to propose major changes to the EITC program, under the rubric of welfare reform.[11] The existing welfare system, Carter declared in 1977, was "anti-work and anti-family."[12] His alternative, the Program for Better Jobs and Income (PBJI), guaranteed employment to the poor who could work and a minimum income to those who could not. The administration estimated that it would have to create as many as 1.4 million public service employment (PSE) jobs in order to ensure that every household had at least one wage earner. These jobs would pay close to the minimum wage, enough to live on but not so much as to discourage recipients from seeking work in the private sector. Refusal to accept government employment would result in termination of welfare benefits. Those who could not reasonably be expected to work (children, the aged, the disabled, and some single parents) would receive a single cash assistance payment in lieu of AFDC, Supplemental Security Income, and Food Stamps.[13]

Though somewhat more generous, PBJI bore a strong resemblance to Russell Long's 1972 workfare proposal. Both proposals classified the poor as deserving or undeserving, and both designed a system that would push welfare recipients to find work, preferably in the private sector. The similarities went deeper. Specific details of PBJI were tailored to win Long's approval because the Finance chairman had blocked welfare reform in the past, as well as many of Carter's recent domestic initiatives. One "apparent concession to Senator Long was the President's recommendation for a significant expansion of the so-called earned income tax credit system."[14] Carter knew that the EITC program was a favorite of Long and hoped that its expansion would cause Long to look favorably upon the entire reform package. An administration spokesman, testifying before Congress, argued that "a major inadequacy of the current hodge-podge of welfare programs is that an insufficient and inequitable amount of total assistance is directed to the working poor, especially two-parent families with dependents."[15] For the first time the tax credit would be adjusted for family size and indexed for inflation. The maximum tax credit for a family of four would increase from $400 to $680. Equally important, PBJI would greatly expand the number of taxpayers eligible for the EITC by doubling the upper end of the phase-out range from $8,000 to $15,600. To make private sector jobs more attractive, those employed in PSE jobs would be ineligible for the EITC. All in all, Carter fashioned quite a carrot for Senator Long.

PBJI never had a chance. The proposed expansion of public service employment and the proposal's overall cost attracted widespread criticism. Organized labor argued that Carter's proposal was inadequate as a full employment policy. Labor officials also worried that additional PSE workers might displace current government workers. Public welfare professionals and the National Urban League claimed that PBJI would create a permanent class of marginal workers. Conservatives expressed similar reservations, though they objected more to the prospect of creating a publicly employed class of marginal workers. Within Congress, Democrats and Republicans harbored serious reservations about building on programs that had a reputation for make-work jobs and abuse.[16] They also questioned whether the PBJI would cost far more than the $3 billion estimated by the administration. Perhaps the fatal flaw was Carter's initial demand that the PBJI not entail any additional spending, one that could not be reconciled with his other demands for comprehensiveness and jobs for all. All these issues overshadowed the proposed changes to the EITC. Carter lost interest in PBJI after the final costs were estimated and passage of Proposition 13 in California was interpreted by many politicians as a demand for fiscal restraint. PBJI died in the Ways and Means Committee in the summer of 1978.

As in 1975, tax reform proved to be a better vehicle for the EITC than welfare reform. The Revenue Act of 1978 increased the maximum tax credit from $400 to $500 and extended the phase-out range to $10,000. These changes were supposed to reflect increases in the cost of living and in the minimum wage, yet benefits were not indexed. The Act also simplified the process by which taxpayers computed the value of the EITC. The single most important change was making the EITC permanent. No longer would it have to be periodically reauthorized. Once again, the scope of conflict remained narrow. Consideration of the EITC was overshadowed by debates over progressivity and the proper mix of tax cuts for individuals and corporations.[17]

Congress made the final version of the Act less progressive and more oriented toward corporate investment than Carter's initial proposal. During the Act's transformation, the revenue committees seized the opportunity to modify the EITC. Members of both committees expressed satisfaction that the EITC had provided tax relief and work incentives, and therefore deserved to be expanded. Ways and Means was a bit more concerned about simplifying the tax forms; Finance favored extending the phase-out range, thus increasing the number of people eligible for the credit.[18] In addition to pushing the EITC on its merits, Long suggested that the EITC would inject a certain amount of equity back into the Act and thereby decrease the likelihood that Carter would veto the entire bill. A veto might suggest to voters that Democrats were incapable of governing, a poor message to send shortly before the off-year elections.

Details aside, the overall pattern is clear: president proposes comprehensive welfare reform, including expansion of EITC; proposal generates widespread and intense opposition; proposal is defeated; president abandons welfare reform; tax committees later expand EITC as part of larger revenue bill; EITC passes with little debate or societal input. The process of amending the EITC in 1978 was a virtual repeat of the program's enactment. The politics of the program had not changed.

TAX EQUITY (PART 1)

The 1980 election set in motion a series of events that transformed the EITC into an object of party competition. The EITC first surfaced in debates over the fairness of President Reagan's tax and budgetary policies.[19] These debates ultimately produced the Tax Reform Act (TRA) of 1986, the most sweeping overhaul of the tax system since 1954. Among its many remarkable features, TRA effectively removed many low-income families from the income tax rolls. This result was achieved partly through the largest single increase in the EITC since its enactment.[20]

Two recent books, *Showdown at Gucci Gulch* and *Taxing Choices*, demonstrate in rich detail the importance of party competition to passage of TRA.[21] Both parties believed that TRA could determine the allegiance of lower- and middle-income voters for years to come. In the words of one Reagan adviser, "Passage of tax reform . . . will erase the cartoon of our party as defender of the rich and privileged. The dramatic relief . . . would reflect well on . . . all Republican candidates for the next generation."[22] For their part, Democrats fought hard to prove that their "roots [still lay] with working families all across the country."[23] No mention of the EITC is made in these two studies of TRA, nor in any other written account. Based on interviews with participants, it now appears that the EITC was part of the glue that held the entire Act together. It allowed legislators to alter the overall distribution of benefits fairly cheaply, and sometimes to offset the impact of measures designed to favor the well-to-do. The process of tax reform in turn reconfigured political support for the EITC program.[24]

Stunned by the 1980 elections, many Democrats searched frantically for Republicans' weaknesses. "Fairness," a complex and ambiguous concept, was the one club Democrats managed to wield successfully during President Reagan's first term. Several Democratic candidates for the House used the fairness issue to defeat their Republican opponents in 1982. Other Democrats directed the General Accounting Office (GAO) and Congressional Budget Office (CBO) to study the distributional effects of Reagan's tax and budgetary policies. Their findings were eye-opening. According to the GAO, cuts in the AFDC program in 1981 had increased the ranks of the working poor by widening the gap between eligibility for public assistance and the poverty line. The CBO study was a more comprehensive evaluation of Reagan's fiscal policies. The good news, as far as the administration was concerned, was that the average family had $840 more in income in 1984 as a result of cuts made in 1981. The bad news was that these benefits were skewed in favor of the affluent. Families earning less than $10,000 per year actually *lost* $390 in income, and those earning between $10,000 and $20,000 basically broke even. Those making more than $80,000 per year, however, pocketed an additional $8,270.

The administration quickly produced its own study purporting to show a more even distribution of benefits. Its findings were overshadowed by studies conducted by the Joint Tax Committee, Ford Foundation, Urban Institute, Center on Budget and Policy Priorities, and Citizens for Tax Justice, all of which provided further evidence of growing income disparities in the 1980s. Even such Reagan stalwarts as Arthur Laffer and the American Enterprise Institute publicly criticized the distributional impact of the administration's policies, particularly on the working poor.[25]

In a series of congressional hearings, Democrats followed up on these studies by publicizing growing income disparities, condemning the administration's policies, and exploring avenues for tax reform. These hearings marked a turning point for public interest groups representing the poor and near-poor. Previously these groups had restricted their lobbying and research activities to direct spending programs. Democrats on the Ways and Means Committee, as well as committee staff, made a conscious effort to demonstrate the importance of tax policy to these groups and to elicit their support for tax reform—a classic instance of government officials mobilizing interest groups around a specific policy.[26] According to a key participant in this effort:

> Prior to the tax reform debate, these groups displayed almost no interest in tax policy. A simple model developed by the [Ways and Means] committee staff was used by Congressman Rangel and other members to persuade these groups to invest heavily in the tax reform debate.

The model calculated the tax burden of a given hypothetical family (for example, a mother with two children or a two-parent family with two children) with earnings equal to the poverty threshold. It demonstrated the large increase in federal taxes paid by families with incomes at the poverty threshold during the 1980s.

The interest groups agreed that it was clearly more salable to urge a $100 per month decrease in federal taxes, than to gain a $100 increase in additional food stamps or other benefit for families near the poverty threshold.[27]

The tactic worked. Since 1984 a number of organizations have supported tax reductions for low-income workers and expansion of the EITC, as well as increases in direct social spending. Of these groups, the Center on Budget and Policy Priorities has become the leading advocate of the EITC.[28] These hearings also helped educate legislators about the impact of seemingly small changes in the tax code—for instance, in the personal exemption, standard deduction, and Earned Income Tax Credit—on low-income workers.[29]

Even before the CBO and GAO studies were published, Republican strategists began to combat, in the words of Republican National Chairman Paul Laxalt, "this unfortunate country club image that makes it appear most Republicans ride around in Mercedes Benz' and eat quiche."[30] Reagan and other Republicans repeatedly portrayed themselves as the party of economic growth. They argued that jobs, not social programs, were the key to prosperity. The problem for Republicans was that the recent recession was the deepest in memory, and many of the working poor were still feeling its effects. Fearing that Democrats would make fairness and tax reform central issues of the 1984 campaign, White House Chief of Staff James Baker urged Reagan to seize the initiative. Reagan announced in his 1984 State of the Union message that the Treasury would conduct a major study of tax reform.[31] During the campaign, Reagan blamed the tax treatment of low-income workers on policies enacted by Carter and Mondale.[32] Aided by economic recovery and the Democrats' failure to capitalize fully on the fairness issue, Republicans succeeded in relegating fairness to a minor theme in the 1984 campaign. Reagan actually won a higher percentage of working-class votes than he had in 1980.[33]

Republicans were less successful in controlling the subsequent direction of tax reform. As discussed in chapter 5, the Treasury study (nicknamed Treasury I) recommended a far more comprehensive revision of the tax code than anyone in the White House expected. Treasury I was an economist's dream and a politician's nightmare. In exchange for lower tax rates, greater equity, and simplicity, it eliminated or reduced most tax expenditures. The proposal's combination of concentrated costs and diffuse benefits was a poor recipe for political success.[34]

Treasury I posed particular difficulties for Republicans, since many of their constituents (i.e., corporations and the affluent) benefited considerably from tax expenditures.

One tax expenditure spared the Treasury knife was the Earned Income Tax Credit. While conceding that the EITC added "considerable complexity to the system, especially for those least able to understand it," Treasury I justified an increase based on equity considerations.[35] The impetus for expanding the EITC came from C. Eugene (Gene) Steuerle, economic coordinator of the Treasury study. Steuerle had been studying the growing tax burdens of low-income families for some time and believed that the government had an obligation to reduce these burdens. Reagan's call for tax reform and the growing attention to tax fairness presented him with a window of opportunity.[36] Of the available options, the EITC was the most attractive because the budget deficit placed a premium on measures that targeted tax relief as efficiently as possible. Steuerle inserted a larger, indexed EITC into Treasury I.[37]

Predictably, Treasury I generated intense opposition from groups threatened with the loss of tax benefits. In contrast, "of all the proposals that led up to the Tax Reform Act of 1986 . . . the suggestion to increase the EITC received almost no public or formal opposition from the day it was first put on the table"[38]—which is not to say that the EITC was ignored. In fact, at several points between Treasury I and passage of the final Act, the EITC was quietly enlarged beyond what Steuerle and the Treasury Department had proposed. The reasons for this expansion had less to do with the intrinsic merits of the EITC than the program's ability to meet the various needs of individual legislators.

Democrats and Republicans agreed that any tax reform package had to be distributionally neutral. Democrats did not want a regressive bill similar to the Economic Recovery and Tax Act (ERTA) of 1981. But with the Senate and White House in Republican hands, Democrats could hardly expect to redistribute much income downward. Neutrality was thought to be the best feasible solution and a big improvement on ERTA. Though some Republicans may have preferred to continue down the ERTA path, many of them wanted to avoid being labeled the party of greed. Distributional neutrality was not a bad compromise as far as Republicans were concerned, for it represented a significant shift away from progressivity in debates over taxation.

The commitment to distributional neutrality meant that anyone interested in amending the tax reform bill in favor of more affluent taxpayers had to add an equal benefit for low-income taxpayers. Because the initial Treasury plan drastically reduced the value of tax expenditures for the affluent, many interest groups and legislators searched for a low-income measure to pair off with their own pet tax preference. Several times they turned to the EITC as a relatively cheap way of preserving distributional neutrality. Unlike increases in, for example, the personal exemption or standard deduction, every dollar added to the EITC program went exclusively to taxpayers at the lower end of the income distribution. The White House never objected to this expansion; Steuerle recalled that "[OMB Director] Darman loved it."[39] Thus legislators were able to support expansion of the EITC as good policy, as a tangible benefit to a significant bloc of voters, or as a means of securing tax benefits that were not otherwise obtainable.

In short, Reagan's election increased the level of party competition, and tax policy was one of the first arenas in which Democrats and Republicans competed. The tax treatment of the working poor was a major concern primarily because of their electoral importance. Because the same committees that have jurisdiction over tax policy also have jurisdiction over tax expenditures, partisan struggles over tax policy affected the EITC.

WELFARE REFORM (PART 2)

Passage of the Tax Reform Act cut short a Democratic attempt to expand the EITC under the guise of welfare reform.[40] The Family Economic Security Act, introduced by Reps. Charles Rangel (D-N.Y.) and Harold Ford (D-Ky.) and Sen. Daniel Patrick Moynihan (D-N.Y.) in 1985, combined higher AFDC benefits and measures designed to ease the transition from welfare to work. Among these measures was a larger Earned Income Tax Credit indexed for inflation, similar to that proposed by Treasury I.[41] The Act did not guarantee all citizens a minimum income (as with FAP), nor did it require a massive increase in public service employment (as with PBJI). Instead it tied work to welfare and increased benefits for the working poor. It was designed to appeal both to the older generation of working-class, urban, socially conservative Democrats and to the newer generation of upper-middle class, suburban, socially liberal Democrats. The proposed reforms appealed to many Reagan Democrats and independent voters as well. It was in part a signal to voters that Democrats could no longer be accused of coddling the poor.[42]

As with tax reform, Reagan officials tried to preempt the Democrats by making welfare reform a top domestic priority of the 1986 State of the Union speech. Reagan charged the White House Domestic Policy Council with performing a study of the entire welfare system and recommending changes. In Congress, Republicans managed to reshape the Democrats' proposal enough to share credit for the final product. After considerable debate and partisan jostling for position, Congress passed the Family Security Act in 1988. The principal difference between the final Act and the original bill was that work incentives were given more prominence, a concession to Republicans and conservative Democrats. Proposed changes to the tax system, including the EITC, were dropped once the Tax Reform Act passed in 1986.[43] Nevertheless, the connection between party competition and the EITC was obvious.

MINIMUM WAGE

Party competition figured prominently during debates over tax reform and welfare reform, and it fueled the expansion of the EITC in 1986. The EITC's subsequent incarnation as an alternative to an increase in the minimum wage introduced an element of *intra*party competition as well. After Republicans lost control of the Senate in 1986, a number of Democratic constituencies began to raise issues that had lain dormant for most of the decade. For example, liberal Democrats, backed by organized labor, civil rights, women's, and church groups, introduced the Minimum Wage Restoration Act in 1987.[44] This Act would have increased the minimum wage from $3.35 to $3.85 in 1988, $4.25 in 1989, $4.65 in 1990, and later indexed the minimum wage to 50 percent of the average hourly wage. Proponents pointed out that the minimum wage had lost one-quarter of its purchasing power since 1981 and linked its erosion to the growing number of working-poor families.[45]

Not surprisingly, this proposal generated strong opposition from Republicans and trade associations, particularly those representing low-wage industries (e.g., the National Federation of Independent Business, the American Hotel and Motel Association, and the American Farm Bureau Federation). They recited the usual arguments against the minimum wage, contending that any increase would fuel inflation, increase unemployment, decrease international competitiveness, and benefit many workers such as middle-class teenagers who were not economically disadvantaged. Opponents did not offer any alternative; the choice was simply whether or not to increase the minimum wage.

One Republican, Rep. Thomas Petri of Minnesota, suggested substituting an increase in the EITC for an increase in the minimum wage. Petri, a member of the moderate Ripon Society, had a reputation as a maverick and innovator.[46] He was the ranking minority member of the House Education and Labor Committee's Labor Standards Subcommittee, the first hurdle for all minimum wage legislation. No fan of the minimum wage, Petri nevertheless recognized that the subcommittee was stacked with Democrats sympathetic to organized labor. He accepted the inevitability of an increase and attempted to minimize its size.

He tried unsuccessfully in the first part of 1988 to amend the Act so that it would include a small increase in the minimum wage, a large increase in the EITC, and an adjustment in the EITC for family size.

Unlike some of his Republican colleagues, Petri believed that government should do more to help the working poor. Increasing the minimum wage was, in his view, an inefficient and ultimately counterproductive solution. Petri and other Republicans persuaded the party to endorse the EITC in its 1988 platform: "As an alternative to inflationary—and job-destroying—increases in the minimum wage, we will work to boost the incomes of the working poor through the earned-income tax credit."[47] Simultaneously, key elements of the print media began editorializing against raising the minimum wage and in favor of enlarging the EITC.[48]

This policy package appealed as well to the Democratic Leadership Council (DLC), a newly formed coalition of moderate and conservative Democrats. DLC members believed that the Democratic Party had become too closely associated with special interests like organized labor and welfare recipients. The party's policies, in their view, had yet to catch up with the rightward shift of the electorate or with the realities of international economic competition. Mondale's drubbing in 1984 was clear proof in their minds that the party had to change. They therefore created an organization outside the Democratic National Committee in order to appeal to "mainstream" voters who were more concerned about economic growth than redistribution.[49]

An increase in the minimum wage was precisely the type of issue that DLC members wanted to avoid. It further tied the Democratic Party to organized labor, fueled the party's image as antibusiness and antigrowth, was economically inefficient, and still left many of the working poor in poverty. For DLC Democrats, the EITC was "a sparkling opportunity to show that their party [was] no longer in thrall to old ideas and the labor Left."[50] They joined Republicans in opposing the bill and favoring instead an increase to the EITC.[51] Supporters of the bill replied that the choice was a false one, that both a higher minimum wage and a larger EITC were needed.[52] They failed, at least initially. Together, DLC Democrats and Republicans prevented the minimum wage bill from coming to a vote on the floor of either chamber by the end of the 1988 session.

Ultimately Congress did enact new minimum wage legislation, though the increases were smaller than originally proposed and were coupled with a new training wage. In the process, both sides agreed to exclude any extraneous matter, including the EITC, from the final bill.[53] This proved to be a temporary setback. Over the long run what mattered was the attraction of new advocates. The minimum wage debates mobilized conservative support for the EITC much as debates over tax fairness prompted liberal antipoverty groups to support the program a few years earlier. The program gained support among congressional Republicans, administration officials (e.g., Council of Economic Advisers chairman Michael Boskin and Labor Secretary Elizabeth Dole), and the U.S. Chamber of Commerce as an alternative to a higher minimum wage. It generated widespread media attention for the first time in its history. Proposals to expand the EITC came from outside the revenue committees. And the EITC became a component of intraparty as well as interparty struggles. These trends continued as policy makers began to link the EITC to family policy in general and child care in particular.

FAMILY POLICY

Much as they did with tax fairness and welfare reform, Democrats and Republicans competed over who would be the "pro-family" party in the 1980s.[54] Republicans, according to Reagan, stood for "traditional" family values, a code word for opposition to abortion, busing, and homosexuality and support for school prayer. This position was calculated to appeal both to conservative Republicans and to working-class Democrats. Although Republicans controlled the legislative agenda during Reagan's first term, they deliberately tabled social issues in order to focus on economic legislation. Their failure to devise a family policy provided Democrats with an opening.

Democrats finally put forward a coherent package of family policies in 1986.[55] *New Choices in a Changing America*, prepared by the Democratic Policy Commission, charted a new, more centrist course for the party. The Commission was the Democratic National Committee's attempt to prevent a split between the party's liberal wing and the newly formed Democratic Leadership Council. Besides urging a harsher line toward the Soviet Union and declining to criticize the Reagan administration's foreign policy in Nicaragua, the report called for a "commitment to stronger families." "Democrats favor pro-family policies that will raise family incomes, help keep families together and provide some assistance to parents in their day-to-day lives."[56] The report made no mention of historically divisive issues like abortion and homosexuality. Instead, it called for larger personal exemptions in the tax code, larger and more targeted child care tax credits, parental leave, flex-time and job-sharing, more job training, portable corporate pensions, and higher-quality education.[57] It placed as much emphasis on changing business practices as it did on government programs, as much on tax-based solutions as on additional spending. Not surprisingly, many liberal Democrats distanced themselves from the report's recommendations.

As several Democratic leaders and strategists pointed out, family issues were good politics and good policy.[58] Opinion polls repeatedly demonstrated the salience of issues like child care and parental leave, as well as widespread support for greater government involvement. In a 1988 Gallup poll, 39 percent of respondents said that child care should be a top priority of the next administration, and another 42 percent identified child care as a medium priority.[59] The media were full of stories about women moving into the labor force, "latchkey" kids, and the difficulties of finding good, affordable child care. The rate of child poverty topped 20 percent. One of the most cited indicators of demographic change was the percentage of employed mothers with children younger than one year old. This figure topped 50 percent in 1987 for the first time in U.S. history. Few Republicans could argue that the government was incapable of addressing family issues. Numerous studies had demonstrated the cost-effectiveness of government health, education, and nutrition programs aimed at poor children.

Democrats pushed family policy along two closely related tracks. Presidential candidate Michael Dukakis and the Democratic Party leadership tried to frame the 1988 election as one of cold, selfish Republicans versus compassionate, family-oriented Democrats. Early on, Dukakis backed up his family rhetoric with specific proposals regarding child care and universal health insurance. The level of detail was unusual in a campaign that otherwise emphasized Dukakis's general competence. Republican strategists tried to round out their image as the party of economic growth and military strength by demonstrating that they understood the plight of working families. Vice President George Bush, the Republican candidate, successfully blunted Dukakis's offensive by pledging more tax credits for families with children and some form of parental leave.

Simultaneously, congressional Democrats introduced several pieces of family legislation, the most important of which was the Act for Better Child Care (ABC). The ABC bill proposed spending an additional $2.5 billion on child care programs and increasing government regulation of child care providers. With the notable exception of Sen. Orrin Hatch (R-Utah), the ABC bill was clearly associated with liberal Democrats and liberal interest groups. The bill's Democratic supporters expected that it would highlight an important policy difference between the two parties in an election year. They did not bank on highlighting fissures within their own party as well. DLC Democrats worried about the program's cost and about favoring two-income families who purchased child care over more "traditional" families in which one parent stayed home. ABC also struck them as more of the same old Democratic politics—throwing money at social problems.[60] Republicans generally shared these concerns and objected as well to what they saw as excessive regulation of child care providers.

These two tracks converged as soon as Bush endorsed family policies in his campaign speeches. His pledge put congressional Republicans opposed to ABC in an awkward position. Senate Democrats tried to add to Republicans' discomfort by bundling the ABC bill with a child pornography bill and a parental leave bill. A "no" vote would surely brand the Republicans as antifamily. The strategy backfired. Business interests opposed to mandatory parental leave now lobbied against the ABC bill. Their opposition helped kill the bill on the Senate floor, though it would not have been decisive without preexisting opposition from many Republicans and DLC Democrats.

ABC supporters could take some comfort in their loss. They now had Bush on record in favor of doing more for working families, and they had made child care a top priority of the 101st Congress. Soon after Congress reconvened, they introduced a modified version of the ABC bill in the Senate. In addition, a number of legislators in both chambers submitted alternative child care bills. Almost all these bills relied on the tax code, either by expanding the existing EITC and dependent care tax credits or by creating a new tax credit for parents of young children. Significantly, some of these measures were proposed by legislators who were not members of either Ways and Means or Finance. President Bush countered with a refundable tax credit for families with children younger than four years old. Because Bush did not want to dictate what child care arrangements parents chose, parents were eligible whether or not they paid others to care for their children. In essence, Bush's proposal was a modified EITC for families with young children. Treasury officials consciously modeled the administration's proposal after the EITC in order to simplify its structure and implementation.

Although legislators continued to debate the creation of quality standards and church-state boundaries, some of the most heated debates concerned the proper mix of tax credits and direct spending for child care. The problem started when ABC supporters on the Senate Labor and Human Resources Committee agreed to combine their bill with a bipartisan tax credit measure sponsored by Senators Moynihan (D-N.Y.) and Packwood (R-Oreg.) of the Finance Committee. This pairing was designed to mollify Republicans and DLC Democrats who felt that the ABC approach entailed too much regulation and too much bureaucracy.

This combination triggered bitter ideological and jurisdictional fights in the House. Democratic members of the Education and Labor Committee, backed by liberal interest groups, insisted that direct spending programs and regulation were the best approach. Tax credits, in their view, did little to address the core problems of affordability, availability, and quality of child care. Tax credits were regressive; they would make child care more affordable for the nonpoor but not the poor. Furthermore, increasing consumers' ability to purchase child care was no guarantee that quality child care centers would locate where they were needed; low-income communities would continue to be underserved. Democrats on the Ways and Means Committee, however, favored almost exclusive reliance on tax credits. Their alternative bill was sponsored by Thomas Downey (D-N.Y.), chairman of the Human Resources Subcommittee and a long-time advocate of children's causes. His bill, the Employment Incentives Act, was a five-year, $16 billion package of tax credits and direct spending. For every dollar in additional funding for Title XX day care programs, it spent nine dollars in tax credits, principally by expanding the EITC and adjusting it for family size.[61] Downey won a key endorsement from another liberal Democrat, Rep. George Miller, a senior member of the Education and Labor Committee and chairman of the Select Committee on Children, Youth, and Families. The EITC component of Downey's proposal gained additional support from the Center on Budget and Policy Priorities whose director, Robert Greenstein, claimed that it would do more to fight poverty than the much heralded Family Support Act of 1988.[62]

The defection of well-respected liberals like Downey and Miller made it all but impossible for ABC's supporters to form a majority in the House. The prevalence of ABC supporters on the Education and Labor Committee, and the intensity of their support, made passage of Downey's alternative equally improbable. Though many House Republicans preferred tax credits to ABC—because tax credits facilitated parental choice of child care arrangements—and some saw the EITC as a way of attracting traditionally Democratic voters, enough Republicans were troubled by the size of the Ways and Means bill to withhold their support. As a result, both committees submitted their bills to the conference committee in charge of the budget reconciliation bill. Although this strategy was supposed to enhance any bill's chances of passage, both measures were stripped from the final package.[63]

During the child care debates of 1989, proponents of ABC gradually resigned themselves to some combination of tax credits and direct spending. They simply did not have the votes, and the EITC continued to receive favorable press. Their acceptance of tax credits paved the way for a compromise in 1990. The House and Senate agreed on a package in October that included $15 billion for a series of tax credits aimed at low-income working families with children and $4 billion for direct child care subsidies. The major sticking point this time was the particular mix of tax credits. Sen. Lloyd Bentsen (D-Tex.), chairman of the Finance Committee, insisted on adding a new tax credit for health insurance purchased for the children of working-poor families. He threatened to bottle up the legislation in committee without these concessions, and won.[64] That tax credit, plus a new tax credit for families with children younger than one year old (deemed nonnegotiable by White House chief of staff John Sununu), came at the expense of the EITC, whose increases were scaled back.

Still, the changes were by no means trivial. The compromise expanded eligibility for the EITC and for the first time adjusted it for family size. It increased the maximum possible credit from $953 in 1990 to $1,702 in 1994. Declared a Ways and Means staff member, "The working poor were made better off by this agreement than by any other piece of legislation passed in the 1980's."[65] These changes were incorporated in the 1990 budget accord. Once again, the EITC served more than one policy objective. Besides addressing child care, policy makers used increases in the EITC to improve the progressivity of a larger tax bill, as they did in 1986.

TAX EQUITY (PART 2)

The most recent period of expansion began during the 1992 presidential campaign.[66] As the Democratic nominee, Bill Clinton struck a nerve during the campaign by highlighting the economic insecurity of ordinary citizens. Much of the labor force had seen the value of their wages erode. Clinton promised voters that he would seek changes in policy that would make their lives more secure. In particular, he declared that no one who worked full-time and had children should be in poverty. He also noted that millions of people lacked health insurance and millions more with insurance feared losing it should they become unemployed. Clinton made specific reference to health reform, deficit reduction, investment in human and physical infrastructure, and the EITC as important steps in improving the economic security of American workers.

Turning those promises into policies proved quite difficult. Clinton won less than half the popular vote, and Democrats enjoyed smaller majorities in the House and Senate than they had under President Carter in the late 1970s (the last time Democrats enjoyed unified control of the government). Congressional Republicans united as the opposition party, vowing to oppose all legislation on which they had any substantial disagreement. Democrats would have to govern alone. Clinton's first economic initiatives exposed some of the major fault lines within the party. His closest aides and key members of the House tended to come from the party's liberal wing; indeed, the 1992 congressional elections produced a record number of women and racial minorities in Congress, almost all of whom were liberal Democrats. They placed less emphasis on deficit reduction than new spending initiatives, and wanted to rely more heavily on tax increases on the rich and corporations to achieve any deficit reduction. In contrast, Clinton appointed a number of fiscally conservative Democrats to key administration posts (for example, Treasury Secretary Lloyd Bentsen and OMB Director Leon Panetta) and had to deal with a number of equally conservative Democrats in the Senate. These officials viewed deficit reduction as the government's top priority and favored greater reliance on spending cuts, particularly of major social programs, to achieve that goal. They viewed additional spending with considerable skepticism.

Several of Clinton's advisers pushed for a major expansion of the Earned Income Tax Credit as part of the administration's first budget, arguing that the president had won in part because of his oft-stated pledge to "make work pay." Clinton believed that "the tax credit had been one of his best applause lines during the campaign. 'I've never seen a program for working poor people be so enthusiastically supported by the middle class and in the suburbs.'"[67] Bentsen did not contradict the president but did argue in favor a much smaller expansion that would add less to the deficit. In the end, proponents for expansion succeeded in including a five-year, $28 billion increase in the EITC in the president's budget proposal. This provision was notable not only because it was one of the very few spending increases in a package filled with hundreds of billions of dollars in spending cuts and tax increases, but also because it extended the credit to working-poor families without dependent children for the first time. Though small, this change in eligibility had the potential to increase substantially the number of people/potential voters receiving the EITC.

Legislators did not spend much time debating the EITC. The relative calm on this front was more an indication of general support for expansion than ignorance or indifference toward the program. More contentious were the administration's mix of spending cuts versus tax increases and a proposed BTU tax on all forms of energy. Democratic leaders in the House tried to dampen business opposition to the package by reducing the increases in corporate taxes, but otherwise passed a bill close to Clinton's initial package. The EITC provisions were almost identical. The more serious difficulties came in the Senate. Democrats there were more intent on reducing spending and limiting tax increases than their colleagues in the House, and were especially hostile to the energy tax. Conservative Democrats from energy-producing states (such as Boren of Oklahoma and Johnston of Louisiana) joined Senate Republicans in insisting that the energy tax, expected to generate more than $70 billion in new revenues, be dropped altogether and replaced with more spending cuts. They also limited the EITC to taxpayers with dependent children and scaled back the total increase to $18 billion. The defection of these Democrats, coupled with Republicans' greater power in the Senate, forced Clinton to capitulate on several key points. A smaller gasoline tax increase replaced the BTU tax, Medicare cuts were increased, and proposed increases in Food Stamps and the EITC were scaled back.

Nevertheless, the final bill (the Omnibus Budget and Reconciliation Act of 1993) represented a major expansion of the Earned Income Tax Credit. While reducing the projected deficit by almost $500 billion over five years, primarily through Medicare cuts and tax increases on the rich, it added $20.8 billion to the EITC. These changes included extending eligibility to higher income levels than before and increasing the dollar value of the tax credit across all incomes. The administration and House also prevailed in extending the credit to those without dependent children.[68] Politically, expanding the EITC became crucial once officials agreed to replace the BTU tax with a more regressive gasoline tax, for the EITC ensured that no one earning less than $30,000 would pay more in taxes. As the final votes drew near, Clinton officials distributed a profile of winners and losers to undecided members of Congress whose districts included large numbers of poor and near-poor people, and to the local media in those districts. The impact of the EITC increase was enormous in these districts, creating far more winners than losers. Increasing the EITC was not enough to win passage: without any Republican votes, Clinton had to cut several last-minute deals with individual Democrats to secure a razor-thin victory. It did, however, enable Democrats to counter charges that they had passed the largest tax increase in history by pointing out that millions of ordinary Americans would not have to pay higher taxes.

This final episode in the development of the Earned Income Tax Credit repeats some familiar themes: as in 1986, expansion of the EITC served to promote greater equity in the distribution of taxes; divisions between the two major parties and within the Democratic Party over tax policy helped shape the final outcome. What set 1993 apart, at least in retrospect, were growing concerns that deficit reduction should take priority over every other domestic program, even the EITC. After taking control of Congress in 1994, some Republicans proposed rolling back several of the changes enacted in 1993 as part of larger plans to balance the budget and eliminate the deficit. Democrats countered that if the Republicans were serious about reforming welfare and promoting work, they would leave the EITC alone. They also pointed out that Republicans were trying to cut the EITC at the same time as proposing tax cuts for the affluent and corporations, making the tax code less equitable than before. In short, Democrats tried to capitalize on the program's ambiguity to prevent retrenchment. The initially sharp criticism of plans to cut the program, in the national media and from liberals as well as some conservatives, suggests that any cuts in the near future will be small.[69]

DISCUSSION

The politics of the Earned Income Tax Credit have changed dramatically since 1975. The EITC is no longer an anonymous tax expenditure. Many more public officials and interest groups are aware of the program and involved in its development. The program's fate no longer rests in the hands of the two revenue committee chairmen. The revenue committees are still central, but proposals for expansion and modification come from a variety of sources in Washington. The EITC's merits are trumpeted in the op-ed pages of major newspapers, not buried in committee reports. Whereas societal actors were once absent, the Center on Budget and Policy Priorities is now an important and consistent advocate. Organized labor, business, antipoverty groups, and children's advocates have likewise promoted the EITC's expansion. These changes were neither a necessary nor an immediate result of enactment. The EITC might have remained obscure but for the 1980 election. Reagan won, and the Earned Income Tax Credit has never been the same.

This transformation yields two hopeful signs for U.S. politics. The Earned Income Tax Credit indicates that it is possible to build a fairly broad coalition on behalf of means-tested programs. Such programs are not destined to occupy some lower tier of social provision; their scope can expand, benefits can increase, and recipients can avoid social stigma. To be sure, programs like Social Security indicate that one can "target within universalism," offering benefits to all and still lifting many needy citizens out of poverty. This may well be the best strategy for helping low-income citizens, but it is not the only politically feasible option. One can also try to replicate the success of the EITC.[70]

By the same token, this case indicates the potential for decisive action during periods of divided government, often depicted as a source of gridlock.[71] Expansion in 1986 and 1990, in conjunction with important tax reform and child care legislation, occurred despite Republican control of the White House and Democratic control of the House of Representatives. Tax reform, welfare reform, the minimum wage, and family policy moved to the top of the policy agenda as Republicans tried to complete a political realignment and Democrats tried to prevent them from succeeding. Competition occurred between the two major parties and between the two major factions of the Democratic Party. Neither party would allow the other to claim sole ownership of the one program clearly aimed at the working poor—the Earned Income Tax Credit.

It would be nice to end on such a positive note. Unfortunately, this episode offers a few sobering insights into U.S. politics as well. For one, the EITC fails to reach the most disadvantaged segments of the population, those who have little or no earned income. It may be touted as antipoverty policy, but it cannot touch the truly disadvantaged. Nor does it offer much help to poor people without dependent children. Even many of those who qualify for the EITC do not receive large enough benefits to move above the poverty line. The other point to note is the importance of historical contingency. A careful reconstruction of the EITC's development indicates that the program was not designed from the beginning to grow in a linear or predictable fashion. Its first ten years suggest that it was not designed to grow at all. The program's remarkable expansion began only after a certain chain of events, far removed from the program's narrow domain, altered the political landscape. While a certain measure of unpredictability makes the EITC interesting to study, it also makes the program vulnerable to comparable shocks in the future. The historic 1994 congressional elections may well be one such shock, enabling Republicans to cut popular programs like the EITC and Medicare. Whatever the outcome, the meteoric rise of the Earned Income Tax Credit will remain one of the more interesting chapters in the history of U.S. social policy.

CHAPTER 8

Targeted Jobs Tax Credit

FOR A NATION supposedly devoted to the values of work and self-sufficiency, the United States has done remarkably little with employment and training programs. The national government spends less on job training than on AFDC, which benefits many people who do not work for wages and is a constant target for cutbacks. As we saw in Table 7.1, while most parts of the visible welfare state grew or held steady between 1980 and 1992, traditional job-training programs suffered substantial cuts. One common explanation for this anomaly hinges on the peculiar structure of U.S. institutions.[1] The effects of fragmented political authority and weak bureaucracies are particularly acute: the executive is divided, as the President's Council of Economic Advisers pushes for macroeconomic policies (e.g., tax cuts and deficit spending) while the Labor Department advocates more targeted employment and training programs; responsibility for a myriad of employment and training programs is divided among a variety of congressional committees and executive agencies; state employment service agencies play a major role in administering these programs; and the U.S. Labor Department has historically wielded little influence in policy debates. A second explanation points to conservative backlashes within the Democratic Party as first Roosevelt and then Johnson tried to expand employment and training programs.[2]

On the surface, the Targeted Jobs Tax Credit (TJTC) seems better suited to thrive than its direct spending counterparts. Responsibility for tax policy is concentrated in the two revenue committees and the Treasury Department and not shared with state-level authorities. Whereas direct expenditures for employment and training are appropriations and not budgetary entitlements, thus making them vulnerable to annual cuts, tax expenditures are usually permanent features of the tax code. As a general rule, conservatives appear to favor tax expenditures over direct expenditures because the former offer incentives and work around existing social welfare bureaucracies. Because the TJTC allowed businesses to deduct a certain fraction of their workers' wages, advocates could portray the program either as a benefit for disadvantaged workers or as a much-needed subsidy to small business, depending on the audience. The program attracted supporters from the liberal Congressional Black Caucus and congressional Republicans, along with interest groups representing veterans, the disabled, and employers.

Despite these advantages, the TJTC has led a fairly marginal existence. Its total cost has fluctuated but remained small, never exceeding $350 million. Though some categories of eligible workers have been added and some of the original categories expanded, other categories have been narrowed or eliminated. Congress deliberately lowered the value of the tax credit to employers in 1986 and again in 1988.[3] The Treasury Department and Labor Department have periodically called for major cuts or outright elimination. The TJTC has remained a temporary tax expenditure, requiring periodic reauthorization, and on a couple of occasions legislators allowed the program to expire. The last such termination occurred at the end of 1994, and as of early 1996 the program no longer exists (though there are efforts in Congress to revive it in modified form). In short, the TJTC developed more like its direct spending counterparts than the other tax expenditures in this study.

The program's political problems, I argue, were rooted in its highly targeted design, which decreased the political clout of beneficiaries and increased the program's complexity. Relative to the EITC, the Targeted Jobs Tax Credit affected a far smaller pool of potential voters, and thus failed to attract much attention from party leaders. Nor could advocates portray the TJTC as a remedy to as many problems as the EITC because the former rewarded a more specific behavior (hiring disadvantaged workers) than did the latter (working for wages). In addition, the creation of very specific categories of disadvantaged workers required the expertise of someone other than the Treasury Department to determine eligibility, and this task fell to an unwieldy network of state and national employment agencies, nonprofit organizations, and private firms. The commitment of the various public agencies was questionable, as some perceived the TJTC as taking away funds from their traditional employment and training programs. The combination of highly specific and often changing definitions of eligible workers drove some employers away from the program. These and related problems came to light in several formal evaluations of the Targeted Jobs Tax Credit, as well as periodic reauthorization hearings in Congress. The more policy makers learned about the TJTC, the more they worried that it basically provided windfall benefits to employers. Considering the growing interest in using tax expenditures to solve social problems, particularly for disadvantaged groups of citizens, this case offers some sobering lessons.

PROPONENTS AND OPPONENTS

Because traditional employment and training programs are often neglected in analyses of U.S. social policy and differ from other means-tested programs in important ways, it may be helpful to sketch out their development at the start of this chapter. From the Manpower Demonstration Training Act and Economic Opportunity Act of the early 1960s to the Job Training Partnership Act (JTPA) of the 1980s, direct expenditure programs have been supported and administered by a (loose) coalition of beneficiaries, service providers, national and state departments of labor, and congressional labor committees.[4] One constant feature of this coalition has been bipartisan support in Congress. Democratic and Republican members of the labor committees, who have polarized around most issues for decades (e.g., the minimum wage), have consistently agreed on the need for some publicly financed job training. Outside these committees, congressional interest in job training has been fairly minimal; other legislators have shown more interest in counter-cyclical public service employment programs. The U.S. Department of Labor and state employment services have been staunch allies of job-training programs, as were the Department of Health, Education, and Welfare and the Office of Equal Opportunity when they administered similar programs in the 1960s. State and local governments became important advocates in the 1970s, as did business interests in the 1980s. Both these actors were responsible for providing employment and training to various groups of disadvantaged workers. The people served by these programs have not been as well represented. The unemployed have seldom organized around more or better job training. Instead, groups like the NAACP, NOW, and the National Urban League have lobbied occasionally on their behalf.

The Targeted Jobs Tax Credit developed a similar coalition of support. As we saw in chapter 4, there is little evidence that anyone representing any of the categories of workers covered by the original Targeted Jobs Tax Credit influenced its enactment. Once it passed, the TJTC triggered a mobilization of these and other interests. Support for the program depended in part on eligibility criteria, which changed frequently. The original legislation included SSI and General Assistance recipients, cooperative education students, and disabled citizens undergoing vocational rehabilitation, as well as economically disadvantaged youth, ex-convicts, and Vietnam veterans younger than thirty-five. The Economic Recovery Tax Act of 1981 added two more target groups: AFDC recipients (formerly covered by the WIN tax credit) and involuntarily terminated CETA and PSE workers.[5] Other legislation in 1981 had slashed funding for CETA and PSE, so extending the credit was a way of minimizing any subsequent rise in unemployment. The Act stipulated further that only economically disadvantaged cooperative education students would be eligible and removed the age limit from Vietnam veterans. The Tax Equity and Fiscal Responsibility Act of 1982 added another target group, economically disadvantaged summer youth (ages sixteen to seventeen), broadened the category of General Assistance recipients, and declared ineligible any involuntarily terminated CETA or PSE workers hired after 1982. As part of a general drive to raise revenue, the Technical and Miscellaneous Revenue Act of 1988 limited the eligibility of economically disadvantaged youth to those aged eighteen to twenty-two, removing twenty-three and twenty-four year olds from the program.[6] With such narrow categories of eligibility, the TJTC was therefore of no benefit to many disadvantaged workers who were eligible for the Earned Income Tax Credit.

Groups claiming to represent the interests of these workers were always present at reauthorization hearings for the TJTC. A quick glance at the transcripts of these hearings reveals a spectrum of interest groups as varied as the TJTC's clientele: the National Urban League, NAACP, National Association for the Deaf, American Council for the Blind, Vietnam Veterans of America, American Legion, National Rehabilitation Association, Chicago Jobs Council, and the Citizens United for Rehabilitation of Errants (CURE), among others. Their appeals before Congress displayed a remarkable uniformity. Typically these groups began by describing the special employment problems facing their constituencies. Some detailed the consequences of budget cuts under Reagan and the resulting importance of the TJTC. Most provided a detailed profile of one or two individuals who had been helped by the tax credit. As criticism of the program became more common, some offered their own cost-benefit studies showing how well the program had worked.[7]

Another source of interest group support were employers in low-wage, low-skill industries where labor costs were a significant fraction of total costs. These firms were more likely to hire disadvantaged workers and to be influenced by a reduction in labor costs. Restaurant chains, hotel chains, and retailers were especially prominent. The Foodservice and Lodging Institute, National Restaurant Association, National Council of Chain Restaurants, American Hotel and Motel Association, and the Association of General Merchandise Chains lobbied on behalf of the TJTC in the 1980s and early 1990s, as did individual corporations such as Marriott, Pepsico (owners of Pizza Hut and Taco Bell), Dayton Hudson, K-Mart, and Kentucky Fried Chicken. All these trade associations and companies had a predictable financial interest in maintaining and expanding the TJTC. Their testimony followed much the same pattern as that of nonprofit advocacy groups.[8]

A second source of business support was unexpected. One unintended consequence of the TJTC was the emergence of a small industry of consultants who helped employers secure the tax credit. While some existing pension and benefits consulting firms added on a TJTC practice, other firms originated directly as a result of the TJTC. In exchange for determining which employees were eligible for the credit and completing the necessary paperwork, these consultants received a fixed percentage of the tax credit (approximately 25 percent)—an arrangement that prompted the business press to label these consultants, "the bounty hunters."[9] This arrangement became a lightning rod for critics of the TJTC, who viewed consultants as evidence that the program was too complex and economically inefficient. It even became a sore point among TJTC advocates. The National Association of Targeted Jobs Consultants (NATJC) was forced to divide its efforts between lobbying for the TJTC and defending its members against charges of profiteering.

Many organizations that did not lobby directly for the TJTC did so indirectly through the Targeted Jobs Tax Credit Coalition, which also formed after the program was created. The TJTC Coalition grew from approximately twelve organizations in 1980 to more than five hundred by the end of the decade. Although consulting firms dominated the Coalition in the early 1980s, they later split off to form the NATJC. The Coalition's membership reflected the remarkable range of interests affected by the credit. It is hard to imagine any other cause uniting large corporations (e.g., Wal-Mart, Hickory Farms, and Chi-Chi's), numerous small businesses (Suddath Van Lines and Cleany-Boppers), community social service agencies (Oregon Human Development Corporation and Shenandoah Valley Independent Living Center), and state departments of rehabilitation. The Coalition served both as a lobby and as a clearinghouse for information about the TJTC. Besides testifying before Congress, many of these interest groups maintained close contact with members of the revenue committees. They continually reminded these legislators about the TJTC's benefits and suggested ways of improving the program.[10]

Interest group opponents to the TJTC were few in number and ineffectual. It is fitting that a program which united such an odd combination of interest groups should be opposed by two groups that rarely saw eye-to-eye on any issue, organized labor and small business. Their criticisms were familiar ones. The TJTC, according to an AFL-CIO official, produced windfall benefits to firms, rewarded only growing firms and industries, and diverted funds from direct spending programs. Through the TJTC, "wages are undercut and employers have an incentive to adopt a revolving-door pattern of laying off subsidized workers as soon as the subsidy ends and displacing current workers for those that are subsidized."[11] The National Federation of Independent Business declared that the TJTC was "terribly cumbersome" for small businesses. Nor were many small firms interested in hiring the types of disadvantaged workers targeted by the program. If Congress really wanted to spur employment in small businesses, the NFIB argued, it should reduce payroll taxes and the minimum wage, or at least create a more general employment tax credit like the expired New Jobs Tax Credit (which the NFIB had supported in 1977).[12] These criticisms were ignored, and the AFL-CIO and NFIB eventually stopped appearing before Congress to oppose the program.

The core of governmental support for the TJTC was located in the congressional revenue committees. Democratic and Republican members of these committees have regularly supported extending and expanding the TJTC, albeit for different reasons. For moderate Republicans like Sen. John Heinz (R-Pa.), a long-time TJTC supporter, the program represented "'a way out of poverty and joblessness for the physically and economically disadvantaged' without causing much of a drain on the federal Treasury."[13] Sen. Pete Domenici (R-N.M.), also a consistent supporter, referred to the TJTC as a rare "win, win program" that worked far better than traditional employment and training programs. "The TJTC Program, in the normal course of business, not by means of some isolated program which takes these disadvantaged people and makes second-class citizens out of them, or makes them public servants, gets them into the mainstream of employment. And this one works."[14] Since the program expired in 1994, Reps. Bill Archer (R-Tex.), the new Ways and Means chairman, and Amo Houghton (R-N.Y.) have introduced legislation to revive the program.[15]

Most Democrats initially intended the TJTC to be a small part of the nation's overall labor market policy, subordinate to CETA, public service employment, and other job-creation programs. As the Reagan administration eliminated public service employment and slashed direct spending on job training, the TJTC became more important by default. No one was more frustrated with this shift than Rep. Charles Rangel (D-N.Y.), a member of the House Ways and Means Committee. Rangel was a cosponsor of the original TJTC and ultimately became its most important advocate in Congress. Nevertheless, he did not exactly offer a ringing endorsement of the program in the mid-1980s: "I only support the [TJTC] concept because there's not much we have to work with under this administration. There is no meaningful job creation program in this administration, so we have to manipulate the tax code to get some of the benefits to the people who have not enjoyed the benefits of the Reagan administration's economic recovery." His sentiments were echoed by Rep. Fortney "Pete" Stark (D-Calif.), then chairman of the Ways and Means Subcommittee on Select Revenue Measures and another advocate of government jobs programs. Said Stark of the TJTC: "It's about the only game in town. But it's a terribly inefficient way to take care of the social and economic needs of the disadvantaged."[16]

Gradually, as the odds of any new government jobs program dropped to zero, Democrats offered more unqualified support for the TJTC. Legislative aides to Reps. Rangel and Stark, for instance, defended the program on its own merits during interviews conducted in 1990. They argued that the TJTC helped meet the employment needs of disadvantaged citizens and that claims of its inefficiency were either outdated or exaggerated. One aide claimed further that the TJTC was not just a second-best solution but an important complement to JTPA and other employment and training programs. In a recent hearing to reauthorize the TJTC, Rangel declared:

> I firmly believe this nation has the responsibility of providing opportunity and employment for all who want to work. In light of the fact that this important credit is scheduled to expire at the end of 1989, it is appropriate that we review its effectiveness in promoting employment among those individuals who have traditionally found it difficult to find jobs. . . . This legislation has benefitted any number of people, and we've proven that it can work.[17]

Their conversion was important because Stark and then Rangel chaired the Ways and Means Subcommittee with jurisdiction over the TJTC program. Rangel was sharply critical of the Clinton administration's willingness to end the program and worked closely with Houghton, the Republican from upstate New York, to revive the TJTC after 1994.[18]

Among government agencies, the chief advocates of the TJTC have been state vocational rehabilitation agencies and especially state employment security agencies (SESAs). The latter administer unemployment insurance, the employment service, and other employment-related programs in conjunction with the U.S. Department of Labor. SESAs were designated the local lead agency for administering the TJTC in 1981. Their tasks include issuing TJTC vouchers, certifying eligible employees, and promoting the TJTC program among local employers. Over the course of the decade, SESA officials from the District of Columbia, Georgia, Iowa, Maryland, Michigan, New York, and South Carolina, as well as the Interstate Conference of Employment Security Agencies, voiced their support before Congress. Some states found that the tax credit interested employers in ways that direct spending programs did not. Others found that the TJTC was "an effective tool in alleviating structural unemployment."[19] State employment officials appealed to Congress to extend the credit and, just as important, increase appropriations for SESAs to administer the credit.

The chief opponent of the TJTC was also partly responsible for its administration—the U.S. Treasury Department. The original legislation designated the Treasury as the lead national agency for the TJTC program. The Treasury's tasks included issuing regulations governing eligibility and processing the tax returns of firms that claimed the credit. Throughout the 1980s, Treasury officials criticized the TJTC program and called for its termination.[20] They claimed that the program was inefficient and ineffective, and with good reason. Early studies indicated that the credit did not change employers' hiring patterns and rewarded many employers for doing what they would have done without the credit. Other evidence suggested that the TJTC displaced existing low-wage workers without creating jobs; it simply redistributed the unemployed without reducing their numbers.[21] Mounting budget deficits magnified these concerns. In explaining why the Treasury favored the JTPA and Job Corps and not the Targeted Jobs Tax Credit, one official stated:

> We believe these direct expenditure programs are superior vehicles for increasing employment of these [disadvantaged] groups. In contrast, we believe the TJTC has been far less effective in increasing targeted employment, and in this budget environment with the large budget deficit, hard choices have to be made, and only the most effective programs can be continued.[22]

Some evidence suggests that the Treasury tried as well to undermine the program covertly by shirking its administrative duties. For example, the IRS did not issue final regulations governing eligibility and procedures for claiming the credit until 1983, five years after enactment. When asked by Congress about the status of these regulations in 1981, the Assistant Secretary for Tax Policy first claimed that they were not required, then corrected himself. He reasoned that because employers had not complained about the lack of regulations, their absence was not a problem and the Treasury was not to blame for the TJTC's difficulties. He somehow neglected to mention that the lack of regulations may have deterred firms from investigating or obtaining the credit in the first place. The Treasury took at least three years to issue regulations governing the 1981 amendments to the TJTC.

Moreover, Treasury estimates of revenue losses appeared to be artificially high during the mid-1980s, possibly to discourage legislators from reauthorizing the TJTC. The Targeted Jobs Tax Credit Coalition pressured the Treasury in 1984 and 1985 to make public its methodology for estimating the costs of the TJTC. After several Freedom of Information requests, the Coalition succeeded in obtaining the details of the Treasury's models and eventually persuaded Treasury officials to scale back their estimates.[23] The Treasury still refused to offset its cost estimate with estimates of potential savings from unemployment insurance, AFDC, and other social programs that advocates claimed were the result of the TJTC.[24] Finally, supporters of the program have charged that the

Treasury has not adequately publicized the availability of TJTC, a charge Treasury officials have denied.[25]

At times the U.S. Labor Department also appears to have opposed the program. It officially opposed extension of the TJTC in 1981, its one and only appearance before Congress concerning this program in the 1980s (at every other hearing the Treasury Department spoke for the administration).[26] After a report by the Department's inspector general concluded that the program was primarily a windfall for large, low-wage employers, Labor Secretary Reich called for its elimination in 1994. The TJTC was a small but clear example of "corporate welfare"; if policy makers were hell-bent on reducing the deficit, they should be just as willing to target these subsidies as they were traditional social programs. Later Reich qualified his statements to suggest that serious reforms to the TJTC were needed.[27] Finally, there have been complaints of bureaucratic shirking. The Labor Department's Employment and Training Administration is responsible for coordinating the activities of state employment service agencies and keeping basic statistics on TJTC program performance. Early in the program, some state employment officials accused the Labor Department of being slow to publicize the availability of the tax credit and disseminate the necessary forms. Many businesses and client groups also felt that Labor could have done more to publicize the program, particularly among smaller firms.

There are several reasons why Labor may have been such an antagonist. Department officials may have resented being shut out of the initial design of the credit nor asked to testify before Congress in 1978. More important, they may have preferred direct spending programs over tax expenditures. Administering a tax credit limited the possibilities for bureaucratic discretion normally available in a program like CETA or JTPA. Second, Labor officials may not have wanted to surrender autonomy and turf. Administrative responsibilities for the TJTC program had to be shared with the Treasury, an agency with a much different organizational culture and outlook on job training than Labor. More traditional employment and training programs only required coordination with like-minded state employment agencies.[28] Third, Labor officials may have opposed the TJTC on grounds of inefficiency, especially after early program evaluations indicated employer windfall and low participation rates for eligible workers. Surprisingly, the lack of bureaucratic support did not prove the TJTC's undoing in its early years.

Just as damaging have been reports of windfall profits for employers and general ineffectiveness. Representatives of employer groups complained initially that state employment agencies responsible for certifying workers as eligible for the TJTC were unaware of the program and had no idea what to do with the relevant forms. Early evaluations of the

TJTC indicated that it was reaching only a tiny fraction of eligible workers, and thus had little impact on unemployment. Most of those workers had been certified as eligible for the TJTC retroactively, which meant that the tax credit could not have affected employers' hiring decisions. The main effect was reducing employers' tax burden and increasing their profitability. A Labor Department official testifying before Congress in 1981 cited such problems as reasons for terminating the program.[29]

Although Congress soon limited the ability of firms to claim the credit retroactively, problems remained. Because Congress failed to appropriate sufficient funds for state employment agencies to administer the program, some SESAs cut back or stopped vouchering TJTC eligibles.[30] Out of necessity, other government agencies began to shoulder the administrative load, including "Comprehensive Employment and Training Act (CETA) prime sponsors (which vouchered only the three economically disadvantaged groups), vocational rehabilitation agencies, Social Security offices, Veterans Administration offices, ex-offender agencies, and state and local welfare agencies."[31] These other agencies could voucher members of their client group only. A 1984 survey of twenty-eight communities in twelve states found that these same agencies accounted for 10 to 50 percent of all vouchers.[32] One might think that by spreading administrative responsibilities across so many agencies, the TJTC program would be guaranteed high participation rates. The more immediate result, particularly early in the program, was administrative confusion.[33]

One of the more damning pieces of evidence came from a controlled experiment in Dayton, Ohio. Researchers there discovered that a control group of job seekers with no wage subsidies was *more* successful in finding employment than a group with a tax credit voucher or a group with a cash rebate voucher. One possible explanation was that employers did not wish to bear the administrative costs of claiming the tax credit or cash rebate. The more disturbing possibility was that these vouchers stigmatized job seekers as "damaged goods," leading individuals to disguise their eligibility for the program and employers not to hire those who did reveal their eligibility.[34] Other studies suggested that employers in low-wage industries were unlikely to use the local employment service to find workers, and thus were unlikely to be aware of the TJTC. Their usual recruitment patterns were more informal, relying on word of mouth from current employees or signs posted in the window of their business. Without considerable outreach by local officials, the program would never have much impact.[35]

These problems surfaced each time the Targeted Jobs Tax Credit came up for reauthorization. In 1989, for example, a Treasury spokesman played up the program's history of windfall profits in calling for its termination. He also pointed to more recent studies that showed little long-term gains in employment and earnings for workers with the TJTC compared to similarly disadvantaged workers without it. The nation would be better served, he argued, by helping such individuals through direct spending programs such as the Job Corps or Job Training Partnership Act. [36] In the face of continual criticism, proponents started to conduct their own evaluations and present the results before Congress. Their main conclusion was that the TJTC saved the government money through reduced spending for AFDC, Medicaid, and Food Stamps.[37]

Based on an audit of the program in nine states, the inspector general of the Labor Department recently found that 92 percent of all TJTC-certified workers would have have been hired without the tax credit. The program was little more than a subsidy to selected companies and industries. He testified in September 1994 that "it was the first time his office found a program so ineffective it was beyond repair," and he, too, called on Congress to end the program. An administrator from the Texas Employment Commission declared at that same hearing that the program was "ripe for fraud" because of its complicated eligibility criteria and vouchering process.[38] Although conceding the need for reform, representatives from Pizza Hut, Marriott, Waffle House, Dayton Hudson, and other national chains nevertheless insisted that the program had changed their hiring practices and helped thousands of needy individuals. They received support, as mentioned above, from an odd coalition of liberal Democrats like Charles Rangel and conservative Republicans like Bill Archer. These legislators were unable to convince enough of their colleagues to extend the program, many of whom felt that deficit reduction and spending restraint were more important than a tax credit with such a checkered history. As of early 1996, Congress is considering whether to reinstate the TJTC in some form.[39]

DISCUSSION

Much of the development of the Targeted Jobs Tax Credit is familiar to students of job-training programs. Such programs have often been enacted from above by government officials and later developed interest group support from below; clients of means-tested programs are seldom represented directly and must rely on others to defend their interests; third-party service providers are an important source of support; changes in rules governing eligibility usually occur incrementally; liberal Democrats like Charles Rangel are important advocates in Congress; and funding trails other types of social programs. In these respects, the TJTC program was no different from CETA or JTPA. What set this tax credit apart were the repeated efforts of executive agencies (Treasury and Labor) to kill the program and the support of conservative Democrats and Republicans, particularly on the revenue committees.

This chapter should stand as a cautionary tale for those who advocate using tax expenditures to address the needs of disadvantaged citizens. This program is targeted far more precisely than the EITC, which means that the Treasury is no longer able to determine eligibility and administer the program on its own. Additional agencies must participate, and the program no longer resembles the "self-executing" ideal of tax expenditures. Agencies and employers must cope with complicated and often changing definitions of eligibility. Narrow targeting may well bring stigma, and third-party providers may be able to sustain a program well after studies have shown it to have structural flaws.

Ironically, as one of the smallest tax expenditures in the hidden welfare state, the Targeted Jobs Tax Credit has been one of the most thoroughly studied. Policy makers know far more about its performance than much larger programs promoting home ownership and employer fringe benefits. This case may prompt readers to wonder how well other tax expenditures would fare if subject to the same level of scrutiny.

PART FOUR

Conclusion

CHAPTER 9

Politics of the Hidden Welfare State

IN THE PROCESS of conducting research for this study, I came across evidence about other tax expenditures that gave me greater confidence in the patterns I observed in the four case studies. There was nothing terribly systematic about this search: finding information concerning the tax treatment of employer pensions might turn up something about employer health benefits; searching for "tax expenditures" in a computer database might yield references to any number of specific programs; and sometimes just staring at the library shelves near the book I wanted could produce interesting results. In retrospect, my somewhat haphazard search process mirrored the unpredictable twists and turns of tax expenditures; perhaps we do become what we study. Nevertheless, most of the additional evidence reinforces the key findings of this study, which were briefly summarized in the introductions to part 2 (Origins) and part 3 (Development) of the book. One purpose of this chapter is to extend those findings with evidence from additional cases and then to suggest explanations for some of the more striking patterns. The primary emphasis is on those patterns that contrast with traditional social programs. Toward the end of the chapter, I speculate about the implications of the hidden welfare state for democratic governance and the study of U.S. social policy.

One of the more obvious contrasts concerns the timing of new social programs. The home mortgage interest deduction was enacted in 1913, the tax expenditure for employer pensions between 1914 and 1926, the Earned Income Tax Credit in 1975, and the Targeted Jobs Tax Credit in 1978. None of these cases fits the prevailing "big bang" pattern of welfare state formation in the United States. Because dating origins is one of the easier tasks in researching the hidden welfare state, it is possible to develop a fairly complete chronology of all tax expenditures with social welfare objectives. Table 9.1 compares the evolution of the visible and hidden welfare states during the twentieth century based on the origins of key programs.

As the left side of this table indicates, the visible welfare state was not created entirely during the 1930s and 1960s; disability insurance (1956) and Section 8 housing vouchers (1974) are notable exceptions to the rule. What matters is that the origins of most direct spending programs coincide with one of the two big bangs, and they do. We would not then

TABLE 9.1
Origins of Major U.S. Social Programs

Year	Direct Expenditures	Year	Tax Expenditures
		1913	Interest on consumer debt (including home mortgage interest), property taxes on homes, interest on life insurance savings, casualty losses
		1914–26	Employer retirement pensions
		1917	Charitable contributions
		1918	Workers' compensation benefits
		1920	Group term life insurance
		1921	Capital gains, capital gains at death
1935	Old Age Insurance, Unemployment Insurance, Old Age Assistance, Aid to Dependent Children, Aid to the Blind	1935	Railroad retirement benefits
1937	Public housing	1938	Unemployment benefits[a]
		1941	Social Security benefits
		1942	Extraordinary medical expenses
		1951	Capital gains on home sales
		1954	Employer health insurance; child and dependent care expenses
1956	Disability Insurance		
1962	Manpower Development and Training Act	1962	Keogh retirement plans for the self-employed
1964	Economic Opportunity Act, Food Stamps, Title XX social services	1964	Capital gains for home sales for age 55+
1965	Medicare, Medicaid, Elementary and Secondary Education Act		

TABLE 9.1 (*cont.*)

Year	Direct Expenditures	Year	Tax Expenditures
		1970	Medicare benefits
		1971	WIN tax credit[b]
1974	Section 8 housing vouchers	1974	Individual Retirement Accounts
		1975	Earned Income Tax Credit
		1978	Targeted Jobs Tax Credit
		1981	Employer-provided child care
		1986	Low-income housing
		1990	Child health insurance tax credit;[a] Young Child Tax Credit[a]

Sources: U.S. Senate, Committee on the Budget, *Tax Expenditures: Relationships to Spending Programs and Background Material on Individual Provisions* (Washington, D.C.: Government Printing Office, 1992); Witte, *Politics and Development of the Federal Income Tax*, pp. 276–82.

Notes: Creation of Supplemental Security Income in 1972 is omitted from the visible welfare state because it largely consolidated existing programs for the aged and disabled. Job-training programs like CETA and JTPA are likewise excluded because they represented a continuation of programs started by the Manpower Demonstration and Training Act of 1962 and the Economic Opportunity Act of 1964.

[a] Later eliminated.
[b] Later combined with TJTC.

expect all major tax expenditures to be created during the 1930s and 1960s, only that most of them follow this pattern. Instead we see that tax expenditures have been created throughout the twentieth century. The United States has been as receptive to new tax expenditures as it has been hostile to new direct expenditures for social welfare.

Table 9.1 suggests three generalizations worth noting. First, whereas the visible welfare state was built in two short, intense bursts, the hidden welfare state was built steadily over nine decades. Consequently, *none* of the extraordinary developments cited in the social policy literature, ranging from economic crises and critical elections to protest movements, has been essential to the formation of the hidden welfare state. Second, we have even more reason to believe that national social programs appeared well before the Social Security Act of 1935. Besides home mortgage interest, important tax expenditures for property taxes and charitable contributions date from before 1920. Although all the tax expenditures created in the 1910s and 1920s may have started small (mostly because so few people paid income taxes), one can make the same observation about Social Security, which initially failed to pay *any* benefits and for years excluded large segments of the workforce. Finally, within the hidden welfare state, new inclusive programs preceded new targeted programs. The most important tax expenditures aimed at the poor—the EITC, TJTC, and low-income housing—have been created since 1970. The prevailing pattern for the visible welfare state, in contrast, has been for new cash transfers to precede in-kind benefits.

Consistent with the routine introduction of new tax expenditures, the scope of conflict has been narrow. This was certainly true of the four cases in this study. In addition, the tax expenditure for property taxes on owner-occupied homes (1913) appears to have been an uncontroversial legacy of the Civil War tax codes. Balch reports that "no explanation was included in either the reports or the debates on the original adoption" of the tax expenditure for ministers' housing costs in 1921.[1] The tax expenditure for employer health benefits generated none of the heat that proposals for national health insurance did immediately after World War II.[2] Favorable tax treatment of IRAs came about quietly while legislators were vigorously debating changes to the existing tax expenditure for employer pensions, culminating in the passage of ERISA in 1974 (chapter 6). The low-income housing tax credit was a minor footnote to the Tax Reform Act of 1986, a last-minute attempt to minimize the impact of various restrictions on real estate development on the supply of affordable housing (chapter 5). Although some tax expenditures (e.g., charitable contributions) appear to have been the product of conscious lobbying by prospective beneficiaries,[3] they were never contested to the extent of Social Security or Medicare. All these tax expenditures were insignificant parts of larger revenue bills.

Why have new tax expenditures been easier to enact than comparable direct expenditures? Here the tax policy literature provides important insights. Although these scholars have overstated the role of business interests in creating tax expenditures, they have correctly noted that certain features of tax expenditures and Congress facilitate passage of tax expenditures.[4] One simple reason is that for much of the twentieth century policy makers had better information about the costs of direct expenditures than about the costs of tax expenditures. As mentioned in chapter 5, the Treasury Department did not produce its first tax expenditure budget until 1969. Anyone who wanted to create a tax expenditure before this point enjoyed the luxury of accenting the program's benefits and ignoring its costs without fear of a serious challenge. Proponents of Social Security, unemployment insurance, Medicaid, and Medicare enjoyed no similar advantage. The availability of cost estimates may help explain why many of the tax expenditures created since 1970 have been targeted at low-income citizens, and thus virtually guaranteed to cost less than inclusive programs for home mortgage interest, Social Security benefits, employer retirement pensions, and employer health benefits, which originated earlier.

A second advantage is that whereas direct spending programs require new legislation, which Congress is not obligated to act upon, tax expenditures can be tucked away in must-pass revenue bills. These advantages help to explain why Senator Long's work bonus failed as part of various social welfare legislation between 1972 and 1974 and succeeded as part of the Tax Reduction Act of 1975. They also help to explain why the Targeted Jobs Tax Credit passed as an amendment to the Revenue Act of 1978 rather than as part of President Carter's urban aid package.

In addition, tax expenditures lend themselves to what Deborah Stone calls "strategic representation."[5] As mentioned in the introduction to this book, part of the political appeal of tax expenditures is that they can be defended on multiple grounds: as aid to individuals in need; subsidies to third-party providers in the private sector; tax relief; and a means of limiting the growth of traditional government programs. Senator Long, for example, promoted his tax credit for the working poor as welfare reform and tax relief. He hoped that his proposal would drain support away from the Family Assistance Plan and proposed increases in AFDC benefits. To House Democrats, many of whom were skeptical of Long's previous workfare bill, the EITC represented not a curb on AFDC but a reduction in the tax burdens of low-income workers. Rep. Charles Rangel supported the Targeted Jobs Tax Credit as much overdue aid to big cities; Rep. Al Ullman viewed the program more as welfare reform. The Nixon administration portrayed the new tax expenditure for IRAs as a source of retirement income and as a brake on demands for tighter regulations on employer pensions.

New tax expenditures enjoy additional advantages over new appropriations. As with many entitlements, jurisdiction over tax expenditures rests with the House Ways and Means and Senate Finance Committees. Richard Fenno, John Manley, and other scholars have shown that these revenue committees have been the most prestigious and powerful committees in Congress for much of the twentieth century. Their chairmen (e.g., Wilbur Mills and Russell Long) have been among the most powerful individuals in Congress. Part of their power derived from the programs under their jurisdiction, which include all tax matters and, since 1935, the major social insurance programs. In the House, Democratic members of the Ways and Means Committee gained added clout by virtue of their responsibility for all Democratic committee assignments between the 1910s and early 1970s. Even after the revenue committees lost some of their formal powers in the late 1960s and early 1970s, and even after budget deficits in the 1980s limited their options, they remained quite influential. The revenue committees certainly wielded more clout than the education and labor committees, the other main source of social welfare legislation in Congress, whose members typically favored new appropriations. When the revenue committee chairmen advocate passage of a new tax expenditure—as Russell Long did with the Earned Income Tax Credit (chapter 3) and Lloyd Bentsen did years later with the tax credit for child health insurance (chapter 7)—chances of enactment are good.[6]

Unlike appropriations, which must be authorized by one congressional committee and funded by another (in each House), tax expenditures are authorized and funded by the same committee in each House. The number of possible veto points in Congress is thereby cut in half. This structure prevents the appropriations committees from imposing the same fiscal discipline on the revenue committees that they do on the authorizing committees. In contrast, when Canada reformed its budget process in 1979, it grouped direct spending and tax expenditures together in ten policy areas, or "envelopes." Budget ceilings are set for each envelope, and any proposed increase in tax expenditures must be accompanied by an equal decrease in direct spending within that same envelope. This system is designed to force policy makers to make explicit trade-offs between equivalent forms of spending.[7]

The irony here, noted earlier in the introduction to part 2 (Origins), is that the structure of Congress and the power of conservative southern Democrats in congressional committees are supposed to be two of the main obstacles to the creation of new social programs. Those features of American politics seem to work against new direct expenditures and in favor of new tax expenditures.

Although the contrast between the development of tax expenditures and direct expenditures is not as sharp as between their respective origins, important differences remain. Targeted tax expenditures developed sources of political support similar to their counterparts in the visible welfare state. The TJTC coalition included the relevant congressional committees, groups representing small businesses and labor-intensive industries, groups representing the various categories of disadvantaged workers, consultants, and state-level employment agencies—not unlike the coalition that supports traditional employment and training programs. For the first decade of the EITC, its main advocates were members of the revenue committees, their staff, and the Center on Budget and Policy Priorities. Both tax expenditures received support from policy experts affiliated with universities or think tanks; neither received organized support from the working poor or disadvantaged workers.

The more inclusive tax expenditures also failed to develop much organized support from the nominal beneficiaries. Organized labor lobbied occasionally concerning the tax treatment of employer pensions, for their members usually received substantial fringe benefits. But this issue tended to take a back seat to other policy concerns such as labor regulations, workplace safety, the minimum wage, and international trade. Home owners have never organized on a national scale. The main lobbying efforts for both inclusive programs were led by third-party providers, even in the case of employer retirement pensions, a cash transfer. Realtors, home builders, savings and loans, Fortune 500 corporations, pension fund managers, actuaries, tax lawyers—these are the main interests that have tried to influence the home mortgage interest deduction and employer pensions. This same pattern appears to hold for the other major tax expenditures benefiting housing and fringe benefits. State and local governments have likewise been the main advocates of retaining the tax expenditure for state and local taxes. It appears, then, that organized groups of beneficiaries like the AARP do not always form around inclusive social programs. Furthermore, it appears that market-like policy tools can generate coalitions of support every bit as strong as those that form around traditional social programs.[8]

As discussed in the introduction to part 3 (Development), social welfare agencies are supposed to be key advocates of the programs they administer, and without their support programs are politically vulnerable.[9] This pattern does not extend to tax expenditures. In all four cases the Treasury Department either opposed or failed to support expansion. The Treasury's attitude is not too surprising, for tax expenditures conflict with its main mission, raising revenue.[10] Tax expenditures by definition create holes in the tax code and lower revenues. They also violate principles of an ideal tax system held by Treasury staff, such as horizontal equity, economic efficiency, and administrative simplicity.[11] Horizontal equity requires that two taxpayers earning the same amount of income incur the same tax liabilities, regardless of how they earned that income and what goods and services they consumed. The existence of a tax expenditure like the home mortgage interest deduction means that if Taxpayers A and B have the same level of income, and Taxpayer A pays off a mortgage while Taxpayer B pays rent, then (*ceteris paribus*) Taxpayer A will owe less tax than B—a violation of horizontal equity. In addition, the current tax system encourages individuals and corporations to overinvest in whatever goods or services are subsidized by tax expenditures, thereby decreasing the pool of capital available for other investments and distorting prices. Treasury officials contend that tax expenditures are also less cost efficient than comparable direct spending programs because many programs reward taxpayers for doing what they would have done anyway, such as purchasing child care or investing in new plants and equipment (i.e., the problem of windfall profits).

Furthermore, tax expenditures greatly complicate the task of collecting revenue. As IRS Commissioner Jerome Kurtz observed in 1977:

> Each of [the tax expenditure] provisions is, in effect, a non-revenue related expenditure program written into the tax law. Each entails its own special set of issues, definitions and limitations. . . . Because of these provisions I find myself, a Commissioner of Internal Revenue, administering programs of many other agencies. If these programs were parceled out to those agencies, the concentration of programs would be diffused and the tax law and administration would be vastly simpler. . . . The administrative problems which result . . . are formidable. To help taxpayers and officials alike, we must provide an inventory of 368 different forms for public use, along with instructions for each. . . . When a provision is placed in the tax law which applies only to a small segment of the taxpaying population, it nevertheless requires additional instructions and lines on the tax return which is distributed to all taxpayers. Thus, each narrowly applicable provision increases the filing burden for everyone, both for those to whom the provision does not apply as well as for those to whom it does.[12]

Treasury and IRS officials routinely point out that such complexity increases the cost of compliance for individuals and corporations, and not just revenue officials, in ways that often go unnoticed or unmentioned by advocates of tax expenditures. Evidence from employer pensions (chapter 6) and the TJTC (chapter 8) indicates that tax expenditures are indeed more cumbersome to administer than many advocates admit.

As specialists in public finance, Treasury officials favor a tax code with a broad base, few loopholes, progressive rates, and a few brackets. As civil servants and political realists, Treasury officials understand that tax expenditures benefit many politicians and powerful interest groups. They know that if they want to do business with the congressional revenue committees, they cannot consistently wage war against tax expenditures. In the colorful words of one former Treasury official: "We'd lose ground on the whole if we acted like a virgin on every piddle-ass thing that comes along. It's a complex tactical game."[13] The Treasury's behavior therefore tends to range from grudging acceptance to conspicuous silence to outright antagonism, depending on the full range of tax issues under consideration. Yet three of the four cases in this study have experienced considerable growth over the last quarter century; only the TJTC, which suffered from a variety of design problems, can be counted as a victim of agency opposition. Social programs administered through the tax code evidently do not require the support of the bureaucracy in order to endure and expand.[14]

Considering the total lack of agency support and occasional periods without interest group support, one might wonder how tax expenditures grow at all. The answer is that their structure as a policy tool makes growth without advocacy possible. As students of tax policy are well aware, tax expenditures function like budgetary entitlements: once embedded in the tax code, these programs can grow without any subsequent changes to eligibility criteria or benefit levels. Demographic changes (e.g., longer life spans) prompt certain tax expenditures to grow, but this is true of many direct expenditure entitlements as well. The peculiar structure of tax expenditures, however, makes their growth depend on a host of public and private decisions. Changes elsewhere in the tax code can have profound ripple effects. As income taxes increase, perhaps because of a larger number of taxpayers or higher tax rates, the size of tax expenditures can increase as well. Fundamental decisions about tax policy can and did have a profound impact on tax expenditures for home mortgage interest and employer pensions, particularly around the time of World War II. We also saw in chapter 5 how changes to the standard deduction and other itemized deductions prompted growth in the home mortgage interest deduction.

In addition, the behaviors rewarded by tax expenditures may become more prevalent, for reasons unrelated to the tax code, causing the size of tax expenditures to increase. Home ownership grew rapidly after World War II, in large part because of greater prosperity, demographic changes, and the availability of mortgages insured by the national government. As home ownership increased, so did the home mortgage interest deduction. When the U.S. government refused to offer national health insurance or expand Social Security immediately after World War II, it effectively encouraged organized labor to demand health insurance and retirement pensions from their employers, which in turn fueled the growth of the tax expenditures for fringe benefits. Stagnating wages and the eroding value of the minimum wage helped fuel the growth of the working poor, and thus the EITC. Tax expenditures are like adolescents, easily influenced by others. Tax rates and the standard deduction, the cost of mortgage credit, collective bargaining, inflation, the minimum wage, failures to enact national health insurance—developments in all these arenas had important and usually unforeseen ripple effects on individual tax expenditures.

The number and range of possible influences make the development of tax expenditures hard to predict. Further complicating this task is the inherent ambiguity of tax expenditures, which appears even more important for their development than it was for their origins. Within the span of a few years, the Earned Income Tax Credit was linked to tax reform, welfare reform, the minimum wage, and child care. Defenders of the home mortgage interest deduction have repeatedly stressed its importance to home owners and to several industries. Though less ambiguous, the TJTC was portrayed as a jobs program for disadvantaged workers and as a wage subsidy to small businesses and labor-intensive industries. The EITC and TJTC were also understood by moderate and conservative members of both parties as a way of curbing demands for AFDC, unemployment insurance, and traditional job training programs. This ambiguity enabled a broad spectrum of policy makers to support the continuation of the TJTC and expansion of the EITC. AFDC and programs covered by the Job Training Partnership Act, on the other hand, were understood primarily as welfare programs. Their advocates, to the extent that they had any, were primarily liberal Democrats whose political influence waned in the 1980s.

Nowhere was this ambiguity more pronounced than in the case of employer pensions. Depending on whom you asked and when, changes to the tax treatment of these pensions have represented a way to guarantee retirees income security, reduce inequities in the distribution of retirement income, defend the gains of organized labor, check the growth of Social Security, reduce the need for public assistance, or ensure the integrity of a massive pool of capital. Some policy makers expect to kill two (or more) birds with one stone. According to the Joint Committee on Taxation, "The policy rationale for this tax expenditure is that the tax benefits for qualified plans encourage employers to provide retirement benefits for their employees. This reduces the need for public assistance and reduces pressure on the social security system."[15]

Ambiguity of purpose increases the likelihood that different interests will have a stake in tax expenditures at different times. When the Earned Income Tax Credit was viewed as antipoverty policy, groups like the Children's Defense Fund and the Center on Budget and Policy Priorities were its main interest group advocates. When the EITC became an alternative to increases in the minimum wage, conservative politicians and business interests joined in singing its praises. Sometimes these changes, as in the case of the EITC, were the result of developments in other policy domains. And sometimes changes in program advocacy resulted from changes to the program's structure. Multiple visions of the government's role in regulating private pensions were embedded in the 1974 ERISA legislation, which in turn dramatically changed the range and number of actors involved in subsequent debates over pension regulations.

The porous and plastic qualities of tax expenditures contributed to important discontinuities in the development of individual programs, meaning that the scope of conflict or growth rates changed significantly. Political support for the EITC, for instance, resembled that for AFDC during the late 1970s and early 1980s, and then became considerably broader and bipartisan; its pattern of growth changed accordingly. The politics of the home mortgage interest deduction changed during the 1980s as persistent deficits prompted a search for revenues and a greater willingness to cut the program. The tax expenditure for employer pensions has undergone three separate phases of development.

It is, of course, possible to make too much of historical contingency and unpredictable outcomes. One can always generalize; the question is at what level of abstraction and with what level of confidence. At this point, the surest generalizations one can make tell the reader where to look rather than what to expect. The starting point is the simple observation that tax expenditures have been more closely wedded to tax policy than to social policy or any decisions over direct expenditures. This link is not inevitable—witness Canada's introduction of budget envelopes—but it does capture the historical experience to date in the United States. This fact has several implications. The first is that wherever we see major overhauls to the nation's tax code, we should look for major effects on the hidden welfare state (indeed, on all tax expenditures). As we have seen, the introduction of corporate (1909) and individual (1913) income taxes, the expansion of income taxes during World War II, and the Tax Reform Act of 1986 were major milestones in the history of the hidden welfare state. We might expect to find comparable results, perhaps of a lesser magnitude, when the U.S. tax code was overhauled in 1954 and 1969, and when tax rates were cut substantially in 1981. Enactment of new tax expenditures for employer-provided health benefits and for child care expenses in 1954 provides some initial evidence for this expectation.

A second implication is that Congress and especially its revenue committees matter. As Sven Steinmo, a leading analyst of tax policy, has noted, "In the United States, Congress, not the president, writes tax law."[16] Of the two core functions of government, the Constitution gives the president more of the power of the sword and Congress more of the power of the purse. Presidents certainly have proposed major changes to the tax code, but the final product always bears the unmistakable imprint of Congress. The Tax Reform Act of 1986 is but one example. Witte calculates that almost 60 percent of all new tax expenditures and almost 80 percent of all modifications to existing tax expenditures originated with Congress.[17]

Some of the reasons why Congress matters have already been mentioned—the formidable powers of the revenue committees, the need for annual revenue bills. One might also argue that the structure of Congress provides both the opportunity and the motive for creating new tax expenditures. Tax expenditures provide members of the revenue committees, who have the politically unenviable task of levying taxes, a valuable opportunity to claim credit for spending money on a specific constituency. In the context of weak political parties and frequent elections (especially in the House), individual legislators must regularly provide constituents with divisible benefits if they hope to be reelected. This task is complicated for members of the revenue committees, who cannot distribute "pork" via the traditional channels of appropriations. Instead, they try to lower the tax burdens on specific individuals and groups.

This study suggests some limits to that generalization. Senator McLean, sponsor of the tax expenditure for employer pensions, was not a member of the Finance Committee. It seems unlikely that architects of the Targeted Jobs Tax Credit were trying to win the support of small business, which after all opposed the TJTC. And the idea that they were vying for the votes of disadvantaged urban youth and the disabled seems far-fetched. More likely they thought that the TJTC would make a dent in structural unemployment, and was therefore worthwhile. We also have evidence from Witte that nearly 40 percent of all new tax expenditures originated in the executive branch, and half of those from administrative rulings by the IRS. Consequently I find it more plausible that the reelection motive applies less to the creation of tax expenditures with social welfare objectives than it does to the creation of other kinds of tax expenditures. This motive may become more salient after the program has been created. Under conditions of fiscal stress, members of the revenue committees may claim credit for keeping existing tax expenditures off the chopping block.

Pointing to Congress suggests that changes to the revenue committees and the budget process should have important consequences for the hidden welfare state. We would expect differences before and after the Budget and Impoundment Control Act of 1974, which capped a historic period of internal reform in Congress.[18] Before passage of the Budget Act, the vast majority of House revenue bills were considered under a closed rule that prohibited House members from deleting or modifying specific provisions on the floor. Since then, revenue bills have been considered under a modified closed rule or open rule, and the frequency of floor amendments has increased. This Act also ended the revenue committees' near monopoly over information and expertise relating to tax matters and required publication of an annual tax expenditure budget. The decentralization of tax policy making may help to explain why the Earned Income Tax Credit and especially the New Jobs Tax Credit generated wider debate at the time of enactment than did the tax expenditures for home mortgage interest and employer pensions. The greater participation of interest groups during enactment of the NJTC and TJTC suggests that opening up the process of making tax policy may have lessened, but by no means eliminated, the role of government officials in creating tax expenditures. The period starting with the release of the first tax expenditure budget in 1969 and ending with the 1974 Budget Act should mark a turning point in the development of the hidden welfare state.

More recent changes in budget procedures have similarly reduced the historical advantages enjoyed by tax expenditures. In an effort to control the deficit, policy makers passed the Budget Enforcement Act (BEA) in 1990 and extended it in 1993. The BEA placed absolute caps on discretionary spending and, more important, mandated that any new increase in mandatory spending or decrease in taxes cannot add to the deficit. This pay-as-you-go rule applied equally to tax expenditures and direct expenditures.[19] It intentionally created more of a zero-sum contest among public programs. Anyone who wanted to expand a tax expenditure or create a new one now had to find the money to do so, meaning that they had to propose cutting someone else's tax expenditure or direct expenditure—an unpleasant and unusually public act for those accustomed to quiet deals and uninterrupted growth.[20] These changes could widen the scope of conflict over tax expenditures in the future and thus help close the gap between the politics of tax expenditures and of direct expenditures.

Finally, if tax expenditures are closely linked to tax policy, then political parties and party competition will likely influence the hidden welfare state. This finding runs counter to much of the existing literature. As I have noted elsewhere, parties are notable in studies of U.S. social policy because of their irrelevance.[21] Lacking the programmatic focus of their European counterparts, U.S. parties have historically specialized in patronage and pork-barrel politics.[22] Tax policy, however, is one domain where parties have consistently and sharply differed. Of particular relevance here are the Democrats' long-standing advocacy of progressive income taxation and Republicans' desire to lower tax rates on corporations and the rich.[23] Party competition was central to the creation of tax expenditures for home mortgage interest and employer pensions, as Democrats and Progressives pushed for income taxes on the affluent and corporations while Republicans tried first to prevent their introduction and later to minimize their impact (chapter 2). Party competition was associated as well with passage of the Young Child Tax Credit in 1990, as Democrats and Republicans competed to be the "pro-family" party (chapter 7). We also have evidence that party competition can fuel expansion of existing tax expenditures, as happened with the Earned Income Tax Credit. During the 1980s, Democrats and Republicans competed for the votes of the working poor, who made up a sizable fraction of the electorate and exhibited no strong attachment to either party. At a minimum, expanding the EITC was in the interest of both parties as a means of preventing the other from winning the label "friend to the working poor."

It is not yet clear under what conditions party competition matters. It may be that when the parties are closely balanced in strength nationally—meaning divided government or rapidly alternating periods of unified control—party competition takes on particular importance as party members extend tax benefits to specific groups that may help the party attain a more stable majority. Parties already enjoying clear majority status would not feel this pressure as heavily, and parties in the minority would lack the power to distribute tax benefits widely. This pattern fits three episodes in this study: Democrats and Republicans alternated control of Congress and the White House between 1908 and 1926 (creating tax expenditures for home mortgage interest and employer pensions), and between 1980 and 1995 (expanding the EITC). It also fits two important examples from the visible welfare state, the expansion of Civil War pensions in the late nineteenth century and Social Security in the late 1960s and early 1970s.[24]

The Meaning of the Hidden Welfare State

Social scientists are fond of using metaphors from the natural sciences. Borrowing from physics, Leman characterized the timing of new social programs in the United States as two "big bangs." More recently, scholars have borrowed the concept of "punctuated equilibrium" from evolutionary biology to describe processes as diverse as industrialization and the emergence of specific issues in Congress and the media.[25] In keeping with this tradition, I was initially attracted to the metaphor of the coral reef to reflect much of what is significant about tax expenditures. The coral reef lies beneath the surface, hard to see unless one knows exactly where to look. Each reef plays host to a fascinating combination of flora and fauna that may be rare in other parts of the ocean. Some reef communities are very large and very old. More important, coral reefs grow at varying rates and in unforeseen directions depending on water temperature, clarity, and salinity, as well as hurricanes and disease.[26]

The coral reef image captures nicely the lack of visibility and predictability I discovered in my research. The unusual combinations of flora and fauna correspond well with the odd coalitions of interest groups and public officials that "inhabit" tax expenditure programs. The main drawback of the coral reef, as with many images borrowed from the natural sciences, is that it conceals human agency. Tax expenditures are not acts of nature; they are created, usually with little foresight or debate, by public officials; their size and shape are sometimes deliberately changed. It seems more accurate to think of tax expenditures as *artificial reefs*. Just as scientists have learned to create reefs by sinking old ships or oil rigs in certain parts of the ocean, policy makers have learned to sink holes in certain parts of the tax code. Although scientists do not know what their new reef will look like, they may periodically add to it or subtract from it, and then let nature again take its course. Tax expenditures operate in much the same way. Once created, their growth is heavily influenced by the tides of tax policy, party competition, inflation, and interest rates, as well as the occasional hurricane of congressional reform. They are deliberately modified on occasion, then subject to the same confluence of forces as before.[27]

While the prevalence of artificial reefs in the tax code provides ample opportunity for recreational and academic study, it also raises troubling issues of accountability and control over public monies. Part of the problem is that tax expenditures routinely escape the same level of scrutiny and evaluation to which direct expenditures are subjected, leaving us practically clueless as to how well they perform. Were policy makers to demand additional studies, the very ambiguity of tax expenditures would make it difficult to establish clear evaluation criteria. In addition, tax expenditures are segregated from direct expenditures in the budget process and budget documents, making informed trade-offs among spending priorities harder to achieve. Considering the hundreds of billions of dollars spent each year through the tax code, and considering the centrality of tax expenditures to the nation's housing, health care, and retirement policies, this is a big problem.

Finally, the benefits of avoiding direct expenditures and traditional bureaucracies come with a price. The costs of administration are not so much eliminated as shifted from government to individuals, corporations, and third-party service providers. These costs are not trivial, and they appear to be growing.[28] The resulting complexity of the tax code generates so much frustration, I suspect, that many individuals embrace quick-fix solutions like the flat tax, even when such solutions will increase their taxes. Just as important, public officials have even less ability to predict and control the growth of tax expenditures than they do with traditional spending entitlements. We have a fairly reasonable idea, several decades from now, who will receive Social Security benefits and how much they will receive; that knowledge makes it possible to address problems early and gradually. We cannot possibly make similar predictions for the home mortgage interest deduction or any tax break for employer fringe benefits.

My final observations concern the links between the visible and hidden welfare states. Almost everything said so far has stressed the ways in which policy making in the hidden welfare state has followed a different path, driven by different forces, than policy making in the visible welfare state. Those differences are the main message of this study. Nevertheless, it is possible to place the hidden and visible welfare states side by side and see some interesting connections. For instance, if you compare Table 9.1 with Table 1.1, you will see an alternating pattern of program origins. The largest tax expenditures today originated in the 1910s (home mortgage interest, property taxes, and charitable contributions), 1920s (employer pensions and capital gains), 1940s (Social Security benefits), and 1950s (employer health benefits). The most important parts of the visible welfare state, in contrast, were created in the 1930s and 1960s. There is little evidence that policy makers consciously chose between two different tools of social policy during the first half of the twentieth century. Rather, the Great Depression interrupted an ongoing series of partisan debates over taxation—how much, paid by whom— that periodically produced tax breaks for specific groups.

Since around 1970, however, policy makers have started to recognize the links between tax expenditures and direct expenditures. The most common response has been to use tax expenditures as a means of slowing the growth or preventing the creation of traditional social programs. The lead practitioners have been moderate Republicans and conservative Democrats who accepted the idea that government should provide certain goods and services but disagreed with liberal Democrats over the nature and extent of aid. Senator Russell Long fashioned his work bonus in part to take support away from proposed increases in AFDC benefits. Later, some advocates portrayed the EITC as a better alternative to increases in the minimum wage and in direct spending for child care. Sen. Herman Talmadge of Georgia, another conservative Democrat, appears to have initiated the WIN tax credit (for employers who hired welfare recipients) as an alternative to increased spending for the Job Corps and other Great Society job-training programs.[29] In 1983 then Senate Finance chairman Robert Packwood (R-Oreg.) offered the following defense for the tax expenditure for employer health insurance:

> Every now and then the ghosts of Stanley Surrey appear before this committee and want to tax all fringe benefits, because they feel the only purpose of the Tax Code is to collect money, not to provide social benefits. I have said this

to you, and I would say it to the administration: I think the one reason we do not have any significant demand for national health insurance in this country among those who are employed is because their employers are paying for their benefits, by and large. And we will never go to the situation in Great Britain so long as that system exists, and I hate to see us nibble at it for fear you are going to have the demand that the Federal Government take over and provide the benefits that would otherwise be lost.[30]

This insight suggests a connection between the failure of national health insurance in the United States since the mid-1950s and the availability of employment-based health insurance underwritten by the tax code. Legislators like Senator Packwood have succeeded in offering enough insurance to middle-class citizens to dampen the demand for universal coverage. President Clinton's health plan foundered in part because he proposed reducing the tax expenditure for employer health benefits in order to pay for broader coverage. This proposal alienated organized labor, a traditional ally of Clinton and the Democrats, because unionized workers had fought long and hard to win comparatively generous health benefits from their employers.[31] There may be a similar explanation for the limits of family policy in the United States, especially the absence of European-style family allowances. The combination of the child care tax credit, the Earned Income Tax Credit, and the tax exemption for dependents (which is not technically a tax expenditure) may have siphoned off support for more direct forms of aid to families with children.[32] One can also imagine how recent efforts to clamp down on the growth of Medicare and Medicaid may have caused doctors and hospitals to pass the costs on to their privately insured patients, thus increasing the cost of health care to employers, thus increasing the size of the tax expenditure for employer health insurance.

It is reasonable to expect closer connections between the hidden and visible welfare states in the future. Policy makers worried about the deficit will continue looking for redundancies or inefficiencies in social welfare spending, whatever form that spending takes. The hidden and visible welfare states are, to paraphrase Willie Sutton, where the money is. Conservatives bent on rolling back Social Security and Medicare will continue proposing tax expenditures for Individual Retirement Accounts and Medical Savings Accounts. Policy makers worried about the future of the Social Security trust fund will have to factor in the availability of private pensions, subsidized by the tax code, before making any substantial cuts in benefits or increases in payroll taxes. By the same token, there is little reason to expect that closer connections will produce better policies. Without better mechanisms for making choices between different types of spending and better information about the actual impact of tax expenditures; and without a frank discussion about the overwhelming bias of social spending in favor of middle- and upper-income citizens, and about public officials' current inability to control tax expenditures, we will continue to make chance and ignorance key ingredients of U.S. social policy.

List of Interviews

Note: Although many of these interviews are cited in specific notes to the chapters, some are not. The latter are listed here to indicate the extent of my research as well as to recognize these individuals for providing me with important background information and copies of hard-to-find documents.

Henry Aaron, August 1990	Economist, Brookings Institution
Scott Barancek, March 1991	Staff, Center on Budget and Policy Priorities
Rosina Barker, August 1990	Tax Staff, Committee on Ways and Means
Helen Blank, August 1990	Director, Child Care, Children's Defense Fund
Albert Buckberg, August 1990	Senior Economist, Joint Committee on Taxation
David Certner, March 1992	Staff, American Association of Retired Persons
Eleanor Chelimsky, August 1990	Assistant Comptroller, Program Evaluation and Methodology, General Accounting Office
Harry Conaway, August 1990	ex-Treasury staff, then with William M. Mercer-Meidinger
Bruce Davie, August 1990	ex-Ways and Means Staff, then with Arthur Andersen & Company
David Ellwood, November 1990	Professor, Kennedy School of Government, Harvard University
Karen Ferguson, March 1992	Director, Pension Rights Center
Seymour Fiekowsky, August 1990	Business Taxation, U.S. Department of the Treasury
Robert Greenstein, August 1990	Director, Center on Budget and Policy Priorities
Ed Hogan, August 1990	Chief of Operations, Employment, and Training Administration, U.S. Department of Labor
Sar Levitan, August 1990	Director, Center for the Study of Social Policy, George Washington University
Paul McDaniel, September 1990	Tax attorney, Hill & Barlow
Meredith Miller, March 1992	Staff, AFL-CIO

Joseph Minarik, February 1991	Executive Director, Joint Economic Committee
Madlyn Morreale, February 1991	Staff, House Select Committee on Children, Youth, and Families
Alicia Munnell, January 1992	Vice President, Federal Reserve Bank of Boston
Wendell Primus, August 1990 and March 1991	Chief Economist, Committee on Ways and Means
Anne Rafaelli, August 1990	Legislative Assistant to Rep. Pete Stark (D-Calif.)
Nancy Reeder, February 1991	Staff, House Select Committee on Children, Youth, and Families
Sylvester Scheiber, March 1992	Staff, Association of Private Pension and Welfare Plans
Bernie Schmitt, August 1990	Assistant Chief of Staff, Joint Committee on Taxation
Isaac Shapiro, August 1990 and September 1991	Senior Research Analyst, Center on Budget and Policy Priorities
Jon Sheiner, August 1990	Legislative Assistant to Rep. Charles Rangel (D-N.Y.)
Mike Sheinfield, February 1991	Legislative Assistant to Rep. Tom Downey (D-N.Y.)
Bill Signer, August 1990	ex-aide to Representative Rangel, then lobbyist, The Keefe Company
Lisa Sprague, March 1992	Staff, U.S. Chamber of Commerce
C. Eugene Steuerle, August 1990, February 1991, and September 1991	ex-Deputy Assistant Secretary for Tax Analysis, U.S. Department of the Treasury, then Senior Visiting Fellow, The Urban Institute
Emil Sunley, August 1990	ex-Deputy Assistant Secretary for Tax Analysis, U.S. Department of the Treasury, then with Deloitte & Touche
Paul Suplizio, August 1990	Lobbyist, Targeted Jobs Tax Credit Coalition
Randy Weiss, February 1991	ex-Staff, Joint Committee on Taxation, then with Deloitte & Touche

Notes

INTRODUCTION

1. Stanley S. Surrey and Paul R. McDaniel, *Tax Expenditures* (Cambridge, Mass.: Harvard University Press, 1985), p. 3. Tax expenditures are not the only way that the tax code is used to make social policy. One might also consider the progressivity of tax rates and the size of personal exemptions and the standard deduction, which are considered part of the baseline tax system and are not tax expenditures.

2. This study focuses exclusively on tax expenditures and social policies of the U.S. government. Although state and local governments have their own tax expenditures, they are far less important in size and scope.

3. This phrase is from Jeffrey P. Owens, "Tax Expenditures and Direct Expenditures as Instruments of Social Policy," in Sijbren Cnossen, ed., *Comparative Tax Studies* (Amsterdam: North-Holland, 1983), pp. 171–97.

4. Kenneth Woodside, "The Political Economy of Policy Instruments: Tax Expenditures and Subsidies in Canada," in Michael M. Atkinson and Marsha A. Chandler, eds., *The Politics of Canadian Public Policy* (Toronto: University of Toronto Press, 1983), p. 175. See also Richard A. Musgrave and Peggy B. Musgrave, *Public Finance in Theory and Practice*, 4th ed. (New York: McGraw-Hill, 1984), and Joseph A. Pechman, *Federal Tax Policy*, 5th ed. (Washington, D.C.: Brookings Institution, 1987).

5. U.S. Senate, Committee on the Budget, *Tax Expenditures: Relationships to Spending Programs and Background Material on Individual Provisions* (Washington, D.C.: Government Printing Office, 1986), p. 1.

6. U.S. Congress, Joint Committee on Taxation (hereafter referred to as JCT), *Estimates of Federal Tax Expenditures for Fiscal Years 1992–1996* (Washington, D.C.: Government Printing Office, 1991), p. 3.

7. Quoted in Alan Ehrenhalt, "Senate Finance: The Fiefdom of Russell Long," *Congressional Quarterly Almanac 1977* (Washington, D.C.: Congressional Quarterly, 1977), p. 178.

8. Richard Rahn, chief economist for the Chamber of Commerce, quoted in "Tax Subsidies: No End to Increases," *U.S. News and World Report*, March 22, 1982, p. 84. A second and less common objection is that the definition of tax expenditures is arbitrary and subject to political manipulation. Boris I. Bittker, "Accounting for Federal 'Tax Subsidies' in the National Budget," *National Tax Journal* 22, 2 (June 1969): 244–61; Aaron Wildavsky, "Keeping Kosher: The Epistemology of Tax Expenditures," *Journal of Public Policy* 5, 3 (August 1985): 413–31.

9. Christopher Howard, "Let's *Not* Talk about Entitlements," paper presented at the 1995 Annual Meeting of the American Political Science Association, Chicago, Ill.

10. Note, for example, how little mention is made of tax expenditures in the major histories of the American welfare state: Mimi Abramovitz, *Regulating the Lives of Women: Social Welfare Policy from Colonial Times to the Present* (Boston: South End, 1988); Edward Berkowitz and Kim McQuaid, *Creating the Welfare State: The Political Economy of 20th-Century Reform*, rev. ed. (Lawrence: University Press of Kansas, 1992); Robert X. Browning, *Politics and Social Welfare Policy in the United States* (Knoxville: University of Tennessee Press, 1986); Michael Katz, *In the Shadow of the Poorhouse: A Social History of Welfare in America* (New York: Basic Books, 1986); Roy Lubove, *The Struggle for Social Security, 1900–1935* (Cambridge, Mass.: Harvard University Press, 1968); Theodore R. Marmor, Jerry L. Mashaw, and Philip L. Harvey, *America's Misunderstood Welfare State* (New York: Basic Books, 1990); James T. Patterson, *America's Struggle Against Poverty, 1900–1985* (Cambridge, Mass.: Harvard University Press, 1986); Theda Skocpol and John Ikenberry, "The Political Formation of the American Welfare State in Historical and Comparative Perspective," *Comparative Social Research* 6 (1983): 87–148; Walter I. Trattner, *From Poor Law to Welfare State: A History of Social Welfare in America*, 4th ed. (New York: Free Press, 1989); Margaret Weir, Ann Shola Orloff, and Theda Skocpol, eds., *The Politics of Social Policy in the United States* (Princeton, N.J.: Princeton University Press, 1988).

11. Based on figures supplied by the Congressional Budget Office, I calculate that the subsidy costs of loan and loan guarantee programs with social welfare objectives equaled approximately $8 billion in fiscal year 1990, a small fraction of the cost of tax expenditures (Congressional Budget Office, *Credit Reform: Comparable Budget Costs for Cash and Credit* [Washington, D.C.: Government Printing Office, 1989], pp. 44–45). Still, it is quite possible that loans and loan guarantees have societal impacts that cannot be measured by their subsidy costs alone.

12. For a good discussion of various definitions of the welfare state and the resulting theoretical muddle, see John Carrier and Ian Kendall, "Categories, Categorizations and the Political Economy of Welfare," *Journal of Social Policy* 15, 3 (July 1986): 315–35, and Gosta Esping-Andersen, *The Three Worlds of Welfare Capitalism* (Princeton, N.J.: Princeton University Press, 1990), pp. 18–26.

13. In many ways we know more about indirect spending in European welfare states than in the United States. See, for example, Esping-Andersen, *Three Worlds of Welfare Capitalism*, ch. 4; Arthur Gould, "The Salaried Middle Class in the Corporatist Welfare State," *Policy and Politics* 9, 4 (October 1981): 401–18; Brian Hogwood, "The Hidden Face of Public Expenditure: Trends in Tax Expenditures in Britain," *Policy and Politics* 17, 2 (1989): 111–30; Jon Kvist and Adrian Sinfield, *Comparing Tax Routes to Welfare in Denmark and the United Kingdom* (Copenhagen: Danish National Institute of Social Research, 1996); Michael O'Higgins, "Public/Private Interaction and Pension Policy," in Martin Rein and Lee Rainwater, eds., *Public/Private Interplay in Social Protection* (Armonk, N.Y.: M. E. Sharpe, 1986), pp. 99–148; Owens, "Tax Expenditures and Direct Expenditures"; Sven Steinmo, "Political Institutions and Tax

Policy in the United States, Sweden, and Britain," *World Politics* 41, 4 (July 1989): 500–535; Gavin Wood, "Housing Tax Expenditures in OECD Countries: Economic Impacts and Prospects for Reform," *Policy and Politics* 16, 4 (1988): 235–50; Woodside, "The Political Economy of Policy Instruments"; Frances Woolley and Julian Le Grand, "The Ackroyds, the Osbornes, and the Welfare State: The Impact of the Welfare State on Two Hypothetical Families over Their Life-times," *Policy and Politics* 18, 1 (1990): 17–30.

14. Titmuss hinted strongly at the interconnections among these three systems but did not develop these ideas fully (Richard Titmuss, *Essays on "The Welfare State"* [New Haven, Conn.: Yale University Press, 1959], pp. 34–55).

15. Peter Flora and Arnold Heidenheimer, "The Historical Core and Changing Boundaries of the Welfare State," in *idem.*, eds., *The Development of Welfare States in Europe and America* (New Brunswick, N.J.: Transaction Books, 1981), p. 26.

16. Edwin Amenta and Theda Skocpol, "Taking Exception: Explaining the Distinctiveness of American Public Policies in the Last Century," in Francis G. Castles, ed., *The Comparative History of Public Policy* (London: Polity Press, 1989), pp. 292–333.

17. Mimi Abramovitz, "Everyone Is on Welfare: The Role of Redistribution in Social Policy Revisited," *Social Work* 28 (November–December 1983): 440–45; Robert J. Lampman, *Social Welfare Spending: Accounting for Changes from 1950 to 1978* (Orlando: Academic Press, 1984); Wallace C. Peterson, "The U.S. 'Welfare State' and the Conservative Counterrevolution," *Journal of Economic Issues* 19, 3 (September 1985): 601–41.

See also P. R. Kaim-Caudle, *Comparative Social Policy and Social Security: A Ten-Country Study* (London: Martin Robinson, 1973); Paul Starr and Gosta Esping-Anderson, "Passive Intervention," *Working Papers for a New Society* 7, 2 (July/August 1979): 15–25; and Judy Temple, "Tax Expenditures," in *Taxation* (Washington, D.C.: Project on the Federal Social Role, 1985), pp. 1–44.

18. Martin Rein and Lee Rainwater, "From Welfare State to Welfare Society," in Gosta Esping-Andersen, Martin Rein, and Lee Rainwater, eds., *Stagnation and Renewal in Social Policy* (Armonk, N.Y.: M. E. Sharpe, 1987), pp. 143–59; Martin Rein and Lee Rainwater, "The Public/Private Mix," in *idem.*, eds., *Public/Private Interplay in Social Protection* (Armonk, N.Y.: M. E. Sharpe, 1986), pp. 3–24; Neil Gilbert and Barbara Gilbert, *The Enabling State: Modern Welfare Capitalism in America* (New York: Oxford University Press, 1989); Beth Stevens, "Blurring the Boundaries: How the Federal Government Has Influenced Welfare Benefits in the Private Sector," in Weir, Orloff, and Skocpol, eds., *The Politics of Social Policy in the United States*, pp. 123–48. My investigation of employer pensions covers a longer period and is more explicitly comparative than Stevens'.

Two good empirical studies by Daniel M. Fox and Daniel C. Schaffer also deserve mention. See their "Health Policy and ERISA: Interest Groups and Semipreemption," *Journal of Health Politics, Policy and Law* 14, 2 (Summer 1989): 239–60, and "Tax Policy as Social Policy: Cafeteria Plans, 1978–1985," *Journal of Health Politics, Policy and Law* 12, 4 (Winter 1987): 609–64.

19. The seminal works are Surrey and McDaniel, *Tax Expenditures;* Stanley Surrey, *Pathways to Tax Reform: The Concept of Tax Expenditures* (Cambridge, Mass.: Harvard University Press, 1973); and John F. Witte, *The Politics and Development of the Federal Income Tax* (Madison: University of Wisconsin Press, 1985).

See also James Alt, "The Evolution of Tax Structures," *Public Choice* 41 (1984): 181–222; R. Douglas Arnold, *The Logic of Congressional Action* (New Haven, Conn.: Yale University Press, 1990), ch. 8; Martin Pfaff and Anita Pfaff, "How Equitable Are Implicit Public Grants? The Case of the Individual Income Tax," and Henry Aaron, "Implicit Transfers to Homeowners in the Federal Budget," in Kenneth E. Boulding and Martin Pfaff, eds., *Redistribution to the Rich and the Poor* (Belmont, Calif.: Wadsworth, 1972), pp. 181–204, 204–19; Theodore J. Eismeier, "The Power Not to Tax: A Search for Effective Controls," *Journal of Policy Analysis and Management* 1, 3 (Spring 1982): 333–45; Donald Kettl, *Government by Proxy: (Mis?)Managing Federal Programs* (Washington, D.C.: CQ Press, 1988); Ronald F. King, "Tax Expenditures and Systematic Public Policy: An Essay on the Political Economy of the Federal Revenue Code," *Public Budgeting and Finance* 4, 1 (Spring 1984), pp. 14–31; JoAnn Klimschot, *The Untouchables: A Common Cause Study of the Federal Tax Expenditure Budget* (Washington, D.C.: Common Cause, 1981); Herman B. Leonard, *Checks Unbalanced: The Quiet Side of Public Spending* (New York: Basic Books, 1986), ch. 4; Paul R. McDaniel, "Tax Expenditures as Tools of Government Action," in Lester M. Salamon, ed., *Beyond Privatization: The Tools of Government Action* (Washington, D.C.: Urban Institute Press, 1989), pp. 167–96; Paul R. McDaniel, "Federal Income Tax Simplification: The Political Process," *Tax Law Review* 34, 1 (Fall 1978): 27–77; Ralph Nader Congress Project, *The Revenue Committees* (New York: Grossman, 1975); Allen Schick, "Controlling Nonconventional Expenditure: Tax Expenditures and Loans," *Public Budgeting and Finance* 6, 1 (Spring 1986): 3–19; Kathy Schroeher, *Gimme Shelters: A Common Cause Study of the Review of Tax Expenditures by the Congressional Tax Committees* (Washington, D.C.: Common Cause, 1978); Stanley S. Surrey, "Tax Incentives as a Device for Implementing Government Policy: A Comparison with Direct Government Expenditures," *Harvard Law Review* 83, 4 (February 1970): 705–38; Wildavsky, "Keeping Kosher: The Epistemology of Tax Expenditures."

Prior to these studies, tax loopholes were a favorite target of modern muckrakers. See Jerome R. Hellerstein, *Taxes, Loopholes and Morals* (New York: McGraw-Hill, 1963); see also two books by Philip M. Stern, *The Great Treasury Raid* (New York: Random House, 1962), and *The Rape of the Taxpayer* (New York: Random House, 1973).

20. The claim that tax expenditures cause taxpayers to overconsume assumes that market distributions of goods and services are somehow natural, appropriate, or fair. Sven Steinmo questions this and other alleged defects of tax expenditures ("So What's Wrong with Tax Expenditures? A Reevaluation Based on Swedish Experience," *Public Budgeting & Finance* 6, 2 [Summer 1986]: 27–44).

21. The notable exception is Witte, *Politics and Development of the Federal Income Tax.*

22. Probably the most notorious and most cited example of such a tax expenditure is the so-called Mayer amendment of 1951. The language of the amendment "provided capital gains treatment for a lump sum distribution to Louis B. Mayer on his retirement from the movie industry. To avoid identifying him by name, the amendment was worded to apply to a movie executive who (1) had been employed for more than 20 years, (2) held his rights to future profits for 12 years, and (3) had the right to receive a percentage of profits for life or for a period of at least five years after the termination of his employment" (Joseph Pechman, "Tax Reform: Theory and Practice," *Journal of Economic Perspectives* 1, 1 [Summer 1987]: 14).

23. See, e.g., Isabel V. Sawhill, "Escaping the Fiscal Trap," *The American Prospect* 1 (Spring 1990): 19–26, and the *New York Times* editorial, "The Right Way to Raise Taxes," July 25, 1990, p. A18.

24. "Studies of social welfare frequently address such questions as: Is it enough? Are we losing ground? How can it improve? But to answer these questions one must first have a reasonably clear picture of what exists. In this regard, the conventional image of the welfare state offers a distorted picture, focusing largely on direct expenditures and disadvantaged populations. It is a view that unwittingly conceals numerous beneficiaries of social transfers in the areas of health, housing, income maintenance, asset maintenance, personal care, and education. Perceptions are so narrow and some of these benefits so difficult to appraise that many recipients decry the rising costs of welfare without realizing the extent to which their own subsidies add to the bill" (Gilbert and Gilbert, *The Enabling State*, p. xii).

25. See the essays by Ann Shola Orloff, Edwin Amenta and Theda Skocpol, Margaret Weir, Kenneth Finegold, and Jill Quadagno in Weir, Orloff, and Skocpol, eds., *The Politics of Social Policy in the United States.* The power of southern Democrats in Congress for much of the twentieth century was the result of their seniority, which was in turn a function of congressional rules and the absence of party competition in the South.

26. Concerning values and social policy, see Nathan Glazer, *The Limits of Social Policy* (Cambridge, Mass.: Harvard University Press, 1988); Anthony King, "Ideas, Institutions and the Policies of Government: A Comparative Analysis," *British Journal of Political Science* 3 (1973): 291–313, 409–23. For a more nuanced analysis, see Gaston Rimlinger, *Welfare Policy and Industrialization in Europe, America, and Russia* (New York: Wiley, 1971). The classic exposition of Lockean liberalism in the United States is Louis Hartz, *The Liberal Tradition in America* (New York: Harcourt, Brace, 1955).

27. Quoted in Joel Havemann, "Tax Expenditures—Spending Money Without Expenditures," *National Journal* 9, 50 (December 10, 1977): 1909.

28. The first and third reasons may appear to overlap. Nevertheless, some people may embrace tax expenditures as a means of lowering taxes and reducing the size of the national government and not care especially what groups or behaviors are rewarded.

29. James Q. Wilson, *Political Organizations* (New York: Basic Books, 1973); Theodore J. Lowi, "American Business, Public Policy, Case Studies, and Political Theory," *World Politics* 16 (1964): 677–715.

30. The emphasis on historical contingency, rooted in a belief in causal complexity, is a distinguishing feature of many studies grouped under the heading of the "new institutionalism" (G. John Ikenberry, "Conclusion: An Institutional Approach to American Foreign Economic Policy," *International Organization* 42, 1 [Winter 1988]: 219–43).

31. Readers who desire to know more about this approach might consult James G. March and Johan P. Olsen, *Rediscovering Institutions: The Organizational Basis of Politics* (New York: The Free Press, 1989).

32. Theda Skocpol, *Protecting Soldiers and Mothers: The Political Origins of Social Policy in the United States* (Cambridge, Mass.: The Belknap Press of Harvard University Press, 1992).

33. For a good survey of the uses of history in political science, see David Brian Robertson, "History, Behavioralism, and the Return to Institutionalism in American Political Science," in Eric H. Monkkonen, ed., *Engaging the Past: The Uses of History Across the Social Sciences* (Durham, N.C.: Duke University Press, 1994), pp. 113–53.

34. This is one strategy discussed in Edwin Amenta, "Making the Most of a Case Study: Theories of the Welfare State and the American Experience," *International Journal of Comparative Sociology* 32, 1–2 (January–April 1991): 172–94.

35. See note 10.

36. Two of the first scholars to differentiate between origins and development were Gosta Esping-Andersen and Walter Korpi, "Social Policy as Class Politics in Post-War Capitalism: Scandinavia, Austria, and Germany," in John Goldthorpe, ed., *Order and Conflict in Contemporary Capitalism* (Oxford: Oxford University Press, 1984), pp. 179–208; see also Flora and Heidenheimer, "The Historical Core and Changing Boundaries of the Welfare State"; Jerald Hage, Robert Hanneman, and Edward T. Gargan, *State Responsiveness and State Activism* (London: Unwin Hyman, 1989), pp. 122–23; and Marmor, Mashaw, and Harvey, *America's Misunderstood Welfare State*, p. 53.

37. Perhaps the most famous statement concerning the importance of the scope of conflict was made by E. E. Schattschneider, *The Semisovereign People* (New York: Holt, Rinehart, 1960).

38. On choosing cases, see Gary King, Robert Keohane, and Sidney Verba, *Designing Social Inquiry* (Princeton, N.J.: Princeton University Press, 1994), ch. 4.

39. I use the adjectives *broad-based* or *inclusive* rather than *universal* because, strictly speaking, no U.S. social program is universal, not even Social Security.

40. To be fair, neither of my inclusive cases covers as many people as Social Security or Medicare. Barely half of all workers are covered by company-based retirement plans, and barely two-thirds of all residential units are owner-occupied homes. Nevertheless, these two tax expenditures benefit far more peo-

ple than any means-tested program and are not restricted to the poor and near-poor.

41. The tax expenditure for employer pensions refers to the net exclusion of pension contributions and earnings from the taxable net income of private corporations. It does not refer to a variety of tax expenditures for employment-based benefits such as retirement plans for the self-employed (Keogh plans), group term life insurance, death benefits, and medical insurance. It also excludes the tax expenditure for Independent Retirement Accounts (IRAs), which are not tied to employment.

42. Some people mistakenly think of the Earned Income Tax Credit (EITC) as a type of negative income tax. The key difference between the two is that the EITC is available only to those with earned income. Negative income tax proposals typically guarantee all citizens, including those entirely dependent on public assistance, a minimum benefit. A more accurate definition of the EITC is wage subsidy.

CHAPTER 1
SIZING UP THE HIDDEN WELFARE STATE

1. A fundamental problem with any cross-national study is the inherent difficulty of comparing tax expenditures. The OECD essentially gave up the one and only time it tried to compare the tax expenditures of member countries. Instead of developing a standard measure of tax expenditures and grouping programs according to function, the OECD grouped programs by country and made no explicit comparisons. It found that the chief obstacle to making meaningful comparisons were the differences among countries' definitions of their normal tax structure and of deviations from that structure. Some countries, for instance, exempt certain foods from sales or value-added taxes and count these exemptions as tax expenditures. Other countries consider only exemptions from income taxes as tax expenditures (Organisation for Economic Cooperation and Development, *Tax Expenditures* [Paris: OECD, 1984]).

One might circumvent these definitional issues by comparing the mix of direct and indirect social spending within various welfare states. However countries choose to define tax expenditures, how much do they spend through the tax code versus appropriations? The aforementioned OECD study indicated enough variation within and across countries to make comparative study worthwhile. Canada, for example, spent almost twice as much on old age and disability programs via tax expenditures as it did via direct transfers in 1979. France, the United Kingdom, and the United States, by contrast, funded the majority of their old-age and disability programs through direct transfers. Interesting differences exist within countries as well. Compared with direct spending, tax expenditures were far more important in the area of old age and disability in Canada than in family allowances or unemployment. The chief impediment to comparisons of this sort is that the data are old and sometimes incomplete. The OECD has not published tax expenditure figures for years after 1980, so researchers must wade through the tax and budget documents of individual countries. In short, it is hard to declare with any certainty whether the United States still merits the laggard label once tax expenditures have been included.

2. The Earned Income Tax Credit and Targeted Jobs Tax Credit are among the few tax expenditures targeted at the poor, so readers who favor a minimalist definition of the welfare state may still be interested in these two cases.

3. This definition is similar to the one used, for example, by Theodore R. Marmor, Jerry L. Mashaw, and Philip L. Harvey in *America's Misunderstood Welfare State* (New York: Basic Books, 1990), and by Fred C. Pampel and John B. Williamson in *Age, Class, Politics, and the Welfare State* (Cambridge: Cambridge University Press, 1989).

4. Peter Flora and Arnold J. Heidenheimer, "The Historical Core and Changing Boundaries of the Welfare State," in idem., eds., *The Development of Welfare States in Europe and America* (New Brunswick, N.J.: Transaction, 1981), pp. 17–34.

5. Laws governing minimum wages, consumer protection, and collective bargaining are sometimes classified by social scientists as social programs but are omitted here as borderline cases that are hard to express in terms of dollars spent.

6. See, for example, Gosta Esping-Andersen, *The Three Worlds of Welfare Capitalism* (Princeton, N.J.: Princeton University Press, 1990), and Norman Furniss and Timothy Tilton, *The Case for the Welfare State* (Bloomington: Indiana University Press, 1977).

7. Both organizations consider the standard deduction and personal exemptions to be part of the tax baseline and not tax expenditures.

8. U.S. Congress, Joint Committee on Taxation, *Estimates of Federal Tax Expenditures, 1995–1999* (Washington, D.C.: Government Printing Office, 1994), p. 8.

9. This classification departs from the JCT list in a couple of ways. It shifts from commerce to income security the preferential tax treatment of investment income on life insurance and annuity contracts, under the assumption that it is analogous to tax expenditures for employer pensions, Social Security, and Individual Retirement Accounts. All of these programs are designed to assist individuals who face a reduction in income resulting from the retirement or death of a wage earner. The deferral of interest on U.S. savings bonds is included under the same rationale. The maximum tax rate on capital gains and especially the exclusion of capital gains at death similarly qualify as income security programs. Totaling almost $22 billion, they protect individual (as opposed to corporate) income and facilitate the transfer of wealth across generations. Readers who disagree with these judgments can subtract out these programs and find that my basic observations about the size and structure of the hidden welfare state remain valid.

Several tax expenditures for employment and training have been shifted to other functions as well. At least among social scientists, this category typically refers to programs that help people become employed (e.g., the Job Training Partnership Act) or support them temporarily when they become unemployed (e.g., unemployment insurance). Retaining this usage requires that we shift cafeteria benefit plans and employee awards to income security. The exclusion of rental allowances for ministers' homes, a very small program, probably belongs in the category of housing. What remain are benefits offered by voluntary employee organizations, usually supplementary unemployment benefits, and the Targeted Jobs Tax Credit.

10. Office of Management and Budget, *Analytical Perspectives, Budget of the United States Government, Fiscal Year 1995* (Washington, D.C.: Government Printing Office, 1994), p. 61.

11. Different assumptions about economic growth, individual and corporate behavior, marginal tax rates, and availability of more recent data can also create gaps between the JCT and Treasury/OMB estimates.

12. Quotation from Neil Gilbert and Barbara Gilbert, *The Enabling State: Modern Welfare Capitalism in America* (New York: Oxford University Press, 1989), p. 30, n. 13. For a more cautious approach, see John F. Witte, *The Politics and Development of the Federal Income Tax* (Madison: University of Wisconsin Press, 1985), pp. 283–84.

13. Ronald F. King, "Tax Expenditures and Systematic Public Policy: An Essay on the Political Economy of the Federal Revenue Code," *Public Budgeting and Finance* 4, 1 (Spring 1984): p. 18; Stanley S. Surrey and Paul R. McDaniel, *Tax Expenditures* (Cambridge, Mass.: Harvard University Press, 1985), p. 52.

14. These sums are based on the JCT list of tax expenditures and assume conservatively that budget outlay equivalent equals revenue loss for programs in which no estimates for budget outlay equivalence are available.

15. Again, some programs have been moved from their traditional place in budget documents. The direct expenditure figures in Table 1.2 do not include military pensions, which appear in budget documents under the category of income security. The figures for housing include a variety of mortgage credit programs that appear in the commerce section of the budget. And unemployment insurance has been moved from income security to employment and training, for reasons cited in note 9.

16. Office of Management and Budget, *Analytical Perspectives, Budget of the United States Government, Fiscal Year 1996* (Washington, D.C.: Government Printing Office, 1995), p. 23.

17. Not all SSI benefits go to the elderly.

18. John Myles, "Postwar Capitalism and the Extension of Social Security into a Retirement Wage," in Margaret Weir, Ann Shola Orloff, and Theda Skocpol, eds., *The Politics of Social Policy in the United States* (Princeton, N.J.: Princeton University Press, 1988), pp. 265–84.

19. But see Arnold J. Heidenheimer, Hugh Heclo, and Carolyn Teich Adams, *Comparative Public Policy*, 3rd ed. (New York: St. Martin's, 1990), ch. 4, for an unusually sophisticated comparison of housing policies.

20. Education in the United States is financed primarily by state and local governments.

21. In some cases the Treasury Department shares administrative responsibilities for tax expenditures with other agencies, especially Labor.

22. Salisbury points out that retirement pensions offered by local, state, and national governments account for a significant fraction of all pension assets,

income, and tax expenditures (Dallas L. Salisbury, "Pension Tax Expenditures: What Do They Buy?" *Benefits Quarterly*, no. 4 [1993]: 66–77).

23. Michael Peter Smith, *City, State, and Market: The Political Economy of Urban Society* (London: Basil Blackwell, 1988), p. 32.

The Gilberts speculate that tax expenditures fit better with the self-image of the middle classes than does direct spending. "Middle-class consumers differ from the traditional low-income clientele of social services insofar as their expectations are higher, their personal resources greater, and their needs more temporal. Middle-class consumers are accustomed to choice; they tend to prefer cash benefits and in-kind services delivered through a variety of providers, including profit-oriented agencies that allow the middle class to distance themselves psychologically and even physically from hard-core problem groups, from the shabbiness of many public service facilities, and from any notion that they are charity or welfare recipients" (Gilbert and Gilbert, *The Enabling State*, p. 39).

24. Technically, the figures in Table 1.3 refer to tax filing units, which could be individuals or households. That is why I refer vaguely to "people" in this paragraph.

25. Cited in Alain Enthoven, "Health Tax Policy Mismatch," *Health Affairs* 4, 4 (Winter 1985): 11.

26. Cited in Barbara L. Wolfe, "Reform of Health Care for the Nonelderly Poor," in Sheldon H. Danziger, Gary D. Sandefur, and Daniel H. Weinberg, eds., *Confronting Poverty: Prescriptions for Change* (Cambridge, Mass.: Harvard University Press, 1994), p. 254.

27. Calculated from U.S. House of Representatives, Committee on Ways and Means, *Overview of Entitlement Programs: 1994 Green Book* (Washington, D.C.: Government Printing Office, 1994), p. 33. Comparable estimates for 1992 can be found in David Pattison, "The Distribution of OASDI Taxes and Benefits by Income Decile," *Social Security Bulletin* 58, 2 (Summer 1995): 21–33.

28. Henry J. Kaiser Family Foundation, *The Medicare Program* fact sheet (December 1995).

29. Many scholars who dispute the origins and function of direct expenditure programs nevertheless agree that the overall structure is bifurcated. See, e.g., Michael K. Brown, "The Segmented Welfare System: Distributive Conflict and Retrenchment in the United States, 1968–1984," in idem., ed., *Remaking the Welfare State: Retrenchment and Social Policy in America and Europe* (Philadelphia: Temple University Press, 1988), pp. 182–210; Linda Gordon, "What Does Welfare Regulate?" *Social Research* 55, 4 (Winter 1988): 609–30; Russell L. Hanson, "The Expansion and Contraction of the American Welfare State," in Robert Goodin and Julian Le Grand, eds., *Not Only the Poor: The Middle Class and the Welfare State* (London: Allen and Unwin, 1987), pp. 169–202; Michael Katz, *In the Shadow of the Poorhouse: A Social History of Welfare in America* (New York: Basic Books, 1986); Jill Quadagno, *The Transformation of Old Age Security: Class and Politics in the American Welfare State* (Chicago: University of Chicago Press, 1988); David Brian Robertson and Dennis Judd, *The Development of American Public Policy: the Structure of Policy Restraint* (Glenview, Ill.:

Scott, Foresman, 1989), ch. 7; Weir, Orloff, and Skocpol, eds., *The Politics of Social Policy in the United States.*

30. Of the major programs in the visible welfare state, workers' compensation and unemployment insurance do not fit easily in the two-tiered model either, a fact seldom noted.

31. Although tax data are not reported by gender or race, it seems fair to infer that the income inequalities found in most tax expenditures mean that women and minorities receive far fewer benefits than their numbers might suggest.

32. Congressional Budget Office, *The Effects of Tax Reform on Tax Expenditures* (Washington, D.C.: Congressional Budget Office, 1988).

PART TWO: INTRODUCTION

1. This oft-used metaphor originated with Christopher Leman, "Patterns of Policy Development: Social Security in the United States and Canada," *Public Policy* 25 (1977): 261–91.

2. For good summaries of these alternative explanations, see Edwin Amenta and Theda Skocpol, "States and Social Policies," *Annual Review of Sociology* 12 (1986): 131–57; Hugh Heclo, "The Political Foundations of Antipoverty Policy," in Sheldon Danziger and Daniel Weinberg, eds., *Fighting Poverty: What Works and What Doesn't* (Cambridge, Mass.: Harvard University Press, 1986), pp. 312–40; and Jill S. Quadagno, "Theories of the Welfare State," *Annual Review of Sociology* 13 (1987): 109–28.

3. Perhaps the best way to capture the intensity and diversity of scholarly opinion is to review the debates over the enactment of the Social Security Act. See, for example, G. William Domhoff, "Corporate Liberal Theory and the Social Security Act: A Chapter in the Sociology of Knowledge," *Politics & Society* 15, 3 (1986–87): 297–330; J. Craig Jenkins and Barbara G. Brents, "Social Protest, Hegemonic Competition, and Social Reform," *American Sociological Review* 54, 6 (December 1989): 891–909; Frances Fox Piven and Richard Cloward, *Regulating the Poor* (New York: Vintage, 1971); Jill S. Quadagno, "Welfare Capitalism and the Social Security Act of 1935," *American Sociological Review* 49, 5 (October 1984): 632–47; Theda Skocpol and John Ikenberry, "The Political Formation of the American Welfare State in Historical and Comparative Perspective," *Comparative Social Research* 6 (1983): 87–148; and the exchange between Quadagno and Skocpol and Amenta in *American Sociological Review* 50, 4 (August 1985): 572–78.

4. E. E. Schattschneider, *The Semisovereign People* (New York: Holt, Rinehart, 1960).

5. A variety of corporate liberal explanations, some more nuanced than others, are represented by Edward Berkowitz and Kim McQuaid, *Creating the Welfare State: The Political Economy of 20th-Century Reform*, rev. ed. (Lawrence: University Press of Kansas, 1992); Domhoff, "Corporate-Liberal Theory and the Social Security Act"; Colin Gordon, "New Deal, Old Deck: Business and the Origins of Social Security, 1920–1935," *Politics & Society* 19, 2 (June 1991):

165–207; Jill S. Quadagno, *The Transformation of Old Age Security: Class and Politics in the American Welfare State* (Chicago: University of Chicago Press, 1988); and James Weinstein, *The Corporate Ideal in the Liberal State, 1900–1918* (Boston: Beacon Press, 1967).

Students of tax policy point out that although business interests are not alone in seeking tax expenditures, they are more successful. Business influence results from greater access to the revenue committees, which is in turn a function of money and expertise in tax matters. Concerning the origins of tax expenditures, see Jeffrey H. Birnbaum and Alan S. Murray, *Showdown at Gucci Gulch* (New York: Vintage, 1987); William L. Cary, "Pressure Groups and the Revenue Code: A Requiem in Honor of the Departing Uniformity of the Tax Code," *Harvard Law Review* 68, 5 (March 1955): 745–80; David G. Davies, *United States Taxes and Tax Policy* (New York: Cambridge University Press, 1986), p. 285; JoAnn Klimschot, *The Untouchables: A Common Cause Study of the Federal Tax Expenditure Budget* (Washington, D.C.: Common Cause, 1981); Ralph Nader Congress Project, *The Revenue Committees* (New York: Grossman, 1975), p. 109; Stanley S. Surrey, "The Congress and the Tax Lobbyist—How Special Tax Provisions Get Enacted," *Harvard Law Review* 70, 7 (May 1957): 1145–82. One scholar who questions the role of special interests in creating tax expenditures is John F. Witte, *The Politics and Development of the Federal Income Tax* (Madison: University of Wisconsin Press, 1985).

6. Concerning the role of Congress in blocking or diluting social welfare legislation, see note 25 in the introduction to this book. Some students of tax policy portray members of the revenue committees as little more than department store clerks: "Seekers of special tax breaks make a quick congressional shopping trip to the tax-writing committees where tax expenditures are designed" (Klimschot, *The Untouchables*, p. ii). Most of the tax policy literature cited in note 5 above also applies here.

CHAPTER 2
HOME MORTGAGE INTEREST AND EMPLOYER PENSIONS

1. The best modern accounts of enactment include John D. Buenker, *The Income Tax and the Progressive Era* (New York: Garland, 1985); Sven Steinmo, *Taxation and Democracy: Swedish, British, and American Approaches to Financing the Modern State* (New Haven, Conn.: Yale University Press, 1993); Jerold L. Waltman, *Political Origins of the U.S. Income Tax* (Jackson: University of Mississippi Press, 1985); and John F. Witte, *The Politics and Development of the Federal Income Tax* (Madison: University of Wisconsin Press, 1985).

2. Richard F. Goode, *The Individual Income Tax*, rev. ed. (Washington, D.C.: Brookings Institution, 1976); Bruce Lee Balch, "Individual Income Taxes and Housing," *National Tax Journal* 11, 2 (June 1958): 168–82; Boris I. Bittker, *Fundamentals of Federal Income Taxation* (Boston: Warren, Gorham & Lamont, 1981).

3. Steven E. Andrachek, "Housing in the United States, 1890–1929," in Gertrude Sipperly Fish, ed., *The Story of Housing* (New York: Macmillan, 1979), pp. 123–76.

4. Witte, *Politics and Development of the Federal Income Tax*, p. 87.

5. In addition to the sources cited in note 1, see Bennett D. Baack and Edward John Ray, "Special Interests and the Adoption of the Income Tax in the United States," *Journal of Economic History* 45, 3 (September 1985): 607–25; Roy G. Blakey and Gladys C. Blakey, *The Federal Income Tax* (London: Longmans, 1940), especially pp. 8–20; Gerald Carson, *The Golden Egg: The Personal Income Tax and Where It Came From, How It Grew* (Boston: Houghton Mifflin, 1977); Susan B. Hansen, "Partisan Realignment and Tax Policy, 1789–1976," in Paul Peretz, ed., *The Politics of American Economic Policy Making* (Armonk, N.Y.: M. E. Sharpe, 1987), pp. 233–57; Cordell Hull, *The Memoirs of Cordell Hull* (New York: Macmillan, 1948), especially pp. 48–71; Ronald Frederick King, "From Hegemonic to Redistributive Logic: The Transformation of American Tax Politics, 1894–1963," *Politics & Society* 12, 1 (1983): 1–52; Randolph E. Paul, *Taxation in the United States* (Boston: Little, Brown, 1954); Sidney Ratner, *A Political and Social History of Federal Taxation 1789–1913* (New York: W. W. Norton, 1942); and Stanley S. Surrey and William C. Warren, *Federal Income Taxation: Cases and Materials* (Brooklyn: The Foundation Press, 1955).

6. Income taxes were collected between 1862 and 1872. Roughly half came from New York, Massachusetts, and Pennsylvania (Baack and Ray, "Special Interests").

7. Although the Civil War income taxes ended in 1872, a few states imposed income taxes between 1872 and 1894.

8. Cited in Paul, *Taxation in the United States*, p. 33.

9. Buenker, *Income Tax and the Progressive Era*, ch. 1; Paul, *Taxation in the United States*, pp. 49–50; Ray M. Sommerfeld, Silvia A. Madeo, Kenneth E. Anderson, and Betty R. Jackson, *Concepts of Taxation* (Fort Worth: Dryden Press, Harcourt Brace College Publishers, 1993), pp. 46–48; Waltman, *Political Origins of the U.S. Income Tax*, p. 4. The *Pollock* ruling overturned *Springer v. United States* (1880), which held that the Civil War income taxes were not direct taxes and were therefore constitutional.

10. Cited in Sommerfeld et al., *Concepts of Taxation*, p. 47.

11. Cited in Waltman, *Political Origins of the U.S. Income Tax*, p. 4.

12. This is not to say that business leaders desired a corporate income tax, for even if they could pass on its cost, the resulting price increase might lower consumer demand. However, given the political necessity of choosing some type of income tax, the corporate tax was preferable.

13. Quoted in Baack and Ray, "Special Interests," p. 624. Aldrich was also the father-in-law of John D. Rockefeller, Jr.

14. By 1910 the sectional divisions started to break down as northern Democrats in Congress, representing middle- and working-class urban constituencies, became supporters of income taxation. In addition, the National Tax Association—composed of academics, corporate executives, and public officials, primarily from the Northeast—advocated national income taxes beginning in 1907 (Buenker, *The Income Tax and the Progressive Era*).

15. Witte, *Politics and Development of the Federal Income Tax*, p. 77.

16. U.S. Bureau of the Census, *Historical Statistics of the United States,*

Colonial Times to 1970, part 1 (Washington, D.C.: Government Printing Office, 1975).

17. Buenker, *The Income Tax and the Progressive Era*, p. 14.

18. "Income Tax Geography and Sectional Analysis," *Wall Street Journal*, December 25, 1914, p. 8. The combination of New York, Massachusetts, Pennsylvania, Ohio, Illinois, and Michigan accounted for 75 percent of individual income tax revenues and 36 percent of the population.

19. Buenker, *The Income Tax and the Progressive Era*, ch. 8.

20. Bittker, *Fundamentals of Federal Income Taxation*, p. 15; Buenker, *The Income Tax and the Progressive Era*, ch. 1; Roger A. Freeman, *Tax Loopholes* (Washington, D.C.: American Enterprise Institute, 1973), p. 71; Clarence F. McCarthy, *The Federal Income Tax: Its Sources and Applications*, 3rd ed. (Englewood Cliffs, N.J.: Prentice-Hall, 1974), p. 359.

21. Lawrence Goodwyn, *The Populist Moment* (New York: Oxford University Press, 1978).

22. This language was included in Treasury Decision 2090, issued December 14, 1914 (U.S. Department of the Treasury, *Treasury Decisions under the Customs, Internal-Revenue, and Other Laws*, vol. 27, no. 25 [Washington, D.C.: Government Printing Office, 1914], p. 47).

23. John J. Broesamle, *William Gibbs McAdoo: A Passion for Change, 1863–1917* (Port Washington, N.Y.: Kennikat Press, 1973); William G. McAdoo, *Crowded Years: The Reminiscences of William G. McAdoo* (Boston: Houghlin Mifflin, 1931).

24. Waltman, *Political Origins of the U.S. Income Tax*, p. 33.

25. Hull, *The Memoirs of Cordell Hull*. Hull (D-Tenn.) was a member of the House at the time.

26. "Alimony Is Subject to the Income Tax," *Wall Street Journal*, December 21, 1914, p. 2.

27. Congressional Budget Office (CBO), *Tax Policy for Pensions and Other Retirement Savings* (Washington, D.C.: Government Printing Office, 1987), pp. 131–32. Again, these provisions failed to generate any mention in the *New York Times*, which reported instead on the proposed changes in tax rates, surtaxes, the personal exemption, and the publicity of tax returns ("Senate Passes Bill Reducing Taxes By $456,261,000," *New York Times*, February 13, 1926, p. 1, and "Taxpayers Reduced 2,300,000 in Number," *New York Times*, February 13, 1926, p. 8).

28. CBO, *Tax Policy for Pensions*; Charles L. Dearing, *Industrial Pensions* (Washington, D.C.: Brookings Institution, 1954); Beth Stevens, "Blurring the Boundaries: How the Federal Government Has Influenced Welfare Benefits in the Private Sector," in Margaret Weir, Ann Shola Orloff, and Theda Skocpol, eds., *The Politics of Social Policy in the United States* (Princeton, N.J.: Princeton University Press, 1988), pp. 123–48.

29. The origins of this tax expenditure have been pieced together from the following sources: Nancy J. Altman, "Rethinking Retirement Income Policies: Nondiscrimination, Integration, and the Quest for Worker Security," *Tax Law Review* 42 (Spring 1987): 435–508; Blakey and Blakey, *The Federal Income Tax*; CBO, *Tax Policy for Pensions*, Appendix A; Dearing, *Industrial Pensions*; Wil-

liam C. Greenough and Francis P. King, *Pension Plans and Public Policy* (New York: Columbia University Press, 1976); King, "From Redistributive to Hegemonic Logic"; Sophie B. Korczyk, *Retirement Security and Tax Policy* (Washington, D.C.: Employee Benefits Research Institute, 1984); Murray Webb Latimer, *Industrial Pension Systems in the United States and Canada* (New York: Industrial Relations Counselors, 1932); Arthur S. Link, *Woodrow Wilson and the Progressive Era, 1900–1917* (New York: Harper & Brothers, 1954), especially pp. 192–96; Alicia H. Munnell, *The Economics of Private Pensions* (Washington, D.C.: Brookings Institution, 1982); Hugh Holleman Macauley, *Fringe Benefits and Their Federal Tax Treatment* (New York: Columbia University Press, 1959); Paul, *Taxation in the United States*; Benjamin G. Rader, "Federal Taxation in the 1920s: A Re-examination," *The Historian* 33, 3 (May 1971): 415–35; Rainard B. Robbins, *Impact of Taxes on Industrial Pension Plans* (New York: Industrial Relations Counselors, 1949); Steinmo, *Taxation and Democracy*; Stevens, "Blurring the Boundaries"; Waltman, *Political Origins of the U.S. Income Tax*; and Witte, *The Politics and Development of the Federal Income Tax*.

30. Altman, "Rethinking Retirement Income Policies," p. 447.

31. Korczyk, *Retirement Security and Tax Policy*, p. 17; Latimer, *Industrial Pension Systems*, p. 42; Greenough and King, *Pension Plans and Public Policy*, pp. 30–31. Add in agricultural workers and the percentage drops below 3 percent for the entire labor force.

32. Jill Quadagno, *The Transformation of Old Age Security: Class and Politics in the American Welfare State* (Chicago: University of Chicago Press, 1988), pp. 79, 83. See also Robbins, *Impact of Taxes*, pp. 3–5, and Greenough and King, *Pension Plans and Public Policy*, pp. 33–38.

33. Robbins, *Impact of Taxes on Industrial Pension Plans*, pp. 11–12, makes this same point.

34. King, "From Redistributive to Hegemonic Logic." Andrew Mellon's treatise, *Taxation: The People's Business* (1924), best articulated the view that the tax system should promote investment rather than income redistribution. Mellon, a wealthy financier and industrialist, served as Treasury Secretary from 1921 to 1932.

35. David Brody, *Workers in Industrial America* (New York: Oxford University Press, 1980), pp. 48–81.

36. Greenough and King, *Pension Plans and Public Policy*, p. 30. See also Quadagno, *Transformation of Old-Age Security*, pp. 91–96.

37. King, "From Redistributive to Hegemonic Logic," p. 22.

38. Waltman, *Political Origins of the U.S. Income Tax*, pp. 34, 35.

39. Blakey and Blakey, *The Federal Income Tax*, p. 191.

40. Steinmo, *Taxation and Democracy*, pp. 93–96. Steinmo also notes that Democrats found the strategy of targeting tax relief to local constituencies appealing as well.

41. Robbins, *Impact of Taxes*, p. 71. Treasury officials may have set a precedent for this move in 1920 when they ruled that premiums paid by employers on group life insurance for their employees were deductible (Macauley, Jr., *Fringe Benefits and Their Federal Tax Treatment*, p. 24).

42. Stevens, "Blurring the Boundaries," p. 128.

43. For evidence that other nations also rolled back taxes on the rich and corporations after the war, see Steinmo, *Taxation and Democracy.*

44. The Ways and Means committee report accompanying the Revenue Act states that "the Nation is now passing through the trying period of liquidation and readjustment. The reduction of the tax burdens is essential to business recovery" (cited in J. S. Seidman, *Seidman's Legislative History of Federal Income Tax Laws, 1938–1861* [New York: Prentice-Hall, 1938], p. 776). See also the *Congressional Record*, August 17, 1921, pp. 5125–46, and August 18, 1921, pp. 5175–92; U.S. House of Representatives, Committee on Ways and Means, *Revenue Bill of 1921*, August 16, 1921; U.S. Senate, Committee on Finance, *Revenue Act of 1921* (Washington, D.C.: Government Printing Office, 1921); U.S. Senate, Committee on Finance, *Internal Revenue Bill of 1921*, part 2, September 26, 1921.

45. *Congressional Record*, February 12, 1926, p. 3853. The general debate over the Revenue Act can be found on pp. 3831–96.

46. As an indication of McLean's leanings, see the *Congressional Record*, October 7, 1921, pp. 6089–94.

47. Michael Katz, *In the Shadow of the Poorhouse: A Social History of Welfare in America* (New York: Basic Books, 1986); James T. Patterson, *America's Struggle Against Poverty, 1900–1985* (Cambridge, Mass.: Harvard University Press, 1986).

48. Edward D. Berkowitz and Kim McQuaid, *Creating the Welfare State: The Political Economy of 20th-Century Reform*, rev. ed. (Lawrence: University Press of Kansas, 1992).

49. The tax expenditure for group term life insurance, created in 1920, functioned in a similar manner. For evidence that the tracks of public and private social provision also crossed at the state level, see Colin Gordon, "New Deal, Old Deck: Business and the Origins of Social Security, 1920–1935," *Politics & Society* 19, 2 (June 1991): 165–207.

50. Greenough and King, *Pension Plans and Public Policy*, p. 42.

51. Latimer estimates that by 1928, 20 percent of unionized workers in the United States and Canada belonged to a union offering retirement pensions, and 12 percent were actually covered (Murray Webb Latimer, *Trade Union Pension Systems* [New York: Industrial Relations Counselors, 1932], pp. 12–33).

52. The emphasis on the structural power of business and indirect influence is more consistent with the arguments of Fred Block and Charles Lindblom than it is with the corporate liberal arguments of James Weinstein and G. William Domhoff, who stress the direct influence of business elites on public policy.

CHAPTER 3
EARNED INCOME TAX CREDIT

1. "A Better Idea on Tax Credits," *New York Times*, July 3, 1990, p. A16.

2. Those who cite Long as the creator of the EITC include Alan Ehrenhalt, "Senate Finance: The Fiefdom of Russell Long," *Congressional Quarterly Almanac 1977* (Washington, D.C.: Congressional Quarterly, 1977), p. 182; Na-

thaniel C. Nash, "Yet Another Incarnation for a Versatile Tax Credit: Child Care Aid," *New York Times*, October 21, 1990, p. 28; Carmen Solomon, *The Earned Income Tax Credit (EITC)* (Washington, D.C.: Congressional Research Service, 1986); James R. Storey, *Refundable Tax Credits to Aid Working Poor Families* (Washington, D.C.: Congressional Research Service, 1989).

3. Regarding AFDC and the WIN program, see Mimi Abramovitz, *Regulating the Lives of Women: Social Welfare Policy from Colonial Times to the Present* (Boston: South End Press, 1988); Congressional Budget Office (CBO), *Employment Subsidies and Employment Tax Cuts* (Washington, D.C.: Government Printing Office, 1977); Frances Fox Piven and Richard Cloward, *Regulating the Poor* (New York: Vintage, 1971); Gilbert Steiner, "Reform Follows Reality: The Growth of Welfare," *The Public Interest* 34 (Winter 1974): 47–64. WIN represented the first official departure from the policy that all AFDC mothers should stay at home with their children.

4. Abramovitz, *Regulating the Lives of Women*, p. 341.

5. FAP guaranteed $500 for each adult and $300 for each child. The penalty for not seeking suitable training and employment was $300.

Regarding FAP, see Evelyn Z. Brodkin, *The False Promise of Administrative Reform* (Philadelphia: Temple University Press, 1986), pp. 24–28; Vincent J. Burke and Vee Burke, *Nixon's Good Deed: Welfare Reform* (New York: Columbia University Press, 1974); Theodore R. Marmor and Martin Rein, "Reforming 'The Welfare Mess': The Fate of the Family Assistance Plan, 1969–72," in Allan P. Sindler, ed., *Policy and Politics in America* (Boston: Little, Brown, 1973), pp. 3–28; Daniel P. Moynihan, *The Politics of a Guaranteed Income* (New York: Random House, 1973); "Nixon Administration Welfare Plan Not Enacted," *Congress and the Nation*, vol. 3, 1969–1972 (Washington, D.C.: Congressional Quarterly, 1973), pp. 622–27; "The Nixon Proposal for Major Public Welfare Revision: Pro & Con," *Congressional Digest* 49, 6–7 (June–July 1970); David A. Rochefort, "Responding to the New Dependency: The Family Assistance Plan of 1969," in Donald T. Critchlow and Ellis W. Hawley, eds., *Poverty and Public Policy in Modern America* (Chicago: Dorsey, 1989), pp. 291–303.

6. Cited in "Nixon Administration Welfare Plan Not Enacted," p. 623.

7. $1,600 − [($2,000 − $720) ∞ 0.50] = $960.

8. One scholar has observed that FAP's structure "reflected, among other things, the Administration's need to build a coalition among diverse interests. Indeed, FAP appeared to have something for everyone" (Brodkin, *False Promise of Administrative Reform*, p. 28).

9. According to Daniel Moynihan, one of the architects of FAP, Nixon was particularly disturbed by an article by Pete Hamill entitled, "The Revolt of the White Lower Middle Classes," which appeared in *New York* magazine in early 1969 (Moynihan, *The Politics of a Guaranteed Income*). For further discussion of the connections between the War on Poverty, white backlash, and the defection of white working-class voters from the Democratic Party, see Thomas Byrne Edsall with Mary Edsall, *Chain Reaction: The Impact of Race, Rights, and Taxes on American Politics* (New York: W. W. Norton, 1991), and Margaret Weir, "The Federal Government and Unemployment: The Frustration of Policy

Innovation from the New Deal to the Great Society," in Margaret Weir, Ann Shola Orloff, and Theda Skocpol, eds., *The Politics of Social Policy in the United States* (Princeton, N.J.: Princeton University Press, 1988), especially pp. 180–86.

10. Mothers with children younger than six years of age were exempted.

11. This discussion of Long's work bonus is based on *Congressional Record*, September 27, 1972, pp. 32470–77; "Nixon Administration Welfare Plan Not Enacted"; Solomon, *The Earned Income Tax Credit (EITC)*; Paul Terrell, "Taxing the Poor," *Social Service Review* 60, 2 (June 1986): 272–86. The estimated annual cost of the wage supplement and work bonus was $1 billion.

12. Personal interview with David Ellwood, November 1990.

13. At the time of Reagan's testimony, welfare reform in California was receiving national attention, much of it favorable. Subsequent evaluations were decidedly more critical.

14. Testimony of Gov. Ronald Reagan before the U.S. Senate, Finance Committee, *Social Security Amendments of 1971*, February 1, 1972, p. 1926. California, however, had not enacted any comparable tax measure as part of its welfare reform package.

15. According to Moynihan, one important result of the FAP debates was that many legislators learned about the connections between tax policy and social policy (*Politics of a Guaranteed Income*).

16. Jeffrey H. Birnbaum and Alan S. Murray, *Showdown at Gucci Gulch* (New York: Random House, 1987).

17. *Congressional Record*, September 30, 1972, pp. S33010, S33011.

18. Daniel Patrick Moynihan, *Family and Nation* (New York: Harcourt Brace Jovanovich, 1986), pp. 156–57.

19. Quoted in "Eleven Per Cent Social Security Increase Approved," *Congressional Quarterly Almanac* 1973 (Washington, D.C.: Congressional Quarterly, 1974), p. 579.

20. Ibid.

21. One can imagine several reasons why a vote for Long's proposal may have demonstrated strategic rather than sincere behavior. Some senators may have voted for Long so as not to anger a powerful committee chairman over a minor amendment; others may have voted for him knowing full well that the House would insist on deletion.

22. "Social Services Programs," *Congress and the Nation*, vol. 4, 1973–1976 (Washington, D.C.: Congressional Quarterly, 1977), pp. 414–16; "Eleven Per Cent Social Security Increase Approved."

23. More precisely, the measure was called the *Earned Income Credit*, a term some continue to use. For simplicity's sake I will refer to the Earned Income Tax Credit throughout this chapter, the name used by most government documents and observers. Initially the EITC was not a permanent tax credit; the overall purpose of the Tax Reduction Act was short-term fiscal stimulus, not long-term tax reform.

This discussion of the enactment of the EITC in 1975 relies on Colin D. Campbell and William L. Peirce, *The Earned Income Credit* (Washington, D.C.:

American Enterprise Institute, 1980); Saul D. Hoffman and Laurence S. Seidman, *The Earned Income Tax Credit: Antipoverty Effectiveness and Labor Market Effects* (Kalamazoo, Mich.: W. E. Upjohn Institute for Employment Research, 1990); Albert R. Hunt, "Conferees Scale Back Tax-Cut Bill; Oil and Some Other Issues Remain," *Wall Street Journal*, May 26, 1975, p. 3; Albert R. Hunt, "Congress Is Expected to Pass Tax Cut of $25 Billion to $27 Billion This Week," *Wall Street Journal*, March 24, 1975, p. 3; "Move Slated to Cut Social Security Tax," *New York Times*, January 6, 1975, p. 30; David E. Rosenbaum, "House Unit Votes Tax Cut of 8-Billion on '75 Income," *New York Times*, February 4, 1975, pp. 1, 23; Eugene Steuerle and Paul Wilson, "The Earned Income Tax Credit," *Focus* 10, 1 (Spring 1987): 1–8; "Tax Policy," *Congress and the Nation*, vol. 4, 1973–1976, pp. 91–96; U.S. Congress, Welfare Reform Subcommittee, *Administration's Welfare Reform Proposal*, part 1, September 20, 1977; U.S. Senate, Finance Committee, *Tax Reduction Act of 1975*, March 17, 1975; Tom Wicker, "The Rich Get Richer and Etc.," *New York Times*, February 11, 1975, p. 39.

24. In 1975 the poverty line was $4,293 for a family of three and $5,500 for a family of four.

25. Between January 1974 and January 1975, unemployment jumped from 5.2 to 8.2 percent, a postwar high. Real GNP fell 2.2 percent in 1974 and a whopping 9.1 percent in the fourth quarter. Inflation topped 12 percent for the year.

26. The payroll tax rate had risen 40 percent over the previous ten years, including a large jump from 5.2 to 5.85 percent in 1973.

27. These measures were favored over exempting more low-income workers from the payroll tax, which might complicate employer record-keeping and reduce the legitimacy of Social Security benefits for low-income workers.

28. "The Nixon Proposal for Major Public Welfare Reform: Pro & Con"; *Congressional Record*, June 22, 1971, pp. 21331–36.

29. "The credit is set at 10 percent in order to correspond roughly to the added burdens placed on workers by both employee and employer social security contributions" (U.S. Senate, Finance Committee, *Tax Reduction Act of 1975*, p. 11).

30. Ibid., p. 33.

31. Neither version of the EITC, however, provided benefits large enough to raise all its eligible population above the poverty line.

32. Charles H. Stewart III, "The Politics of Tax Reform in the 1980s," in Alberto Alesina and Geoffrey Carliner, eds., *Politics and Economics in the 1980s* (Chicago: University of Chicago Press, 1991), pp. 155, 156. See also Catherine E. Rudder, "Tax Policy: Structure and Choice," in Allen Schick, ed., *Making Economic Policy in Congress* (Washington, D.C.: American Enterprise Institute, 1983), pp. 196–220.

33. "Ways and Means Panel: No Longer Pre-eminent," *Congress and the Nation*, vol. 4, 1973–1976 (Washington, D.C.: Congressional Quarterly, 1977), p. 100.

34. Ehrenhalt, "Senate Finance: The Fiefdom of Russell Long."

35. John Kingdon, *Agendas, Alternatives, and Public Policies* (Boston: Little, Brown, 1984).

36. Catherine Rudder, "The Policy Impact of Reform of the Committee on Ways and Means," in Leroy N. Rieselbach, ed., *Legislative Reform: The Policy Impact* (Lexington, Mass.: Lexington Books, 1978), pp. 73–89.

37. Brodkin, *False Promise of Administrative Reform*; Ronald Randall, "Presidential Power versus Bureaucratic Intransigence: The Influence of the Nixon Administration on Welfare Policy," *American Political Science Review* 73, 3 (September 1979): 795–810.

CHAPTER 4
TARGETED JOBS TAX CREDIT

1. The best account of the origin of the New Jobs Tax Credit is Emil M. Sunley, "A Tax Preference Is Born: A Legislative History of the New Jobs Tax Credit," in Henry J. Aaron and Michael J. Boskin, eds., *The Economics of Taxation* (Washington, D.C.: Brookings Institution, 1980), pp. 391–408. See also Congressional Budget Office, *Employment Subsidies and Employment Tax Credits* (Washington, D.C.: Government Printing Office, 1977); Judy Gardner and Mary Eisner Eccles, "Carter Stimulus Plan: Some Questions Remain," *Congressional Quarterly Weekly Report* 35, 3 (January 15, 1977): 95–98; John Pierson, "That Controversial Job Tax Credit," *Wall Street Journal*, February 8, 1977, p. 20; Robert J. Samuelson, "Carter's Early Economic Choices—It's as Simple as 2 + 2 = 5," *National Journal* 9, 2 (January 8, 1977): 59–65; Eileen Shanahan, "A Plan for Aid in Many Fields," *New York Times*, January 8, 1977, p. A1; Herbert Stein, *Presidential Economics*, 2nd ed. (Washington, D.C.: American Enterprise Institute, 1988); U.S. Departments of Labor and Treasury, *The Use of Tax Subsidies for Employment* (Washington, D.C.: Government Printing Office, 1986); U.S. Senate, Finance Committee, *Summary of Testimony on H.R. 3477 and the Administration's Economic Stimulus Program*, March 14, 1977; U.S. Senate, Finance Committee, *Tax Reduction and Simplification Act of 1977*, March 8–11, 1977; U.S. Senate, Select Committee on Small Business, *Impact of the Administration's Tax Stimulus Package on Small Business and Examination of Employment Tax Credit Alternatives*, February 22, 1977; John F. Witte, *The Politics and Development of the Federal Income Tax* (Madison: University of Wisconsin Press, 1985).

2. State and local governments became prime advocates of targeted employment and training programs, which they administered, as spending by the national government increased in the 1960s and 1970s (Gary Mucciaroni, *The Political Failure of Employment Policy, 1945–1982* [Pittsburgh: University of Pittsburgh Press, 1990]).

3. Sunley, "A Tax Preference Is Born," p. 392.

4. Shanahan, "Plan for Aid in Many Fields," p. A1.

5. Sunley, "A Tax Preference Is Born," p. 394.

6. Pierson, "That Controversial Job Tax Credit," p. 20.

7. Charles Schultze, *The Public Use of Private Interest* (Washington, D.C.: Brookings Institution, 1977).

8. *Congressional Record*, May 16, 1969, pp. 12875–79; "Tax Credit Pros and Cons," *Congress and the Nation*, vol. 2, 1965–1968 (Washington, D.C.: Congressional Quarterly, 1969), p. 737.

9. Some of these latter economists were familiar with recent experiments with wage subsidies in Western Europe, some of which relied on the tax code. See, for example, John Bishop and Robert Haveman, "Selective Employment Subsidies: An Assessment of NJTC and TETC," in U.S. Senate, Finance Committee and Select Committee on Small Business, *Jobs Tax Credit*, July 26, 1978; Daniel Hamermesh, "Subsidies for Jobs in the Private Sector," in John Palmer, ed., *Creating Jobs: Public Employment Programs and Wage Subsidies* (Washington, D.C.: Brookings Institution, 1978), pp. 87–122; Robert H. Haveman and Gregory B. Christainsen, "Public Employment and Wage Subsidies in Western Europe and the U.S.: What We're Doing and What We Know," in National Commission for Manpower Policy, *European Labor Market Policies* (Washington, D.C.: National Commission for Manpower Policy, 1978), pp. 261–345; and Beatrice G. Reubens, *The Hard-to-Employ: European Programs* (New York: Columbia University Press, 1970), ch. 7.

10. "Labor Letter," *Wall Street Journal*, January 7, 1975, p. 1. These recommendations probably resulted from a Labor Department experiment with wage subsidies conducted between 1969 and 1975 (Hamermesh, "Subsidies for Jobs in the Private Sector," pp. 96–97).

11. *Congressional Record*, March 11, 1976, pp. 6170, 6172, 6356–57, and May 6, 1976, p. 12917.

12. Congressional Budget Office, *Employment Subsidies and Employment Tax Credits*, p. 62. However, the model used to generate these predictions included several questionable assumptions that contributed to their optimistic forecast: no cyclical economic fluctuations or short-term employer adjustments; no windfall benefits to employers; and a uniformly high demand for labor.

An interesting study published in 1977 suggested that had an employment tax credit been enacted in 1962 rather than the investment tax credit, the number of jobs created would have been greater (Jonathan R. Kesselman, Samuel H. Williamson, and Ernst R. Berndt, "Tax Credits for Employment Rather Than Investment," *American Economic Review* 67 [June 1977]: 339–49).

13. During December 1976, business executive Irving Shapiro of DuPont unsuccessfully tried to persuade Carter to target employment tax incentives at firms that hired disadvantaged workers and even suggested imposing a quota for hiring such workers (Eileen Shanahan, "Candidates for Next Cabinet," *New York Times*, December 3, 1976, p. A20).

14. U.S. Senate, Select Committee on Small Business, *Impact of the Administration's Tax Stimulus Package on Small Business and Examination of Employment Tax Credit Alternatives*, February 22, 1977. See also Sunley, "A Tax Preference is Born"; and O'Neill, "Employment Tax Credit Programs."

15. This section of the bill incorporated parts of the proposed Handicapped Employment Act of 1977, sponsored by Rep. Harold Ford (D-Tenn.), which was modeled explicitly after the WIN tax credit passed in 1971 (*Congressional Record*, February 17, 1977, pp. 4683–84 and March 7, 1977, p. 6553).

16. Regarding the origins of the TJTC, see "Carter Urban Policy: A 'Smorgasbord' . . .," *Congress and the Nation*, vol. 5, 1977–1980 (Washington, D.C.: Congressional Quarterly, 1981), pp. 440–41; Edward Cowan, "Tax Cut in 1979 of $16.3 Billion Gains in House," *New York Times*, July 28, 1978, pp. A1, D2; Martha V. Gottron, ed., *Budgeting for America* (Washington, D.C.: Congressional Quarterly, 1982); David McKay, *Domestic Policy and Ideology: Presidents and the American State 1964–1987* (Cambridge: Cambridge University Press, 1989); "1978 Tax Cut Bill," *Congress and the Nation*, vol. 5, 1977–1980 (Washington, D.C.: Congressional Quarterly, 1981), pp. 238–44; John Pierson, "Ways and Means Panel Approves $16 Billion Tax Cut; Including Capital-Gains Relief Carter Vowed to Veto," *Wall Street Journal*, July 28, 1978, p. 3; U.S. House of Representatives, Conference Report, *Revenue Act of 1978*, October 15, 1978; U.S. Senate, Finance Committee, *Revenue Act of 1978*, August 17, 21–25, September 6, and October 1, 1978; U.S. Senate, Finance Committee, Subcommittee on Administration of the Internal Revenue Code and Senate Select Committee on Small Business, *Jobs Tax Credit*, July 18 and 26, 1978; U.S. Senate, Finance Committee, Subcommittee on Economic Growth, Employment and Revenue Sharing, *Targeted Jobs Tax Credit*, April 3, 1981; Sunley, "A Tax Preference Is Born"; Gordon L. Weil, *The Welfare Debate of 1978* (White Plains, N.Y.: Institute for Socioeconomic Studies, 1978); Witte, *Politics and Development of the Federal Income Tax.*

17. Statement of Emil M. Sunley, Deputy Assistant Secretary of the Treasury for Tax Policy, before the U.S. Senate, Finance Committee, *Jobs Tax Credit*, July 26, 1978, p. 95.

18. Oddly, no one mentioned lessons learned from the WIN tax credit, which had been in effect since 1971.

19. Subsequent analysis of Proposition 13 indicated that voters in California wanted lower taxes but no reduction in the level of public services. Politicians in Washington heard only the first part of this message (David O. Sears and Jack Citrin, *Tax Revolt: Something for Nothing in California* [Cambridge: Harvard University Press, 1982]).

20. In retrospect one can see that the Revenue Act of 1978 served as an important transition from the tax policies of the New Deal era to the Economic Recovery and Tax Act of 1981.

21. See, for example, Rangel's comments in U.S. Congress, Welfare Reform Subcommittee, *Administration's Welfare Reform Proposal*, part 1, September 21, 1977, pp. 475–78, and part 2, September 29, 1977, pp. 753–62.

22. In a memo to President Carter, HEW Secretary Califano observed in 1978 that "Ullman does not like paying government cash to individuals who are employed. I think he recognizes the need [for welfare reform] in terms of preserving incentives to work, but he prefers trying to do this by additional tax credits for employers (along the lines of the tax credit [i.e., the TJTC] he placed in your fiscal stimulus legislation) or by paying cash to employers to pay employees" (quoted in Laurence E. Lynn, Jr., and David deF. Whitman, *The President as Policymaker: Jimmy Carter and Welfare Reform* [Philadelphia: Temple University Press, 1981], p. 222).

23. Personal interview with Bill Signer, August 1990.

24. For evidence that ex-offender groups did not lobby at any point to be included in the TJTC, see James B. Jacobs, Richard McGahey, and Robert Minion, "Ex-Offender Employment, Recidivism, and Manpower Policy: CETA, TJTC, and Future Initiatives," *Crime and Delinquency* 30, 4 (October 1984): 486–506.

25. Some authors also mention the Area Redevelopment Act of 1961 and Public Works Acceleration Act of 1962 as triggers for this second burst of employment and training programs. However, both these programs were short-lived and poorly funded compared with the MDTA and EOA, and neither was incorporated into CETA.

26. This discussion of the origins of the MDTA is based largely on Mucciaroni, *Political Failure of Employment Policy, 1945–1982*, and James L. Sundquist, *Politics and Policy: The Eisenhower, Kennedy, and Johnson Years* (Washington, D.C.: Brookings Institution, 1968).

27. Organized labor did sponsor a march on Washington in 1958 demanding that officials do something about unemployment, but they were more interested in aggregate demand policies than targeted employment and training programs.

28. See, for example, Frances Fox Piven and Richard A. Cloward, *Regulating the Poor* (New York: Vintage 1971); and Carl M. Brauer, "Kennedy, Johnson, and the War on Poverty," *Journal of American History* 69, 1 (June 1982): 98–119.

PART THREE: INTRODUCTION

1. Although some readers may want to read only one or two cases of specific interest, it helps to read all of them in sequence. For example, some of the more important developments to employer pensions (chapter 6) also affected home mortgage interest and are explained more fully in chapter 5.

2. See, for example, Michael K. Brown, "The Segmented Welfare System: Distributive Conflict and Retrenchment in the United States, 1968–1984," in idem., ed., *Remaking the Welfare State: Retrenchment and Social Policy in America and Europe* (Philadelphia: Temple University Press, 1988), pp. 182–210; Theda Skocpol, "Targeting Within Universalism: Politically Viable Policies to Combat Poverty in the United States," in Christopher Jencks and Paul E. Peterson, eds., *The Urban Underclass* (Washington, D.C.: Brookings Institution, 1991), pp. 411–36. To see this process at work in European welfare states, see Gosta Esping-Andersen, *Politics Against Markets* (Princeton, N.J.: Princeton University Press, 1985).

3. Inclusive programs thus fall in the category James Q. Wilson calls "majoritarian politics." An early version of Wilson's typology of policies appears in *Political Organizations* (New York: Basic Books, 1973). A more recent application, focusing on public agencies, appears in *Bureaucracy* (New York: Basic Books, 1989), especially ch. 5.

4. Martha Derthick, *Policymaking for Social Security* (Washington, D.C.: Brookings Institution, 1979). For a more critical appraisal of bureaucrats' actions, see Jerry Cates, *Insuring Inequality: Administrative Leadership in Social*

Security, 1935–54 (Ann Arbor: University of Michigan Press, 1983); and Carolyn Weaver, "The Social Security Bureaucracy in Triumph and in Crisis," in Louis Galambos, ed., *The New American State: Bureaucracies and Policies since World War II* (Baltimore: The Johns Hopkins University Press, 1987), pp. 54–84.

5. Paul Pierson, *Dismantling the Welfare State? Reagan, Thatcher, and the Politics of Retrenchment* (Cambridge: Cambridge University Press, 1994); Michael Weisskopf and David Maraniss, "Republican Leaders Win Battle by Defining Terms of Combat; Medicare Pitch Became 'Preserve and Protect,'" *Washington Post*, October 29, 1995, p. A1.

6. Sidney Verba, Kay Lehman Schlozman, and Henry Brady, *Voice and Equality* (Cambridge, Mass.: Harvard University Press, 1995).

7. Helene Slessarev, "Racial Tensions and Institutional Support: Social Programs during a Period of Retrenchment," in Margaret Weir, Ann Shola Orloff, and Theda Skocpol, eds., *The Politics of Social Policy in the United States* (Princeton, N.J.: Princeton University Press, 1988), pp. 357–79; R. Kent Weaver, "Controlling Entitlements," in John Chubb and Paul Peterson, eds., *The New Direction in American Politics* (Washington, D.C.: Brookings Institution, 1985), pp. 307–41.

8. Herman B. Leonard, *Checks Unbalanced: The Quiet Side of Public Spending* (New York: Basic Books, 1986); Stanley S. Surrey and Paul R. McDaniel, *Tax Expenditures* (Cambridge, Mass.: Harvard University Press, 1985).

9. Witte found interesting variations among tax expenditures after their enactment. Based on a sample of eighty-nine tax expenditures, he found that "need-based" tax expenditures were less likely to be modified than "general economic stimulus" or "specific economic incentive" tax expenditures, meaning that those targeted at the poor tended to be more insulated than those targeted at corporations (John F. Witte, *The Politics and Development of the Federal Income Tax* [Madison: University of Wisconsin Press, 1985], pp. 311–21).

CHAPTER 5
HOME MORTGAGE INTEREST

1. The size of the home mortgage interest deduction also varies with interest rates. Because I am interested in accounting for the overall growth of the program over almost a century, I pay little attention to the short-run fluctuations in growth that occur as interest rates rise and fall. It is also, frankly, hard to know without rigorous quantitative analysis what the net effect of interest rates might be, for higher rates could mean higher interest costs for fewer home owners and lower rates could mean lower interest costs for more home owners.

2. Paul Pierson, *Dismantling the Welfare State? Reagan, Thatcher, and the Politics of Retrenchment* (Cambridge: Cambridge University Press, 1994), p. 45.

3. Social scientists have discovered that groups protecting benefits tend to be more successful than groups seeking benefits in the United States because the fragmented nature of political institutions favors the status quo and because individuals are more sensitive psychologically to losses than to gains.

4. *A Summary of the Evolution of Housing Activities in the Federal Government* (Washington, D.C.: U.S. Housing and Home Finance Agency, 1950).

5. C. Harry Kahn, *Personal Deductions in the Federal Income Tax* (Princeton, N.J.: Princeton University Press, 1960).

6. Ibid., p. 111.

7. Henry Aaron, *Shelter and Subsidies: Who Benefits from Federal Housing Policies?* (Washington, D.C.: Brookings Institution, 1972); Gertrude Sipperly Fish, "Housing Policy during the Great Depression," in idem., ed., *The Story of Housing* (New York: Macmillan, 1979), pp. 177–241; Barbara Miles, "Housing Finance: Development and Evolution in Mortgage Markets," in Congressional Research Service, *Housing—A Reader* (Washington, D.C.: Government Printing Office, 1983), pp. 45–65.

8. Sven Steinmo, *Taxation and Democracy: Swedish, British, and American Approaches to Financing the Modern State* (New Haven, Conn.: Yale University Press, 1993), p. 101.

9. Harry C. Bredemeier, *The Federal Public Housing Movement* (New York: Arno Press, 1980); Josephine Hedges Ewalt, *A Business Reborn: The Savings and Loan Story, 1930–1960* (Chicago: American Savings and Loan Institute Press, 1962); Fish, "Housing Policy during the Great Depression"; R. Allen Hays, *The Federal Government and Urban Housing*, 2nd ed. (Albany: State University of New York Press, 1995); Kenneth T. Jackson, *Crabgrass Frontier: The Suburbanization of the United States* (New York: Oxford University Press, 1985); Nathaniel S. Keith, *Politics and the Housing Crisis since 1930* (New York: Universe Books, 1973).

10. Cited in Jackson, *Crabgrass Frontier*, p. 204.

11. Fish, "Housing Policy during the Great Depression"; Keith, *Politics and the Housing Crisis since 1930*.

12. Committee on Ways and Means, *Overview of the Federal Tax System* (Washington, D.C.: Government Printing Office, 1990); William F. Hellmuth and Oliver Oldman, eds., *Tax Policy and Tax Reform: 1961–1969. Selected Speeches and Testimony of Stanley S. Surrey* (New York: Commerce Clearing House, 1973); Randolph Paul, *Taxation in the United States* (Boston: Little, Brown, 1954); Steinmo, *Taxation and Democracy*; John F. Witte, *The Politics and Development of the Federal Income Tax* (Madison: University of Wisconsin Press, 1985). There were also significant increases in corporate income taxes during World War II.

13. Kahn, *Personal Deductions in the Federal Income Tax*, p. 111.

14. Witte, *Politics and Development of the Federal Income Tax*, p. 123.

15. Kahn, *Personal Deductions in the Federal Income Tax*, p. 111.

16. Bredemeier, *Federal Public Housing Movement*; Leo Grebler, "Stabilizing Residential Construction—A Review of the Postwar Test," *American Economic Review* 39, 5 (September 1949): 898–910; Jackson, *Crabgrass Frontier*; Mary K. Nenno, "Housing in the Decade of the 1940s—The War and Postwar Periods Leave Their Marks," in Gertrude Sipperly Fish, ed., *The Story of Housing* (New York: Macmillan, 1979), pp. 242–67.

17. "These groups wanted to keep the organizational structure of federal housing activities splintered so that they could more easily control the individual

units without threat of interference from above by a strong administrator" (William E. Pemberton, *Bureaucratic Politics: Executive Reorganization during the Truman Administration* [Columbia: University of Missouri Press, 1979], p. 57).

18. Alvin H. Hansen, *The American Economy* (New York: McGraw-Hill, 1957), p. 32. Other stabilizers included unemployment insurance, deposit insurance for banks and savings and loans, and the progressive income tax. Hansen was the most important early proponent of Keynesian thought in the United States. For an earlier statement of Hansen's views toward residential construction and economic recovery, see his *Fiscal Policy and Business Cycles* (New York: Norton, 1941), especially pp. 83–95.

19. It increased slightly to 64 percent in 1980 and has since leveled off. U.S. Bureau of the Census, *Historical Statistics of the United States, Colonial Times to 1970*, part 2 (Washington, D.C.: Government Printing Office, 1975), p. 646; U.S. Bureau of the Census, *Statistical Abstract of the United States 1995* (Washington, D.C.: Government Printing Office, 1995), p. 733.

20. Albert Chevan, "The Growth of Home Ownership: 1940–1980," *Demography* 26, 2 (May 1989): 249–66, and studies cited therein; Richard Goode, *The Individual Income Tax*, rev. ed. (Washington, D.C.: Brookings Institution, 1976).

21. Kahn, *Personal Deductions in the Federal Income Tax*, p. 111.

22. Jack Walker, *Mobilizing Interest Groups in America: Patrons, Professions, and Social Movements* (Ann Arbor: University of Michigan Press, 1991).

23. For summaries of several of these criticisms, see Bruce Lee Balch, "Individual Income Taxes and Housing," *National Tax Journal* 11, 2 (June 1958): 168–82.

24. Boris I. Bittker, "Accounting for Federal 'Tax Subsidies' in the National Budget," *National Tax Journal* 22, 2 (June 1969): 244–61; Joseph A. Pechman, "Tax Reform: Theory and Practice," *Journal of Economic Perspectives* 1, 1 (Summer 1987): 11–28.

25. It also helped that Walter Heller, Kennedy's senior economic adviser, had earlier expressed similar concerns about tax preferences in his contribution to the *Tax Revision Compendium*. For evidence of continuing criticism of the deduction by public finance experts, see Melvin White and Anne White, "Horizontal Inequality in the Federal Income Tax Treatment of Homeowners and Tenants," *National Tax Journal* 18, 3 (September 1965): 225–39; Henry Aaron, "Income Taxes and Housing," *American Economic Review* 60 (1970): 789–806.

26. Hellmuth and Oldman, *Tax Policy and Tax Reform: 1961–1969.*

27. Cited in ibid., p. 30.

28. Cathie J. Martin, *Shifting the Burden: The Struggle over Growth and Corporate Taxation* (Chicago: University of Chicago Press, 1991); Herbert Stein, *The Fiscal Revolution in America*, rev. ed. (Washington, D.C.: American Enterprise Institute, 1990), ch. 17; "United States Tax Policy," *Congress and the Nation, 1945–1964* (Washington, D.C.: Congressional Quarterly, 1965), pp. 397–442.

29. Hellmuth and Oldman, *Tax Policy and Tax Reform: 1961–1969*, p. 40.

30. "Builders Oppose Exemption Limit," *New York Times*, February 9, 1963, p. 9; "Realty Men Call Tax Bill a Blow to the Homeowner," *New York Times*, February 20, 1963, p. 1; Stanley S. Surrey, *Pathways to Tax Reform: The Concept of Tax Expenditures* (Cambridge, Mass.: Harvard University Press, 1973), pp. 232–36.

31. Hellmuth and Oldman, *Tax Policy and Tax Reform: 1961–1969*, p. 59.

32. *Federal Income Tax Policy Positions of National Association of Home Builders* (Washington, D.C.: National Association of Home Builders, 1961).

33. William Lilley III, "The Homebuilders' Lobby," in Jon Pynoos, Robert Schafer, and Chester W. Hartman, eds., *Housing Urban America* (Chicago: Aldine, 1973), pp. 30–48.

34. Pierson also discusses this type of lock-in effect, based on previously established networks and knowledge acquired, in chapter 2 of *Dismantling the Welfare State?*.

35. Joseph Minarik, *Making America's Budget Policy: From the 1980s to the 1990s* (Armonk, N.Y.: M. E. Sharpe, 1990), pp. 156–57; Thomas J. Reese, *The Politics of Taxation* (Westport, Conn.: Quorum Books, 1980), pp. 14, 22–30; Surrey, *Pathways to Tax Reform*.

36. These details are recounted later in the *Congressional Record*, November 14, 1975, pp. 36778–80. The Tax Reform Act of 1969 made substantial changes to many tax expenditures, in part to address the kinds of problems raised by Surrey and Secretary Barr.

37. Skocpol argues that "widespread federated interests," like home builders, realtors, and lenders, are well positioned to influence public policy because of their "fit" with geographically fragmented political institutions (Theda Skocpol, *Protecting Soldiers and Mothers: The Political Origins of Social Policy in the United States* [Cambridge, Mass.: Harvard University Press, 1992], especially pp. 54–57).

38. Lilley, "The Homebuilders' Lobby."

39. An interesting note is that when the Treasury Department submitted a comprehensive tax reform plan in 1977, it recommended eliminating the tax expenditure for local property taxes on owner-occupied homes and keeping the home mortgage interest deduction. The Treasury study was started during the Ford administration and largely ignored during the Carter administration (David F. Bradford and the U.S. Treasury Tax Policy Staff, *Blueprints for Basic Tax Reform*, 2nd ed. rev. [Arlington, Va.: Tax Analysts, 1984], especially pp. 77–81).

40. In terms of revenues lost, the Joint Committee on Taxation estimated that the home mortgage interest deduction grew from about $3 billion in 1970 to $25 billion in 1985.

41. Hays, *The Federal Government and Urban Housing*, pp. 235–36. Housing programs aimed at the poor are not budgetary entitlements and thus are more vulnerable to annual cuts in appropriations than are tax expenditures like the home mortgage interest deduction.

42. Pierson, *Dismantling the Welfare State?*, pp. 87–89.

43. "Most Federal Help for Housing Goes to the Rich, Study Says," *Bureau of National Affairs Daily Report for Executives*, April 3, 1985, p. G-8.

44. Pechman, "Tax Reform: Theory and Practice," p. 11. The following discussion of the Tax Reform Act also relies on Jeffrey H. Birnbaum and Alan S. Murray, *Showdown at Gucci Gulch: Lawmakers, Lobbyists, and the Unlikely Triumph of Tax Reform* (New York: Vintage, 1987); "Congress Enacts Sweeping Overhaul of Tax Law," *Congressional Quarterly Almanac 1986* (Washington, D.C.: Congressional Quarterly, 1987), pp. 491–524; Timothy J. Conlan, Margaret T. Wrightson, and David R. Beam, *Taxing Choices: The Politics of Tax Reform* (Washington, D.C.: Congressional Quarterly, 1990); Kenneth R. Harney, "Don't Panic, Senate Tax Bill Isn't Set in Stone . . . Yet," *Washington Post*, May 17, 1986, p. E12; "Home Builders' Poll," *National Journal* 17, 21 (May 25, 1986): 1253; Martin, *Shifting the Burden*; Wendy Swallow, "Era of Special Benefits Seen Ending in Real Estate Industry," *Washington Post*, August 18, 1986, p. A8.

45. For some individuals and many companies, the deliberate cuts to tax expenditures offset the gains resulting from lower tax rates, producing higher effective tax rates.

46. Pechman, "Tax Reform: Theory and Practice," p. 19.

47. Brian P. Smith, "Mortgage Interest Deduction Reform Merits Analysis," *Savings & Loan News* 104, 3 (March 1983): 112–13.

48. Birnbaum and Murray, *Showdown at Gucci Gulch*, p. 57.

49. Swallow, "Era of Special Benefits Seen Ending."

50. James R. Follain and David C. Ling, "The Federal Tax Subsidy to Housing and the Reduced Value of the Mortgage Interest Deduction," *National Tax Journal* 44, 2 (June 1991): 147–68.

51. Congressional Budget Office, *The Effects of Tax Reform on Tax Expenditures* (Washington, D.C.: Congressional Budget Office, 1988).

52. Quoted in Wendy Swallow, "Proposal Would Affect Home Investment Plans," *Washington Post*, August 23, 1986, pp. E1, E6.

53. John Cranford, *Budgeting for America*, 2nd ed. (Washington, D.C.: Congressional Quarterly, 1989), p. 109; Jeannine B. McCrady, "Home Mortgage Interest: Recent Developments Complicate the Tax Maze," *The Tax Adviser* 19, 7 (July 1988): 488–91; Susan E. Woodward and John C. Weicher, "Goring the Wrong Ox: A Defense of the Mortgage Interest Deduction," *National Tax Journal* 42, 3 (September 1989): 301–13.

54. Robert Stowe England, "A Crack in the Foundation," *Mortgage Banking* 52, 6 (March 1992): 56.

55. It appears that realtors knew of the proposed cap on mortgage debt and chose to fight other parts of the reconciliation bill that affected their interests, a choice they later called a mistake (Phil Kuntz, "Mortgage-Interest Deduction: Still Sacrosanct?" *Congressional Quarterly Weekly Report* 47, 4 [January 28, 1989]: 155–60).

56. Quoted in John Betz Willmann, "The Washington Scene: Mortgage Tax Benefit Is Threatened," *Los Angeles Times*, September 11, 1988, p. 2. See also "Home Mortgage Interest Deduction Challenged," *National Mortgage News*, August 15, 1988, p. 2.

57. Kenneth R. Harney, "Forces rally over home deductions," *St. Petersburg Times*, December 11, 1988, p. 1H; Kuntz, "Mortgage-Interest Deduction: Still

Sacrosanct?"; Stephanie Saul, "Downey's Tale of Pressure Politics," *Newsday* (February 26, 1989), p. 13.

58. Louis Gerhardstein, Debra Cope, and Robert Trigaux, "Housing Groups Rally to Save Deduction," *The American Banker*, July 26, 1990, p. 4.

59. "Budget Adopted after Long Battle," *Congressional Quarterly Almanac 1990* (Washington, D.C.: Congressional Quarterly, 1990), pp. 111–66; England, "A Crack in the Foundation," pp. 52–62.

60. Michael Barone and Grant Ujifusa, *The Almanac of American Politics 1992* (Washington, D.C.: National Journal, 1991), p. 983.

61. Fellow Democrats from California, New Jersey, and New York were less enthused because many of their constituents had large mortgages and large itemized deductions.

62. England, "A Crack in the Foundation."

63. Peter Dreier and John Atlas, "Housing's Moment of Truth," *The American Prospect* 22 (Summer 1995): 68–77. For an earlier critique of the home mortgage interest deduction, see their article, "Deductio Ad Absurdum," *The Washington Monthly* (February 1990): 18–20.

64. "Mortgage Deduction Plays Essential Role," *Nation's Building News* 11, 8 (July 17, 1995): 1, 6.

65. Don DeBat, "Builders Relieved by Clinton Plan," *Chicago Sun-Times*, February 23, 1993, p. 33; "Bank Notes," *Bureau of National Affairs Banking Report* 61, 16 (November 1, 1993): 675. Remarkably, Bob Dole and then Bill Clinton proposed making tax free the first $500,000 in capital gains from the sale of a home. No lobbyist had suggested such a generous benefit for home owners, but a presidential election can make candidates do the unusual (Kenneth Harvey, "Tax Breaks for the Well-Off," *The Washington Post*, October 2, 1996, p. A17).

66. "A Flat Tax Could Wallop Home Equity," *Nation's Building News* 11, 8 (July 17, 1995): 1, 7.

67. Office of Management and Budget, *Analytic Perspectives. Budget of the United States Government, Fiscal Year 1996* (Washington, D.C.: Government Printing Office, 1995).

68. Its name notwithstanding, the recently formed Alliance for America's Homeowners is essentially a coalition of real estate and lending organizations (Peter Weaver, "Tax Tampering: Mortgage Deductions Targeted?" *St. Louis Post-Dispatch*, April 18, 1989, p. 7D).

CHAPTER 6
EMPLOYER PENSIONS

1. Important secondary works chronicling the development of private pensions, some of which mention their tax treatment, include Nancy J. Altman, "Rethinking Retirement Income Policies: Nondiscrimination, Integration, and the Quest for Worker Security," *Tax Law Review* 42 (Spring 1987): 435–508; Robert L. Clark and Ann A. McDermed, *The Choice of Pension Plans in a Changing Regulatory Environment* (Washington, D.C.: American Enterprise Institute, 1990); Congressional Budget Office (CBO), *Tax Policy for Pensions*

and Other Retirement Savings (Washington, D.C.: Government Printing Office, 1987); Charles L. Dearing, *Industrial Pensions* (Washington, D.C.: Brookings Institution, 1954); William Graebner, *A History of Retirement* (New Haven, Conn.: Yale University Press, 1980); Michael S. Gordon, "Overview: Why Was ERISA Enacted?" in U.S. Senate, Select Committee on Aging, *The Employee Retirement Income Security Act of 1974: The First Decade* (Washington, D.C.: Government Printing Office, 1984), pp. 1–25; William C. Greenough and Francis P. King, *Pension Plans and Public Policy* (New York: Columbia University Press, 1976); Alicia H. Munnell, *The Economics of Private Pensions* (Washington, D.C.: Brookings Institution, 1982); Jill Quadagno, *The Transformation of Old Age Security: Class and Politics in the American Welfare State* (Chicago: University of Chicago Press, 1988); Rainard B. Robbins, *Impact of Taxes on Industrial Pension Plans* (New York: Industrial Relations Counselors, 1949); and Beth Stevens, "Blurring the Boundaries: How the Federal Government Has Influenced Welfare Benefits in the Private Sector," in Margaret Weir, Ann Shola Orloff, and Theda Skocpol, eds., *The Politics of Social Policy in the United States* (Princeton, N.J.: Princeton University Press, 1988), pp. 123–48.

Although this tax expenditure covers pensions in the private and public sectors, the private sector is stressed far more in past studies of pensions, government documents, and this chapter.

2. Cited in Earl S. MacNeill, "Trends in the Pension Field: Legal, Functional, and Economic Developments," *Trusts and Estates* 80, 1 (January 1945): 65.

3. For the early history of Social Security, see Martha Derthick, *Policymaking for Social Security* (Washington, D.C.: Brookings Institution, 1979). Statistics taken from U.S. House of Representatives, Committee on Ways and Means, *Overview of Entitlement Programs* (Washington, D.C.: Government Printing Office, 1991), pp. 111, 113, 117 (hereafter known as *1991 Green Book*). Old Age Insurance (OAI) was renamed Old Age and Survivors' Insurance (OASI) after amendments made in 1939.

4. As a proxy for revenue losses or budget outlay equivalents, I will look at changes in the availability of pensions and in corporate tax rates. The size of this tax expenditure should be positively correlated with both these measures. I found no estimates for the early size of this program like those for interest on personal debt mentioned in the last chapter.

5. It also appears that the tax incentives were not large enough to change employers' behavior. According to Stevens, "Most employers were indifferent to the tax advantages. As late as the 1930s annuity salesmen, accountants, and pension counselors were finding that many employers were slow to see the advantages of pensions" (Stevens, "Blurring the Boundaries," p. 128). For a contrary view of corporate pensions during the Depression, see Frank R. Dobbin, "The Origins of Private Social Insurance: Public Policy and Fringe Benefits in America, 1920–1950," *American Journal of Sociology* 97, 5 (March 1992): 1416–50.

6. Congressional Budget Office, *Tax Policy for Pensions and Other Retirement Savings*, p. 132.

7. After being declared unconstitutional, this program was redesigned as part of the 1937 Railroad Retirement Act.

8. Study cited in Quadagno, *Transformation of Old Age Security*, p. 118. In addition, many plans unexpectedly switched from employer financing to shared financing between employers and employees ("Effect of Social Security Act on Company Pensions," *Monthly Labor Review* 50, 3 [March 1940]: 642–47).

9. Stevens, "Blurring the Boundaries," p. 129.

10. A few years prior to debate over the Clark amendment, a handful of corporate executives (e.g., Gerald Swope of General Electric and Henry Harriman of New England Power) proposed a mandatory system of private pensions as part of a larger program of economic recovery. They hoped to prevent the national government from providing such pensions and to ensure that all companies in a given industry had to bear the same costs that they did. Their plans were never implemented (Jill Quadagno, "Welfare Capitalism and the Social Security Act of 1935," *American Sociological Review* 49 [1984]: 632–47).

11. Roy G. Blakey and Gladys C. Blakey, *The Federal Income Tax* (London: Longmans, 1940); Ronald Frederick King, "From Redistributive to Hegemonic Logic: The Transformation of American Tax Politics, 1894–1963," *Politics & Society* 12, 1 (1983): 1–52; James T. Patterson, *Congressional Conservatism and the New Deal* (Lexington: University of Kentucky Press, 1967), pp. 58–76; Randolph E. Paul, *Taxation in the United States* (Boston: Little, Brown, 1954); Robbins, *Impact of Taxes on Industrial Pension Plans*; Herbert Stein, *The Fiscal Revolution in America* (Chicago: University of Chicago Press, 1969), pp. 74–90; Sven Steinmo, "Rethinking American Exceptionalism," prepared for the Conference on the Dynamics of American Politics, Boulder, Colo., February 20–22, 1992.

12. Paul, *Taxation in the United States*, p. 202.

13. Morgenthau quoted in Robbins, *Impact of Taxes*, p. 54. Treasury officials uncovered the potential for abuse by accident when they happened across articles in various trade magazines that touted the creative possibilities of pension trusts.

14. Robert R. Frei and James G. Archer, "Taxation and Regulation of Pension Plans under the Internal Revenue Code," *University of Illinois Law Forum* (Winter 1967): 699–700; Alicia H. Munnell, "Employee Benefits and the Tax Base," *New England Economic Review* (January/February 1984): 46, fn. 21.

15. Altman, "Rethinking Retirement Income Policies"; John K. Dyer, Jr., "Concept of Pension-Social Security Integration," in Dan M. McGill, ed., *Social Security and Private Pension Plans: Competitive or Complementary?* (Homewood, Ill.: Richard D. Irwin, 1977), pp. 123–33; Greenough and King, *Pension Plans and Public Policy*, pp. 60–63; Munnell, *Economics of Private Pensions*, pp. 10–15; Robbins, *Impact of Taxes*, pp. 15–23; Stevens, "Blurring the Boundaries"; John F. Witte, *The Politics and Development of the Federal Income Tax* (Madison: University of Wisconsin Press, 1985), pp. 110–20.

16. Stevens, "Blurring the Boundaries," p. 130.

17. Greenough and King, *Pension Plans and Public Policy*, p. 62.

18. "The Treasury Department argued: 'There are in our tax system certain provisions which grant relatively few of our people special advantages and privileges at the expense of the great mass who must pay what is thereby lost. . . . They are bad enough in time of peace—they are intolerable in time of war.' . . .

" 'The country will not tolerate retention of undue profits at a time like this, when millions are pledging their very lives to save and perpetuate our freedom' " (cited in Stevens, "Blurring the Boundaries," p. 132).

19. Stevens, "Blurring the Boundaries." This ruling created similar exemptions for vacation pay and contributions to life insurance policies. Jensen argues that the NWLB was legally prohibited from requiring companies to establish pension plans (Vernon H. Jensen, "Pensions and Retirement Plans as a Subject of Collective Bargaining," *Industrial and Labor Relations Review* 2, 2 [January 1949]: 229).

20. Munnell, *Economics of Private Pensions*, p. 10.

21. For an explicit contrast of the United States and the United Kingdom, see Edwin Amenta and Theda Skocpol, "Redefining the New Deal: World War II and the Development of Social Provision in the United States," in Margaret Weir, Ann Shola Orloff, and Theda Skocpol, eds., *The Politics of Social Policy in the United States* (Princeton, N.J.: Princeton University Press, 1988), pp. 81–122.

22. Nelson Lichtenstein, "From Corporatism to Collective Bargaining: Organized Labor and the Eclipse of Social Democracy in the Postwar Era," in Steve Fraser and Gary Gerstle, eds., *The Rise and Fall of the New Deal Order, 1930–1980* (Princeton, N.J.: Princeton University Press, 1989), pp. 122–52; Munnell, *Economics of Private Pensions*, p. 13; Quadagno, *Transformation of Old Age Security*, pp. 153–71; Stevens, "Blurring the Boundaries."

23. Munnell, *Economics of Private Pensions*, pp. 11–12; Stevens, "Blurring the Boundaries"; Beth Stevens, "Labor Unions, Employee Benefits, and the Privatization of the American Welfare State," *Journal of Policy History* 2, 3 (1990): 233–60.

24. Munnell, *Economics of Private Pensions*, pp. 11–12. At issue in this case was whether Inland Steel had the right to establish a pension unilaterally, outside its collectively bargained agreements with the union.

Before the NLRB ruling, several smaller unions had established pension plans through collective bargaining. Among these were Local 3 of the International Brotherhood of Electrical Workers (1941), garment workers (1944–45), and New York painters, photoengravers, and textile dyers (1946–48) (Robert Tilove, "Social and Economic Implications of Private Pensions," *Industrial and Labor Relations Review* 14, 1 [October 1960]: 26).

25. Stevens, "Labor Unions," pp. 235, 249.

26. Jeremy Rifkin and Randy Barber, *The North Will Rise Again: Pensions, Politics and Power in the 1980s* (Boston: Beacon Press, 1978), pp. 98–103.

27. Witte, *Politics and Development of the Federal Income Tax*, pp. 131–44; U.S. House of Representatives, Committee on Ways and Means, *Overview of the Federal Tax System* (Washington, D.C.: Government Printing Office, 1990).

28. Committee on Ways and Means, *Overview of the Federal Tax System*, p. 57.

29. "Appendix 1: Tables of Selected Aspects of Pensions," in John A. Turner and Daniel J. Beller, eds., *Trends in Pensions* (Washington, D.C.: U.S. Department of Labor, 1989), p. 357; Lichtenstein, "From Corporatism to Collective Bargaining." Using slightly different methodology, Woods estimates that pen-

sion coverage peaked at 50 percent in 1979 and declined to 46 percent by 1988 (John R. Woods, "Pension Coverage among Private Wage and Salary Workers: Preliminary Findings from the 1988 Survey of Employee Benefits," *Social Security Bulletin* 52, 10 [October 1989]: 17). In either case, the leveling off of pensions was unexpected. As a conservative guess, Tilove predicted in 1960 that pension coverage would reach 50 to 60 percent of the labor force by 1970 ("Social and Economic Implications of Private Pensions," p. 29).

30. Dearing, *Industrial Pensions*, pp. 45–54; Lichtenstein, "From Corporatism to Collective Bargaining"; Quadagno, *Transformation of Old Age Security*, pp. 162–71. In general, unions affiliated with the CIO were more interested in using corporate pensions to provoke employer support for Social Security than were unions affiliated with the AFL.

31. In addition, the Treasury issued several rulings clarifying the meaning of nondiscrimination rules between 1942 and 1954 (Alicia H. Munnell, "ERISA—The First Decade: Was the Legislation Consistent with Other National Goals?" *University of Michigan Journal of Law Reform* 19, 1 [Fall 1985]: 54).

32. Greenough and King, *Pension Plans and Public Policy*, p. 66.

33. Both quotations are from Greenough and King, *Pension Plans and Public Policy*, p. 66. See also "Employee Benefit Security Act of 1974," *Congressional Record* 120 (February 25, 1974): 3977–4001; Gordon, "Overview: Why Was ERISA Enacted?"; "Pension Plans," *Congressional Quarterly Almanac 1968* (Washington, D.C.: Congressional Quarterly, 1968), p. 529; Rifkin and Barber, *The North Will Rise Again*, p. 102.

34. The following account of events leading up to passage of ERISA is indebted to Gordon, "Overview: Why Was ERISA Enacted?" See also Merton C. Bernstein, "Private Pensions in the United States: Gambling with Retirement Security," *Journal of Social Policy* 2, 1 (January 1973): 1–12; Charles Culhane, "Industry, Labor Push Conflicting Approaches to Pension Legislation as Congress Nears Action," *National Journal* 4, 37 (September 9, 1972): 1415–26; Michael S. Gordon, "Introduction: The Social Policy Origins of ERISA," in Barbara S. Gutmann et al., eds., *Employee Benefits Law* (Washington, D.C.: Bureau of National Affairs, 1991), pp. lxiii-lxxxix; Peter Henle and Raymond Schmitt, "Pension Reform: The Long, Hard Road to Enactment," *Monthly Labor Review* 97, 11 (November 1974): 3–12; Sar A. Levitan and Martha R. Cooper, *Business Lobbies: The Public Good & the Bottom Line* (Baltimore, Md.: The Johns Hopkins University Press, 1984), ch. 5; "Private Pension Plans," *Congressional Quarterly Almanac 1971* (Washington, D.C.: Congressional Quarterly, 1972), pp. 683–85; Ray Schmitt, *Major Issues Facing the Private Pension System* (Washington, D.C.: Congressional Research Service, 1978), pp. 6–7.

35. The question of labor mobility arose because many pension plans required employees to remain with the same employer for many years, sometimes until retirement, in order to receive their pensions. These restrictions limited employees' ability to change jobs.

Gordon argues that Kennedy was influenced by the Commission on Money and Credit, a private organization whose report, *Money and Credit* (1961), called attention to the impact of pension funds on the economy ("Overview: Why Was ERISA Enacted?" pp. 7–8).

36. Charles Culhane, "Administration, Congress Feel Pressures for Tough Regulation of Private Pension Plans," *National Journal* 3, 21 (May 22, 1971): 1096–1105.

37. Henle and Schmitt, "Pension Reform," p. 3.

38. "The idea of public pension insurance . . . was apparently the brainchild of the United Auto Workers (UAW), whose president held a seat on the committee. The UAW experienced 113 pension plan terminations in the previous fifteen years, capped by its most celebrated termination at the Studebaker Corp" (Richard I. Ippolito, "A Study of the Regulatory Effect of the Employment Retirement Security Act," *Journal of Law and Economics* 31 [April 1988]: 117, n. 46).

39. Gordon, "The Social Policy Origins of ERISA," p. lxvii. Gordon was appointed by Javits in 1970 as minority counsel for pensions on the Senate Labor and Public Welfare Committee and served until 1975. Javits was one of the Republicans mentioned in chapter 4 who suggested in the late 1960s creating tax credits for employers who hired and trained disadvantaged workers.

40. Quoted in Julie Kosterlitz, "Promises to Keep," *National Journal* 19, 35 (August 29, 1987): 2138.

41. "Finance Committee Reports Gutted Private Pension Bill," *Congressional Quarterly Almanac 1972* (Washington, D.C.: Congressional Quarterly, 1972), p. 151. Critics argued that the sample taken in the study was too small to be meaningful.

42. Multiemployer plans covered all employees in a given industry. They were most common in industries like construction and trucking in which there were many small companies and considerable job mobility.

43. Henle and Schmitt, "Pension Reform," p. 4.

44. Bernstein, "Private Pensions in the United States," p. 11.

45. David Vogel, *Fluctuating Fortunes: The Political Power of Business in America* (New York: Basic Books, 1989), p. 137.

46. Martin Feldstein, "Toward a Reform of Social Security," *The Public Interest* 40 (Summer 1975): 75–95. Both *U.S. News and World Report* and the *Wall Street Journal* ran articles in the summer of 1974 suggesting the possibility of collapse. Feldstein argues that these fears were unfounded.

47. U.S. House of Representatives, Committee on Ways and Means, *Private Pension Tax Reform*, February 21, 1974, p. 104.

48. For a discussion of the major features of ERISA, see Clark and McDermed, *The Choice of Pension Plans*; Gordon, "Introduction: The Social Policy Origins of ERISA"; Ippolito, "A Study of the Regulatory Effect of the Employment Retirement Security Act"; Michael I. Richardson, "Employee Benefits Law: Securing Employee Welfare Benefits through ERISA," *Notre Dame Law Review* 61, 3 (1986): 551–71; Schmitt, *Major Issues Facing the Private Pension System*; U.S. Congress, conference report, *Employee Retirement Income Security Act of 1974*, August 12, 1974.

49. U.S. House of Representatives, Education and Labor Committee, *Employee Retirement Income Security Act of 1974* (Washington, D.C.: Government Printing Office, 1973), p. 1.

50. Gordon, "Overview: Why Was ERISA Enacted?" p. 18.

51. Quoted in James W. Singer, "New Pension Reform Enacted; Law Gets Mixed Reaction," *National Journal* 6, 35 (August 31, 1974): 1318.

52. ERISA also increased the significance of the judicial arena. Although these cases are far too numerous and complex to include here, the courts have clearly had a strong influence on the development of this program over the last two decades.

53. The most important of these regulations stipulated the minimum percentage of employees within a company that must be eligible for pensions; the minimum percentage of employees actually covered; vesting standards (i.e., the number of years of employment required to entitle employees to their pension, even if they change jobs); the extent of allowable discrimination in favor of higher-paid employees; the maximum annual contribution (in dollars) for defined contribution plans; the maximum annual benefit for defined benefit plans; the rate at which benefits can accrue over time; minimum funding standards; the taxation of pension benefits received by employees; penalties for early withdrawal of benefits; and penalties for receiving benefits that exceed the annual maximum. In addition, Labor Department regulations governing fiduciary standards and reporting requirements run about two hundred pages, as do regulations issued by PBGC. *Employee Benefits Plans under ERISA Federal Regulations* (New York: Prentice Hall, 1989).

54. U.S. Congress, Joint Committee on Taxation (JCT), *Present-Law Rules Relating to Qualified Pension Plans* (Washington, D.C.: Government Printing Office, 1990), p. 2.

55. Ethan Lipsig, Nancy E. Hezlep, and Nicolle R. Nelson, "A Comprehensive Approach to Qualified Plan Antidiscrimination Testing," *Tax Notes* 50, 6 (February 11, 1991): 649–61.

56. Personal interviews with David Certner, March 1992; Karen Ferguson, March 1992; Meredith Miller, March 1992; Sylvester Scheiber, March 1992; and Lisa Sprague, March 1992. Their frustration was echoed by the secretary of the retirement committee at a large university, who remarked: "I've been in the pension business twenty years, and we're reaching the point where I can't understand my actuary." Said one attorney specializing in ERISA, "The effort to decipher and comply with the standards has employers in a state of chronic discontent. . . . It's hard for me to articulate this stuff without getting people seriously upset." Both are quoted in Stephen Clark, "The Unintended Cost of Fairness," *Institutional Investor* 23, 12 (October 1989): 273.

57. Concerning the post-ERISA era, see Timothy B. Clark, "Congress Wonders Whether Uncle Sam Should Keep Subsidizing Fringe Benefits," *National Journal* 15, 26 (June 25, 1983): 1332–37; Clark and McDermed, *The Choice of Pension Plans*; Congressional Budget Office, *Tax Policy for Pensions and Other Retirement Savings*; Martin Donsky, "Congress Opens New Debate on Private Pension System," *Congressional Quarterly Weekly Report* 37, 11 (March 17, 1979): 450–56; Levitan and Cooper, *Business Lobbies*, pp. 80–90; Munnell, "ERISA—The First Decade"; Utgoff, "Proliferation of Pension Regulations"; personal interviews with David Certner, Karen Ferguson, Meredith Miller, Sylvester Scheiber, and Lisa Sprague, all in March 1992.

58. Vogel, *Fluctuating Fortunes.* Cathie J. Martin argues that this mobilization started earlier and was triggered by the efforts of Kennedy and Johnson officials to build business support for their economic and social policies (*Shifting the Burden: The Struggle over Growth and Corporate Taxation* [Chicago: University of Chicago Press, 1991]).

59. The Association of Private Pension and Welfare Plans, which represents large employers, actuaries, and pension consultants, was created in 1967 as soon as comprehensive reform seemed likely. The Association both lobbies and commissions studies concerning pensions.

60. U.S. Senate, Governmental Affairs Committee, *Department of Labor's Enforcement of ERISA,* June 25, 1985, p. 5. This statement was made by Robert Monks of the Labor Department.

61. "The 1990 Pensions Directory," *Institutional Investor* 24, 1 (January 1990) (supplement): 3–110.

62. Terry Moe, "The Politics of Bureaucratic Structure," in John E. Chubb and Paul E. Peterson, eds., *Can the Government Govern?* (Washington, D.C.: Brookings Institution, 1989), pp. 267–329.

63. Under 401k plans, companies match whatever contributions employees make. Because many employees cannot afford to make such contributions, these plans serve primarily higher-paid workers.

64. Archie Parnell, *Congress and the IRS: Improving the Relationship* (Washington, D.C.: Fund for Public Policy Research, 1980), pp. 9–10, 30–33.

65. President's Commission on Pension Policy, *Coming of Age: Toward a National Retirement Policy* (Washington, D.C.: President's Commission on Pension Policy, 1981). The House Select Committee on Aging also failed in a bid to make pension coverage mandatory (Warren Weaver, Jr., "Pension Laws Sought to Avert Social Security Gap," *New York Times,* March 30, 1981, p. B11).

66. Congressional Budget Office, *The Effects of Tax Reform on Tax Expenditures* (Washington, D.C.: Congressional Budget Office, 1988).

Chapter 7
Earned Income Tax Credit

1. David T. Ellwood, *Poor Support: Poverty in the American Family* (New York: Basic Books, 1988); Isaac Shapiro and Robert Greenstein, *Making Work Pay: A New Agenda for Poverty Policies* (Washington, D.C.: Center on Budget and Policy Priorities, 1989). For general arguments linking values and social policy, see Gaston Rimlinger, *Welfare Policy and Industrialization in Europe, America, and Russia* (New York: Wiley, 1971); Anthony King, "Ideas, Institutions, and the Policies of Governments: A Comparative Analysis," *British Journal of Political Science* 3 (1973): 291–313, 409–23; and Nathan Glazer, *The Limits of Social Policy* (Cambridge, Mass.: Harvard University Press, 1988), especially chs. 9 and 10.

2. For evidence that AFDC mothers believe strongly in the work ethic and act on it, see Christopher Jencks and Katherine Edin, "The Real Welfare Problem," *The American Prospect* 1 (Spring 1990): 31–50.

3. Benjamin I. Page and Robert Y. Shapiro, *The Rational Public* (Chicago: University of Chicago Press, 1992).

4. Analysts disagree over whether the 1980 election signaled a political realignment, a split realignment, or dealignment. This is not the place to evaluate those arguments. I am convinced that party leaders believed at the time that major electoral changes were under way and am persuaded by analysts, like Ladd, who see a profound weakening of party ties: "The New Deal realignment was accompanied by an unambiguous strengthening of Democratic loyalties in the electorate. In contrast the present one finds more and more people splitting their tickets and deciding their votes on grounds related to the candidates and issues in specific elections, rather than going down the line for their party. Party ties count for less today than at any point since a mature party system took shape in the United States in the 1830s" (Everett Carll Ladd, "The National Election," *Public Opinion* 11, 5 [January/February 1989]: 60). See also Walter Dean Burnham, "The 1980 Earthquake: Realignment, Reaction, or What?" in Thomas Ferguson and Joel Rogers, eds., *The Hidden Election: Politics and Economics in the 1980 Presidential Campaign* (Armonk, N.Y.: Pantheon, 1981), pp. 98–140.

5. Benjamin Ginsberg and Martin Shefter, *Politics by Other Means: The Declining Importance of Elections in America* (New York: Basic Books, 1990). Generally speaking, both parties chose not to mobilize new voters.

6. Harold W. Stanley and Richard G. Niemi, *Vital Statistics on American Politics*, 2nd ed. (Washington, D.C.: Congressional Quarterly, 1990), pp. 100–101.

7. Stanley B. Greenberg, "Plain Speaking: Democrats State Their Minds," *Public Opinion* 9, 2 (Summer 1986): 44–50. See also Thomas Byrne Edsall with Mary Edsall, *Chain Reaction: The Impact of Race, Rights, and Taxes on American Politics* (New York: Norton, 1991).

8. "Reagan's Polarized America," *Newsweek* (April 5, 1982): 16–19; Linda E. Demkovich, "Fairness Issue Will Be Campaign Test of Reagan's Record on Budget Policies," *National Journal* 16, 36 (September 8, 1984): 1648–53; U.S. House of Representatives, Committee on Ways and Means, Subcommittee on Oversight, *Federal Tax Treatment of Low Income Persons*, April 12, 1984.

9. Politicians also played up cultural issues such as race and abortion in order to appeal to the working poor.

10. John B. Gilmour, *Strategies of Disagreement in American Politics* (Pittsburgh: University of Pittsburgh Press, 1995), p. 54. This kind of party competition—two major parties competing for the same bloc of voters on the basis of specific issues and programs—differs from that discussed in chapter 2 with respect to the origins of tax expenditures for home mortgage interest and employer pensions. There, Democrats and Republicans competed to confer tax benefits on separate constituencies.

11. The EITC was extended by the Revenue Adjustment Act of 1975 and the Tax Reform Act of 1976, both times as minor amendments to larger revenue bills. Neither bill altered the basic structure of the tax credit.

12. David E. Rosenbaum, "Carter Asks New Welfare System with Emphasis on Required Work; New York Could Save $527 Million," *New York Times*, August 7, 1977, p. 1.

13. For PBJI, see David H. McKay, *Domestic Policy and Ideology: Presidents and the American State, 1964–1987* (Cambridge: Cambridge University Press, 1989); David A. Rochefort, "Responding to the New Dependency: The Family Assistance Plan of 1969," in Donald T. Critchlow and Ellis W. Hawley, eds., *Poverty and Public Policy in Modern America* (Chicago: Dorsey, 1989), pp. 291–303; U.S. Congress, Welfare Reform Subcommittee, *Administration's Welfare Reform Proposal*, part 1, September 20, 1977; part 2, September 29 and 30, and October 12, 1977; and part 3, October 14, 1977; Gordon L. Weil, *The Welfare Debate of 1978* (White Plains, N.Y.: Institute for Socioeconomic Studies, 1978); and "Welfare Reform," *Congress and the Nation*, vol. 5, 1977–1980 (Washington, D.C.: Congressional Quarterly, 1981), pp. 685–88.

14. Rosenbaum, "Carter Asks New Welfare System," p. 40.

15. Testimony of Laurence N. Woodworth, Assistant Secretary of the Treasury for Tax Policy, before the U.S. Congress, Welfare Reform Subcommittee, *Administration's Welfare Reform Proposal*, part 1, September 20, 1977, p. 377.

16. Harrison H. Donnelly, "House Votes Sharp Cuts in CETA Jobs Program," *Congressional Quarterly Weekly Report* 36, 32 (August 8, 1978): 2106–7.

17. This discussion of the EITC and the Revenue Act of 1978 is based on Edward Cowan, "Tax Cut in 1979 of $16.3 Billion Gains in House," *New York Times*, July 28, 1978, pp. A1, D2; Martha V. Gottron, ed., *Budgeting for America* (Washington, D.C.: Congressional Quarterly, 1982), pp. 180–82; McKay, *Domestic Policy and Ideology*; "1978 Tax Cut Bill," *Congress and the Nation*, vol. 5, 1977–1980 (Washington, D.C.: Congressional Quarterly, 1981), pp. 238–44; John Pierson, "Ways and Means Panel Approves $16 Billion Tax Cut; Including Capital-Gains Relief Carter Vowed to Veto," *Wall Street Journal*, July 28, 1978, p. 3; "Senate Panel Raises Personal Tax Exemption," *Wall Street Journal*, September 15, 1978, p. 3; U.S. Senate, Finance Committee, *Revenue Act of 1978*, October 1, 1978; U.S. House of Representatives, conference committee, *Revenue Act of 1978*, October 15, 1978.

18. According to Gene Steuerle, the changes proposed by Ways and Means stemmed from recommendations made by staff from its Subcommittee on Oversight and from the Treasury Department (phone interview, September 1991).

19. This theme was first picked up by the media during the 1981–82 recession. *Newsweek*, for instance, featured the anxious face of a young child on its cover of April 5, 1982. The headline read, "Reagan's America: And the Poor Get Poorer."

20. Removing low-income workers from the income tax rolls was one of four unconditional requirements Reagan made of any tax reform bill. The other three were reductions in corporate tax rates from 50 to 35 percent, retention of the home mortgage interest deduction, and revenue neutrality (Jeffrey H. Birnbaum and Alan S. Murray, *Showdown at Gucci Gulch* [New York: Vintage, 1987], pp. 116–17).

21. Birnbaum and Murray, *Showdown at Gucci Gulch*; Timothy J. Conlan, Margaret T. Wrightson, and David Beam, *Taxing Choices: The Politics of Tax Reform* (Washington, D.C.: Congressional Quarterly, 1990).

22. Mitch Daniels quoted in David R. Beam, Timothy J. Conlan, and Margaret T. Wrightson, "Solving the Riddle of Tax Reform: Party Competition and the Politics of Ideas," *Political Science Quarterly* 105, 2 (Summer 1990): 201.

23. Ways and Means Chairman Dan Rostenkowski (D-Ill.), cited in Conlan, Wrightson, and Beam, *Taxing Choices*, p. 94.

24. For the connections between the EITC and tax reform, see Beam, Conlan, and Wrightson, "Solving the Riddle of Tax Reform"; Birnbaum and Murray, *Showdown at Gucci Gulch*; Dom Bonafede, "Democratic Party Takes Some Strides Down the Long Comeback Trail," *National Journal* 15, 41 (October 8, 1983): 2053–55; Conlan, Wrightson, and Beam, *Taxing Choices*; Linda E. Demkovich, "Fairness Issue Will Be Campaign Test of Reagan's Record on Budget Policies," *National Journal* 16, 36 (September 8, 1984): 1648–53; Greenberg, "Plain Speaking"; Karlyn H. Keene, "Who's the Fairest of Them All?" *Public Opinion* 7, 2 (April/May 1984): 47–51; Robert Pear, "Budget Study Finds Cuts Cost the Poor as the Rich Gained," *New York Times*, April 4, 1984, p. A1; "The Poor Pay More," *Washington Post*, April 19, 1984, p. A20; Wendell E. Primus, "Children in Poverty: A Committee Prepares for an Informed Debate," *Journal of Policy Analysis and Management* 8, 1 (Winter 1989): 23–34; Susan Smith, "New GOP Leadership Readies Grassroots Organizing Effort," *Congressional Quarterly Weekly Report* 41, 10 (March 12, 1983): 519–22; C. Eugene Steuerle, "Tax Credits for Low-Income Workers with Children," *Journal of Economic Perspectives* 4, 3 (Summer 1990): 201–12; U.S. House of Representatives, Committee on Ways and Means, Oversight Subcommittee, *Federal Tax Treatment of Low-Income Persons*, April 12, 1984; U.S. Senate, Finance Committee, *Tax Reform Proposals—IV (People below Poverty Line)*, June 17, 1985; personal interviews with Robert Greenstein, August 1990; Wendell Primus, August 1990 and March 1991; Gene Steuerle, February 1991; and Randy Weiss, February 1991.

25. According to Jack Mayer of the American Enterprise Institute, "The working poor are 'an egregious example of people who have been hurt' by the Administration's social policies. . . . 'I am very much in favor of the austerity Reagan advocated . . . but I do not think he distributed it fairly.'" As a remedy, Mayer suggested greater cuts in middle-class entitlements. Quoted in Demkovich, "Fairness Issue," p. 1651.

26. Cathie J. Martin describes a similar process in *Shifting the Burden: The Struggle over Growth and Corporate Taxation* (Chicago: University of Chicago Press, 1991).

27. Primus, "Children in Poverty: A Committee Prepares for an Informed Debate," p. 30. Primus was the Ways and Means staff economist. Robert Greenstein, director of the Center on Budget and Policy Priorities, confirmed that it was Primus who first brought the EITC to his attention. The two had known each other since the late 1970s when Primus was a staff member of the Agriculture Committee and Greenstein administered the Food Stamps program (personal interview with Greenstein, August 1990).

President Clinton later appointed Primus to be Deputy Assistant Secretary of Human Services at the Department of Health and Human Services.

28. Other groups in this category include Bread for the World, the Children's Defense Fund, Coalition on Block Grants and Human Needs, the Lutheran Council, and the American Federation of State, County, and Municipal Workers (AFSCME). The Center on Budget and Policy Priorities also became instrumental in coordinating a nationwide campaign to publicize the EITC in working-poor communities. For more detail about the implementation of the EITC, see Christopher Howard, "Happy Returns: How the Working Poor Got Tax Relief," *The American Prospect* 17 (Spring 1994): 46–53.

29. See, for example, the testimony of Joseph Minarik, then an economist with the Brookings Institution, and of Robert Greenstein, in U.S. House of Representatives, Committee on Ways and Means, *Federal Tax Treatment of Low-Income Workers*. Greenstein estimated that the real value of the EITC in 1985 would be less than half its original value in 1975 unless Congress acted.

30. Quoted in Smith, "New GOP Leadership," p. 521. Republicans' efforts to change their image increased visibly after the 1982 elections. Their loss of twenty-six House seats was the largest midterm setback in more than half a century.

31. Birnbaum and Murray, *Showdown at Gucci Gulch*; Conlan, Wrightson, and Beam, *Taxing Choices*. Conlan, Wrightson, and Beam (pp. 46–49) argue that Reagan did not view tax reform simply as a defensive maneuver to hold the Democrats in check. Reagan also equated tax reform with further reductions in tax rates.

32. To be fair, the Carter administration did increase payroll taxes in 1977. On the other hand, so did Reagan in 1983.

33. Mondale tried to make fairness a key theme of the 1984 presidential election. He referred to Republicans as the party "of the rich, by the rich, and for the rich" (cited in Demkovich, "Fairness Issue," p. 1648) and appealed directly to Reagan Democrats on grounds of economic self-interest. Many voters found it difficult to square Mondale's commitment to fairness with his pledge to raise taxes and avid courtship of special interest groups. Moreover, to many white, working-class ears, *fairness* was a code word for affirmative action and preferential treatment of minorities. By the same token, the Democratic leadership did not pay more than lip service to Reagan Democrats or independents. Mondale and the Democratic National Committee bet that increasing their support among traditional bases—organized labor, blacks, Hispanics, women, and the elderly—would be enough to win.

34. James Q. Wilson, *Political Organizations* (New York: Basic Books, 1973), ch. 16.

35. U.S. Department of the Treasury, *Tax Reform for Fairness, Simplicity, and Economic Growth* (Washington, D.C.: Department of the Treasury, 1984), p. 71.

36. For a discussion of how problems, solutions, and politics come together to form "policy windows," see John Kingdon, *Agendas, Alternatives, and Public Policy* (Boston: Little, Brown, 1984).

37. Less efficient options included increases in the standard deduction and personal exemption, which would benefit all taxpayers regardless of need (personal interview with Gene Steuerle, February 1991).

38. Gene Steuerle, "The Integration of Tax and Transfer Systems Part 2: A Negative Earnings Tax (NET)," *Tax Notes* 50, 1 (January 7, 1991): 89–90.

39. Personal interview with Gene Steuerle, February 1991.

40. "After Years of Debate, Welfare Reform Clears," *Congressional Quarterly Almanac 1988* (Washington, D.C.: Congressional Quarterly, 1988), pp. 349–64; *Congressional Record*, May 22, 1985, pp. S6861–75; U.S. House of Representatives, Committee on Ways and Means, Subcommittee on Public Assistance and Unemployment Compensation, *Welfare Reform*, March 13, 1987; U.S. Congress, Joint Committee on Taxation, "Federal Tax Treatment of Individuals below the Poverty Line," in Senate Finance Committee, *Tax Reform Proposals— IV (People below Poverty Line)*.

41. The Act also tried to make it easier for recipients to move off AFDC and into the labor force by extending their Medicaid coverage, making permanent the WIN and WIN Demonstration programs, and increasing the standard deduction and personal exemption.

42. On the salience of welfare reform to working-class whites, see Edsall, *Chain Reaction*.

43. However, the Family Support Act of 1988 did require states to disregard the EITC when calculating AFDC eligibility and benefits.

44. Timothy B. Clark, "Raising the Floor," *National Journal* 19, 12 (March 21, 1987): 702–5; Nadine Cohodas, "Minimum Wage Getting Maximum Attention," *Congressional Quarterly Weekly Report* 45, 10 (March 7, 1987): 403–7; "Minimum-Wage Impasse Finally Ended," *Congressional Quarterly Almanac 1989*, vol. 45 (Washington, D.C.: Congressional Quarterly, 1990), pp. 333–40; "Minimum Wage Increase," *Congress and the Nation*, vol. 7, 1985–88 (Washington, D.C.: Congressional Quarterly, 1990), pp. 705–6; Macon Morehouse, "Senate Opens Debate on Minimum-Wage Hike," *Congressional Quarterly Weekly Report* 46, 38 (September 17, 1988): 2587; "Raising the Minimum Wage," *Congressional Digest* 66, 8–9 (August–September 1987): 193–224; Jonathan Rauch, "Paycheck Politics," *National Journal* 21, 27 (July 8, 1989): 1746–49; personal interview with Joe Flader, legislative assistant to Rep. Tom Petri, March 1991.

In addition to the minimum wage, organized labor pushed for plant closing and parental leave legislation.

45. The minimum wage had equaled between 45 and 60 percent of the average hourly wage since the late 1940s. It slipped from 48 percent in 1981 to 38 percent in 1987 (Clark, "Raising the Floor").

46. Phil Duncan, ed., *Politics in America, 1990: The 101st Congress* (Washington, D.C.: Congressional Quarterly, 1989), pp. 1643–45. Tom Tauke of Iowa, a moderate Republican member of the Education and Labor Committee, was another advocate of expanding the EITC in lieu of the minimum wage.

47. Cited in Rauch, "Paycheck Politics," p. 1747.

48. Howard Banks, "A Better Way to Help the Low-Paid," *Forbes* 141, 14 (June 27, 1988): 43; "Better Than $3.35, $4.25, or Even $5.05," *New York Times*, July 11, 1988, p. A16.

49. E. J. Dionne, Jr., "Democrats Fashion Centrist Image In New Statement of Party Policy," *New York Times*, September 21, 1986, pp. 1, 28; Jon F. Hale,

"Party Factionalism in Congress: A Study of the Democratic Leadership Council's Membership in the House," paper presented at the annual meeting of the American Political Science Association, Washington, D.C., August 28–September 1, 1991; Janet Hook, "Officials Seek Moderation in Party's Image," *Congressional Quarterly Weekly Report* 43, 10 (March 9, 1985): 457; Robert Kuttner, *The Life of the Party: Democratic Prospects in 1988 and Beyond* (New York: Viking, 1987).

50. Rauch, "Paycheck Politics," p. 1746.

51. Rep. Buddy MacKay (D-Fla.) editorial, "Raise the Minimum Wage? No, There's a More Sensible Approach," *Washington Post*, May 5, 1988, p. A23; Robert J. Shapiro, "Work and Poverty: A Progressive View of the Minimum Wage and the Earned Income Tax Credit," Progressive Policy Institute, *Policy Report No. 1* (June 1989). The Progressive Policy Institute is the research arm of the DLC.

Ironically, a Gallup poll taken in 1987 indicated across-the-board support for an increase in the minimum wage from $3.35 to $4.65 per hour, phased in over three years. Seventy-seven percent of all respondents favored such an increase, including 66 percent of Republicans, 78 percent of independents, and 79 percent of those earning between $15,000 and $25,000 per year—some of the very groups targeted by DLC Democrats (George Gallup, Jr., *The Gallup Poll: Public Opinion 1987* [Wilmington, Del.: Scholarly Resources, 1988], pp. 125–28).

52. Robert Greenstein and Isaac Shapiro, "A Higher Minimum Wage *Would* Help the Poor," *Washington Post*, August 15, 1989, p. A19.

53. This decision appealed to organized labor, since any increase to the EITC might have come at the expense of the minimum wage. And it appealed to President Bush, who wanted to deal with the minimum wage issue quickly so Congress could move on to other business such as his proposed cut in capital gains taxes, which some congressional Republicans insisted on tying to any increase in the minimum wage.

54. This discussion of the EITC and family policy is based on "Child-Care Bill Caught in House Spat," *Congressional Quarterly Almanac 1989*, vol. 45 (Washington, D.C.: Congressional Quarterly, 1990), pp. 203–17; "Child-Care Bill Dies amid Partisan Sniping," *Congressional Quarterly Almanac 1988*, vol. 44 (Washington, D.C.: Congressional Quarterly, 1989), pp. 365–68; Jason DeParle, "Poor Families Gain under Tax Accord," *New York Times*, October 31, 1990, p. A20; Dionne, "Democrats Fashion Centrist Image"; Thomas B. Edsall, "Consensus Builds to Expand Aid for Working Poor," *Washington Post*, August 21, 1989, pp. A1, A10; Elaine Ciulla Kamarck and William A. Galston, *Putting Children First: A Progressive Family Policy for the 1990s* (Washington, D.C.: Progressive Policy Institute, 1990); Julie Kosterlitz, "Family Fights," *National Journal* 22, 22 (June 2, 1990): 1333–37; Julie Rovner, "Child-Care Debate Intensifies as ABC Bill Is Approved," *Congressional Quarterly Weekly Report* 47, 11 (March 18, 1989): 585–87; Julie Rovner, "Congress Shifts Its Attention to the Working Poor," *Congressional Quarterly Weekly Report* 47, 7 (February 18, 1989): 326–28; Julie Rovner, "Consensus Grows on Dual Path to Boosting Child-Care Aid," *Congressional Quarterly Weekly Report* 47, 16 (April

22, 1989): 902; William A. Schambra, "Turf Battles: The Parties Clash over Community," *Public Opinion* 11, 2 (July/August 1988): 17–19+; U.S. House of Representatives, Committee on Ways and Means, Subcommittee on Human Resources, *How to Help the Working Poor; and Problems of the Working Poor*, February 28, March 21, and April 27, 1989.

The written record is supplemented by personal interviews with Helen Blank, August 1990; David Ellwood, November 1990; Robert Greenstein, August 1990; Wendell Primus, March 1991; Nancy Reeder and Madlyn Morreale, February 1991; and Michael Scheinfield, February 1991.

55. Before 1986, individual Democrats tried to reclaim the pro-family label in disparate ways. One positive step was the creation of the House Select Committee on Children, Youth, and Families in 1982. The Committee was the brainchild of Rep. George Miller, a liberal Democrat from California, who wanted to create a forum in which Democrats could rethink family policy. Governor Mario Cuomo of New York made extensive and passionate use of family imagery in his speech at the Democratic National Convention in 1984, to little effect. Various Democrats made disparaging remarks about the administration's treatment of families in conjunction with hearings about poverty and tax reform.

56. Quoted in Dionne, "Democrats Fashion Centrist Image," p. 28.

57. Many of these policies were also justified in the name of improving American competitiveness in the world economy, another site of interparty competition in the 1980s.

58. Party strategist Robert Kuttner argued that "the working-family issues of the 1980s are the counterpart to the issues of the 1940s that made the Democrats the majority party of working Americans" (cited in Kosterlitz, "Family Fights," p. 1333). In a similar vein, the Democratic National Committee issued a strategy paper, *Kids as Politics*, which declared that "kids are now the dominant form of expression for the politics of '88 . . . Kids are an umbrella that Democrats should embrace to recreate their majority" (quoted in Schambra, "Turf Battles," p. 17).

59. George Gallup, Jr., *The Gallup Poll: Public Opinion 1988* (Wilmington, Del.: Scholarly Resources, 1989), pp. 219–20.

60. Besides the DLC, a few liberal Democrats and the ACLU expressed reservations about any bill that extended aid to church-based child care centers.

61. It also included smaller increases in the dependent care tax credit and made that credit refundable for the poor. The initial version of Downey's bill was twice as large. It would cost an estimated $34 billion over five years. Of this, approximately $25 billion would go the EITC, $7 billion to the dependent care tax credit, and $2 billion for Title XX day care programs. Downey suggested that eliminating the "bubble" in the income tax rates (i.e., increasing the top rate from 28 to 33 percent) would generate more than enough revenue to fund his bill.

62. Downey's proposal was also more acceptable to the National Governors Association, which had gone on record as being opposed to nationwide quality standards and in favor of additional tax credits and deductions.

63. Reconciliation bills are voted up or down as a package, with no opportunity for amendment. Thus "copious and relatively veto-proof reconciliation bills often have been the vehicles of social legislation in recent years" ("All-Purpose Increase for the Poor," *Washington Post*, July 5, 1989, p. A16).

In this episode, Senate conferees objected to attempts by House conferees to purge the bill of numerous special interest measures inserted by the Senate Finance Committee. Senate conferees demanded that the House give up both child care proposals in exchange for a "cleaner" bill.

64. Some proponents of the EITC suspect that Bentsen was motivated less by good policy concerns than a desire to establish a positive record on family issues in the event he ran for president in 1992 or 1996. They also suspect that his staff leaked evidence of problems in the EITC program to a reporter at the *Washington Post* in order to erode support for the EITC.

65. Quoted in DeParle, "Poor Families Gain under Tax Accord," p. A20. The staff member was referring as well to increases in Medicaid passed as part of the same budget package.

66. This discussion of expansion in 1993 draws on material from "Deficit-Reduction Bill Narrowly Passes," *Congressional Quarterly Almanac 1993* (Washington, D.C.: Congressional Quarterly, 1994), pp. 107–24; Guy Gugliotta, "How to Aid 'Working Poor'?" *Washington Post*, April 15, 1993, p. A1; Marshall Ingwerson, "Tax Credit Geared for Working Poor Stays in Budget Mix," *Christian Science Monitor*, August 5, 1993, p. 8; Timothy Noah and Laurie McGinley, "Advocate for the Poor, Respected on All Sides, Secures a Pivotal Role in Expanding Tax Credit," *Wall Street Journal*, July 26, 1993, p. A12; Paul J. Quirk and Joseph Hinchliffe, "Domestic Policy: The Trials of a Centrist Democrat," in Colin Campbell and Bert A. Rockman, eds., *The Clinton Presidency: First Appraisals* (Chatham, N.J.: Chatham House, 1996), pp. 262–89; and Bob Woodward, *The Agenda: Inside the Clinton White House* (New York: Simon & Schuster, 1994).

67. Woodward, *The Agenda*, p. 128.

68. The Center on Budget and Policy Priorities estimated that the average EITC for taxpayers without children would be around $175. Working largely behind the scenes, the Center persuaded the Clinton administration to modify its initial proposal so that working-poor families earning less than $20,000 would receive more of the increase. The final bill also eliminated tax credits for health insurance for children and for young children that had been created in 1990. Eligibility for these tax credits had been linked to the EITC, making implementation of all three tax credits quite complicated.

69. Concerning recent GOP proposals to cut the EITC, see Albert R. Hunt, "The GOP on the Working Poor: Let Them Eat Cake," *Wall Street Journal*, September 28, 1995, p. 21; Amy Kaslow, "Critics Say GOP Tilts Toward Rich," *Christian Science Monitor*, November 2, 1995, p. 8; Clarence Page, "Keeping the Poor Poorer," *Chicago Tribune*, October 25, 1995, p. 17; Robert J. Samuelson, "Pouncing on Working Poor," *Boston Globe*, October 3, 1995, p. 72; and Dave Skidmore, "House May Cut Earned-Income Credit for Poor," *Washington Post*, September 15, 1995, p. A4.

70. It does not appear that designing programs to reinforce the work ethic is enough, otherwise the United States would have done much more in the way of employment and training. My hunch is that it is equally important to avoid programs that restrict benefits to those below or well below the poverty line—who also tend to be disproportionately black and Hispanic. As we will see in the next chapter, the Targeted Jobs Tax Credit was more narrowly targeted than the EITC, and it never achieved the growth or popularity of the EITC. Politically, it would seem smarter to create programs that serve the poor and near-poor so as to increase the program's political clout among policy makers and avoid the taint of race. Here one might want to compare the EITC to programs like Food Stamps and Medicaid, which have also grown in recent years and which also extend benefits to people above the poverty line, to determine how much support is needed to form a critical mass.

71. See, for example, Ginsberg and Shefter, *Politics by Other Means*, and James Sundquist, "The Crisis of Competence in Our National Government," *Political Science Quarterly* 95 (1980): 183–208. For evidence that policy making is roughly equal during periods of divided and unified government, see David R. Mayhew, *Divided We Govern* (New Haven, Conn.: Yale University Press, 1991).

CHAPTER 8
TARGETED JOBS TAX CREDIT

1. Gary Mucciaroni, *The Political Failure of Employment Policy, 1946–1982* (Pittsburgh: University of Pittsburgh Press, 1990); Theda Skocpol, *Social Policy in the United States* (Princeton, N.J.: Princeton University Press, 1994), ch. 7; Margaret Weir, *Politics and Jobs* (Princeton, N.J.: Princeton University Press, 1992).

2. Skocpol, *Social Policy in the United States*, pp. 245–49.

3. The Tax Reform Act of 1986 limited the tax credit to 40 percent of the first $6,000 in wages and eliminated the credit for employment in the second year. The Technical and Miscellaneous Revenue Act of 1988 limited the credit for summer youth to 40 percent of the first $3,000 in wages.

4. Donald C. Baumer and Carl E. Van Horn, *The Politics of Unemployment* (Washington, D.C.: Congressional Quarterly, 1985); Roger H. Davidson, *The Politics of Comprehensive Manpower Legislation* (Baltimore, Md.: The Johns Hopkins University Press, 1972); Grace A. Franklin and Randall B. Ripley, *CETA: Politics and Policy 1973–1982* (Knoxville: University of Tennessee Press, 1984); Mucciaroni, *The Political Failure of Employment Policy, 1945–1982*.

5. CETA, the Comprehensive Employment Training Act, replaced MDTA as the major job training program, and was in turn replaced by JTPA, the Job Training Partnership Act.

6. For changes in eligibility, see U.S. Department of Labor, "Targeted Jobs Credit (TJTC) Program: Legislative History," mimeo, n.d.; John Bishop, ed., *Targeted Jobs Tax Credit: Findings from Four Employer Surveys* (Columbus, Ohio: National Center for Research in Vocational Education, 1985); Linda

LeGrande, *The Targeted Jobs Tax Credit, 1978–1987* (Washington, D.C.: Congressional Research Service, 1987); personal interview with Bill Signer, August 1990.

7. For testimony of other nonprofit advocacy groups, see U.S. Senate, Finance Committee, Subcommittee on Economic Growth, Employment and Revenue Sharing, *Targeted Jobs Tax Credit*, April 3, 1981; U.S. House of Representatives, Committee on Ways and Means, Subcommittee on Select Revenue Measures, *Targeted Jobs Tax Credit Extension*, April 10, 1984; U.S. House of Representatives, Committee on Ways and Means, Subcommittee on Select Revenue Measures, *Targeted Jobs Tax Credit Extension*, March 19, 1985; U.S. House of Representatives, Committee on Ways and Means, Subcommittee on Select Revenue Measures, *Targeted Jobs Tax Credits*, June 6, 1989; U.S. House of Representatives, Committee on Ways and Means, Subcommittee on Oversight, *Extending Targeted Tax Credits*, May 9, 1995.

8. In addition to the sources cited above in note 7, see Robin Lee Allen, "Operators fight Clinton to retain TJTC," *Nation's Restaurant News* 28, 41 (October 17, 1994): 3; National Employment Opportunities Network, "Usage of Targeted Jobs Tax Credit," mimeo, February 23, 1990; Joan Oleck, "The Party's Over; Targeted Jobs Tax Credit Is Slated to Expire," *Restaurant Business* 94, 1 (January 1, 1995): 36.

9. Jane Carmichael, "The Bounty Hunters," *Forbes* 128, 2 (July 20, 1981): 82.

10. Targeted Jobs Tax Credit Coalition, "Fact Sheet," mimeo, 1989; Targeted Jobs Tax Credit Coalition, "Members of the TJTC Coalition," mimeo, n.d.; personal interview with Paul Suplizio, August 1990.

11. Testimony of Arnold Cantor, Assistant Director, Department of Economic Research, AFL-CIO, in U.S. Senate, Finance Committee, *Targeted Jobs Tax Credit*, April 3, 1981, p. 191. Cantor reiterated these criticisms in 1984 (U.S. House of Representatives, Committee on Ways and Means, *Targeted Jobs Tax Credit Extension*, April 10, 1984, pp. 95–105).

12. Testimony of John Motley III, Deputy Director of Federal Legislation, National Federation of Independent Business, in U.S. Senate, Finance Committee, *Targeted Jobs Tax Credit*, April 3, 1981, pp. 50–53.

13. Quoted in Janet Hook, "Tax Credit Could Be Only 'Jobs' Bill in 1984," *Congressional Quarterly Weekly Report* 42, 16 (April 21, 1984): 929.

14. U.S. House of Representatives, Committee on Ways and Means, *Targeted Jobs Tax Credits*, June 6, 1989, p. 6.

15. Deborah Billings, "Houghton, Rangel Join Forces to Reform Targeted Jobs Tax Credit," *Bureau of National Affairs Daily Labor Report* (May 10, 1995), p. D6; "Panel Approves Tax Plan Extending Pension Reversions, Hiring Credit," *Bureau of National Affairs Daily Labor Report* (September 21, 1995), p. D23.

16. Both quoted in Hook, "Tax Credit Could Be Only 'Jobs' Bill in 1984," p. 929.

17. Charles Rangel in U.S. House of Representatives, Committee on Ways and Means, *Targeted Jobs Tax Credits*, June 6, 1989, pp. 2, 5.

18. U.S. House of Representatives, Committee on Ways and Means, *Targeted Jobs Tax Credit*, March 2, 1984, pp. 12–15, 79; Targeted Jobs Tax Credit Coalition, "Lobbying Plans for TJTC Campaign," mimeo, July 17, 1990; Billings, "Houghton, Rangel Join Forces to Reform Targeted Jobs Tax Credit"; personal interviews with Jon Sheiner, August 1990; and Ann Rafaelli, August 1990.

19. Statement of Robert E. David, Executive Director, South Carolina Employment Security Commission, in U.S. House of Representatives, Committee on Ways and Means, *Targeted Jobs Tax Credits*, June 6, 1989, p. 80.

According to one state official, the TJTC "provides employers with a worthwhile incentive to seriously consider hiring targeted group people who need that opportunity. . . . We have consistently found that, where people are given the opportunity because of the incentive of the tax credit to get on a private payroll, they might not have otherwise been seriously considered by the employers" (testimony of Donald Grabowski, Director, Employer Relations, New York State Department of Labor, in U.S. House of Representatives, Committee on Ways and Means, *Extension of the Targeted Jobs Tax Credit*, March 19, 1985, p. 130).

20. Testimony of John E. Chapoton, Assistant Secretary of the Treasury for Tax Policy, before the Senate Finance Committee, Subcommittee on Economic Growth, Employment, and Revenue Sharing, *Targeted Jobs Tax Credit*, April 3, 1981; testimony of Charles E. McLure, Jr., Deputy Assistant Secretary for Tax Policy, Department of the Treasury, before the House Ways and Means Committee, Subcommittee on Select Revenue Measures, *Targeted Jobs Tax Credit Extension*, April 10, 1984; testimony of Mikel M. Rollyson, Tax Legislative Counsel, Department of the Treasury, before the House Ways and Means Committee, Subcommittee on Select Revenue Measures, *Extension of the Targeted Jobs Tax Credit*, March 19, 1985; testimony of Thomas S. Neubig, Director and Chief Economist, Office of Tax Analysis, Department of the Treasury, before the House Ways and Means Committee, Subcommittee on Select Revenue Measures, *Targeted Jobs Tax Credits*, June 6, 1989.

21. A spokesperson from the Congressional Budget Office reiterated this point, though she admitted that there was no concrete estimate of the displacement effect (testimony of Nancy M. Gordon, Assistant Director for Human Resources and Community Development, Congressional Budget Office, in U.S. House of Representatives, Committee on Ways and Means, *Extension of the Targeted Jobs Tax Credit*, March 19, 1985, pp. 24–31).

22. Testimony of Thomas S. Neubig, Director and Chief Economist, Office of Tax Analysis, Department of the Treasury, *Targeted Jobs Tax Credits*, June 6, 1989, p. 19.

23. Statements of Paul E. Suplizio, Targeted Jobs Tax Credit Coalition, and Rep. Pete Stark in U.S. House of Representatives, Committee on Ways and Means, *Targeted Jobs Tax Credit Extension*, April 10, 1984 pp. 167 and 10, respectively.

24. Statement of Paul E. Suplizio, Targeted Jobs Tax Credit Coalition, in U.S. House of Representatives, Committee on Ways and Means, *Targeted Jobs*

Tax Credit Extension, April 10, 1984; statements of Joseph W. Arwady and Richard A. Lacey, in U.S. House of Representatives, Committee on Ways and Means, *Targeted Jobs Tax Credits*, June 9, 1989.

25. Testimony of John E. Chapoton in U.S. Senate, Finance Committee, *Targeted Jobs Tax Credit*, April 3, 1981, pp. 27–28; testimony of William H. Kolberg, President, National Alliance of Business, in U.S. House of Representatives, Committee on Ways and Means, *Targeted Jobs Tax Credit*, March 2, 1984, pp. 85–92.

It is not unusual for the Treasury to take one or two years to translate legislation into the tax code. But five years for a relatively straightforward bill suggests a certain amount of foot-dragging.

26. Testimony of Albert Angrisani, Assistant Secretary for Employment and Training, Department of Labor, in U.S. Senate, Finance Committee, Subcommittee on Economic Growth, Employment, and Revenue Sharing, *Targeted Jobs Tax Credit*, April 3, 1981, pp. 35–46. The Labor Department's silence on the TJTC was a continual source of frustration to legislators who wanted more information about the program's effectiveness and efficiency.

Other than these hearings, the Labor Department briefly mentioned in passing efforts to inform employers about the TJTC during hearings on youth employment programs in 1979. But it clearly placed more emphasis on its CETA and Job Corps programs (U.S. Senate, Education and Labor Committee, Subcommittee on Employment Opportunities, *Youth Employment Act of 1979*, part 1, June 20, 26, 27, and July 18, 1979).

27. Allen, "Operators Fight Clinton to Retain TJTC"; U.S. House of Representatives, Committee on Ways and Means, Subcommittee on Select Revenue Measures, *Targeted Jobs Tax Credit*, September 29, 1994.

28. On the importance of autonomy and turf to bureaucracies, see James Q. Wilson, *Bureaucracy* (New York: Basic Books, 1989).

29. U.S. Senate, Finance Committee, *Targeted Jobs Tax Credit*, April 3, 1981.

30. Sar A. Levitan and Frank Gallo, "The Targeted Jobs Tax Credit: An Uncertain and Unfinished Experiment," *Labor Law Journal* 38, 10 (October 1987): 641–49; personal interview with Ed Hogan, August 1990.

31. Departments of Labor and Treasury, *The Use of Tax Subsidies for Employment*, p. 65. See also Robert Crosslin, Kevin Hollenbeck, and Phillip Richardson, *Impact Study of the Implementation and Use of the Targeted Jobs Tax Credit: Overview and Summary* (Columbus, Ohio; Macro Systems, in conjunction with the National Center for Research in Vocational Education, 1986).

32. Crosslin, Hollenbeck, and Richardson, *Impact Study*. The twelve states were California, Colorado, Florida, Georgia, Illinois, Indiana, Kansas, Missouri, Oregon, Pennsylvania, South Carolina, and Tennessee.

33. U.S. Congress, Joint Committee on Taxation, "Background on Tax Incentives for Employment," in U.S. Senate, Finance Committee, *Targeted Jobs Tax Credit*, April 3, 1981, pp. 16–18.

34. Gary Burtless, "Are Targeted Wage Subsidies Harmless? Evidence from a Wage Voucher Experiment," *International Labor Relations Review* 39, 1 (1985): 105–14. See also John Bishop and Suk Kang, "Applying for Entitle-

ments: Employers and the Targeted Jobs Tax Credit," *Journal of Policy Analysis and Management* 10, 1 (Winter 1991), pp. 24–45.

35. John Bishop, "The Targeted Jobs Tax Credit: What Has Been Learned," in U.S. Senate, Finance Committee, *Targeted Jobs Tax Credit*, March 2, 1984, pp. 103–42.

36. Testimony of Thomas Neubig, Department of the Treasury, before the Committee on Ways and Means, *Targeted Jobs Tax Credits*, June 6, 1989, pp. 19–36.

37. See, e.g., studies by Borg-Warner and Price Waterhouse in Committee on Ways and Means, *Targeted Jobs Tax Credits*, June 6, 1989.

38. David R. Sands, "Reich backs tax credits for jobs," *The Washington Times*, September 30, 1994, p. B9; David R. Sands, "Employer tax credit draws ire, no action," *The Washington Times*, September 21, 1994, p. B7.

39. Allen, "Operators fight Clinton to save TJTC"; Sands, "Employer tax credit draws ire, no action"; U.S. Congress, Committee on Ways and Means, *Extending Targeted Tax Credits*, May 9, 1995.

CHAPTER 9
POLITICS OF THE HIDDEN WELFARE STATE

1. Bruce Lee Balch, "Individual Income Taxes and Housing," *National Tax Journal* 11, 2 (June 1958): 180.

2. Alain Enthoven, "Health Tax Policy Mismatch," *Health Affairs* 4, 4 (Winter 1985): 10.

3. Sven Steinmo, *Taxation and Democracy: Swedish, British, and American Approaches to Financing the Modern State* (New Haven, Conn.: Yale University Press, 1993), pp. 74–76; Jerold Waltman, *The Political Origins of the U.S. Federal Income Tax* (Jackson: University of Mississippi Press, 1985), p. 51.

4. In addition to the works cited in note 19 of the introduction, see Thomas J. Reese, *The Politics of Taxation* (Westport, Conn.: Quorum Books, 1980); Catherine E. Rudder, "Tax Policy: Structure and Choice," in Allen Schick, ed., *Making Economic Policy in Congress* (Washington, D.C.: American Enterprise Institute, 1983), pp. 196–220.

5. Deborah A. Stone, *Policy Paradox and Political Reason* (Glenview, Ill.: Scott, Foresman, 1988), p. 106.

6. Richard F. Fenno, Jr., *Congressmen in Committees* (Boston: Little, Brown, 1973); John F. Manley, *The Politics of Finance* (Boston: Little, Brown, 1970); Randall Strahan, *New Ways and Means: Reform and Change in a Congressional Committee* (Chapel Hill: University of North Carolina Press, 1990).

7. Congressional Budget Office, *Tax Expenditures: Budget Control Options and Five-Year Budget Projections for Fiscal Years 1983–1987* (Washington, D.C.: Congressional Budget Office, 1982). In Britain, however, the lack of co-ordination is even more pronounced than in the United States. There, "decisions about totals for public expenditure programmes for the next financial year are announced in the Autumn Statement in November of the previous year. Tax changes, including changes affecting tax expenditures, are announced in the Budget in March or April as a result of a quite separate process of decision-

making" (Brian W. Hogwood, "The Hidden Face of Public Expenditures: Trends in Tax Expenditures in Britain," *Policy and Politics* 17, 2 [1989]: 114).

8. For evidence of similar effects with the contracting out of social services, see Steven Rathgeb Smith and Deborah A. Stone, "The Unintended Consequences of Privatization," in Michael Brown, ed., *Remaking the Welfare State* (Philadelphia: Temple University Press, 1988), pp. 232–52.

9. Cates shows how bureaucrats at the Social Security Administration consciously built up the more inclusive old age insurance program at the expense of the means-tested old age assistance program (Jerry Cates, *Insuring Inequality: Administrative Leadership in Social Security, 1935–54* [Ann Arbor: University of Michigan Press, 1983]).

An interesting aside is that some agencies (HUD, HEW, and Energy) have proposed new tax expenditures even though the Treasury would administer them (Reese, *Politics of Taxation*, pp. 48–50).

10. Concerning the importance of mission to government agencies, see James Q. Wilson, *Bureaucracy* (New York: Basic Books, 1989). Regarding the Treasury Department and tax expenditures, see Timothy J. Conlan, Margaret T. Wrightson, and David Beam, *Taxing Choices: The Politics of Tax Reform* (Washington, D.C.: Congressional Quarterly, 1990); Jonathan Barry Forman, "Origins of the Tax Expenditure Budget," *Tax Notes* 30, 6 (February 10, 1986): 537–45; Daniel M. Fox and Daniel C. Schaffer, "Tax Policy as Social Policy: Cafeteria Plans, 1978–1985," *Journal of Health Politics, Policy and Law* 12, 4 (Winter 1987): 632, n. 58; Donald Lubick and Gerard Brannon, "Stanley S. Surrey and the Quality of Tax Policy Argument," *National Tax Journal* 38, 3 (September 1985): 256–58; Paul R. McDaniel, "Tax Expenditures as Tools of Government Action," in Lester M. Salamon, ed., *Beyond Privatization: The Tools of Government Action* (Washington, D.C.: Urban Institute, 1989), pp. 167–96; Reese, *The Politics of Taxation*, pp. 52–54; Surrey, *Pathways to Tax Reform*, pp. 150–51; Surrey and McDaniel, *Tax Expenditures*; personal interviews with Seymour Fiekowsky, Gene Steuerle, and Emil Sunley, all in August 1990.

11. Unlike many fields of economics, there is considerable methodological and normative consensus within the field of public finance concerning the criteria for an ideal tax system. One of the major unresolved issues hinges on how progressive tax rates should be.

12. Quoted in Surrey and McDaniel, *Tax Expenditures*, p. 95.

13. Quoted in Ralph Nader Congress Project, *The Revenue Committees*, p. 129.

14. Someone familiar with principal-agent models might investigate how Congress, which creates most tax expenditures and has an interest in distributing benefits through the tax code, monitors the performance of the Treasury and the IRS, which have strong incentives to limit the amount of revenue lost through special exceptions. The potential for noncompliance (i.e., "shirking") is considerable. Congress relies on the Treasury's Office of Tax Policy to translate general legislative mandates into specific provisions of the tax code. At the "street level," IRS field agents apply the tax code to an almost limitless variety of individual and corporate taxpayers. Their "basic instinct . . . is to interpret the

tax expenditure program as narrowly as possible in order to maximize government revenues" (McDaniel, "Tax Expenditures," p. 175). Nevertheless, one former Treasury official suggested to me that most Treasury and IRS officials faithfully perform whatever tasks Congress assigns them (interview with Emil Sunley, August 1990). This case is particularly intriguing because the potential for noncompliance arises not out of a conflict between the public interest and the private interests of bureaucrats. It arises because Congress asks the Treasury and IRS to pursue conflicting objectives and to administer social programs in which they have no substantive expertise.

15. U.S. Congress, Joint Committee on Taxation, *Present-Law Tax Rules Relating to Qualified Pension Plans* (Washington, D.C.: Government Printing Office, 1990), p. 4.

16. Steinmo, *Taxation and Democracy*, p. 101.

17. John F. Witte, *The Politics and Development of the Federal Income Tax* (Madison: University of Wisconsin Press, 1985), pp. 321–23.

18. These reforms have been repeatedly analyzed. One of the best discussions is Rudder, "Tax Policy: Structure and Choice."

19. The BEA does not affect the growth of existing entitlements, however, as long as there are no statutory changes to eligibility or benefits. This exception weakens its ability to control the deficit.

20. Some evidence indicates that Ways and Means started to insist informally on deficit neutrality for any changes to tax expenditures shortly before the 1990 Budget Act formally instituted PAYGO rules (Carol Matlack, "Zap! You're Taxed," *National Journal* 22, 5 [February 3, 1990]: 267–69).

21. Christopher Howard, "Protean Lure for the Working Poor: Party Competition and the Earned Income Tax Credit," *Studies in American Political Development* 9 (Fall 1995): 404–36.

22. This generalization applies to the national level. At the state level, parties have long been considered an important determinant of social policy. See, for example, V. O. Key, Jr., *American State Politics: An Introduction* (New York: Knopf, 1956); Charles F. Cnudde and Donald J. McCrone, "Party Competition and Welfare Policies in the American States," *American Political Science Review* 63, 3 (September 1969): 858–66; Edward T. Jennings, "Competition, Constituencies, and Welfare Policies in American States," *American Political Science Review* 73, 2 (June 1979): 414–29; and Robert D. Plotnick and Richard F. Winters, "Party, Political Liberalism, and Redistribution," *American Politics Quarterly* 18, 4 (October 1990): 430–58.

23. Susan B. Hansen, "Partisan Realignment and Tax Policy, 1789–1976," in Paul Peretz, ed., *The Politics of American Economic Policy Making* (Armonk, N.Y.: M. E. Sharpe, 1987), pp. 233–57; Charles H. Stewart III, "The Politics of Tax Reform in the 1980s," in Alberto Alesina and Geoffrey Carliner, eds., *Politics and Economics in the 1980s* (Chicago: University of Chicago Press, 1991), pp. 143–70; Witte, *Politics and Development of the Federal Income Tax*.

24. Concerning Civil War pensions, see Theda Skocpol, *Protecting Soldiers and Mothers: The Political Origins of U.S. Social Policy* (Cambridge, Mass.: Harvard University Press, 1992). Concerning Social Security, see Martha Derthick, *Policymaking for Social Security* (Washington, D.C.: Brookings Institution,

1979); and John B. Gilmour, *Strategies of Disagreement: Stalemate in American Politics* (Pittsburgh: University of Pittsburgh Press, 1995).

25. Michael J. Piore and Charles F. Sabel, *The Second Industrial Divide: Possibilities for Prosperity* (New York: Basic Books, 1984); Frank R. Baumgartner and Bryan D. Jones, *Agendas and Instability in American Politics* (Chicago: University of Chicago Press, 1993).

26. W. David Liddell, "Reefs," in Frank N. Magill, ed., *Magill's Survey of Science. Earth Science Series* vol. 4 (Pasadena, Calif.: Salem Press, 1990), pp. 2158–65.

27. It should be clear that I do not expect to see any grand theory explaining the politics of the hidden welfare state, and anyone trying to apply a model of comprehensive rationality to the process of creating, expanding, and reducing tax expenditures will be sorely disappointed. Understanding the politics of tax expenditures requires an appreciation for historical contingency and unintended consequences. I would expect mid-range theories, bounded by specific eras and limited to specific tax expenditures, to be the most fruitful.

28. One survey found that individuals spent an average of twenty-seven hours per year complying with the income tax system in 1989, and that despite efforts at simplification this figure had grown since 1982. About half of them also paid for professional assistance, at an average cost of $132 each (Marsha Blumenthal and Joel Slemrod, "The Compliance Cost of the U.S. Individual Income Tax System: A Second Look after Tax Reform," *National Tax Journal* 45, 2 [June 1992]: 185–202).

29. *Congressional Record*, November 11, 1969, pp. 35053–55; U.S. Senate, Finance Committee, *Revenue Act of 1971*, November 9, 1971.

30. Cited in Fox and Schaffer, "Tax Policy as Social Policy," p. 615, n. 15.

31. David S. Cloud, "Congress Takes on the Explosive Issue of Taxing Health Care Benefits," *Congressional Quarterly Weekly Report* 52, 19 (May 14, 1994): 1218–19.

32. Sheila B. Kamerman and Alfred J. Kahn, "Social Policy and Children in the United States and Europe," in John L. Palmer, Timothy Smeeding, and Barbara Boyle Torrey, eds., *The Vulnerable* (Washington, D.C.: Urban Institute Press, 1988), pp. 351–80.

Index

PRINCETON STUDIES IN AMERICAN POLITICS:
HISTORICAL, INTERNATIONAL, AND
COMPARATIVE PERSPECTIVES

The Origins of the Urban Crisis: Race and Inequality in Postwar Detroit
by Thomas J. Sugrue

*The Road to Nowhere: The Genesis of President Clinton's Plan
for Health Security* by Jacob Hacker

*Imperiled Innocents: Anthony Comstock and Family Reproduction
in Victorian America* by Nicola Beisel

Morning Glories: Municipal Reform in the Southwest by Amy Bridges

*The Hidden Welfare State: Tax Expenditures and Social Policy
in the United States* by Christopher Howard

About the Author

CHRISTOPHER HOWARD is Assistant Professor of Government at the
College of William and Mary.